D1235549

THE NOTION OF THE STATE

Oxford University Press, Ely House, London W. 1

GLASGOW NEW YORK TORONTO MELBOURNE WELLINGTON
CAPE TOWN SALISBURY IBADAN NAIROBI LUSAKA ADDIS ABABA
BOMBAY CALCUTTA MADRAS KARACHI LAHORE DACCA
KUALA LUMPUR HONG KONG TOKYO

THE NOTION OF
THE STATE

AN INTRODUCTION TO
POLITICAL THEORY

BY

ALEXANDER PASSERIN D'ENTRÈVES

PROFESSOR OF POLITICAL THEORY
IN THE UNIVERSITY OF TURIN

OXFORD
AT THE CLARENDON PRESS
1967

© *Oxford University Press 1967*

PRINTED IN GREAT BRITAIN

'Am Ende hängen wir doch ab
Von Kreaturen, die wir machten.'

GOETHE, *Faust*

PREFACE

THIS book was first published in Italian in 1962. I have been planning to rewrite it ever since, with a view to publishing an English edition which might be definitive. Here, at long last, is the fruit of my labours.

Miss Margaret Carlyle greatly eased my task by providing me with a literal translation of the original text and by revising my English. It gives me particular pleasure that her name should once again be associated with one of my books. *The Notion of the State* would probably never have been written had its author not had the good fortune of sitting at her father's feet forty years ago in those unforgettable tutorials at 29 Holywell.

Nor would it have been written but for the stimulus of teaching my own subject again after resigning the chair of Italian Studies at Oxford. I therefore wish to record a special debt of gratitude to my old Faculty in Turin for welcoming me back after a long absence, as well as to the Department of Philosophy and to the Law School at Yale for entrusting me year after year with a course on political and legal philosophy which proved to be one of the most enjoyable experiences of my career as a teacher.

I should find it hard to say which of these three different settings—British, Italian, American—has had most influence on the views set forth in these pages. There is so much that is personal in them, and what little scholarship there is is of secondary importance. If there is one point which I am particularly anxious to emphasize, it is that *The Notion of the State* is not a treatise of political science, nor a history of political thought, nor an exercise in linguistic analysis. The only purpose of this book is to defend a certain type of approach to political theory.

I am well aware that, only a few years ago, such an approach would have seemed out of fashion, at any rate in Oxford. But the wheel seems to have come full circle since the 'heyday of Weldonism'. 'Rolling the classics round the tongue like old brandy' may be sneered at by the young. But the questions which old-time political philosophers used to ask are no longer brushed aside as pointless or meaningless. Indeed, as Sir Isaiah Berlin has remarked,

political theory will not perish from the earth 'so long as rational
curiosity exists—a desire for justification and explanation in terms
of motives and reasons'.

Needless to say, I fully share this conviction.

Turin, *November 1966*   A. P. d'ENTRÈVES

CONTENTS

INTRODUCTION   *page* 1

PART I. MIGHT

1. The Argument of Thrasymachus   15
2. Realism and Pessimism   21
3. The State—a Neologism   28
4. The 'New Principality' and the Method of 'Effectual Truth' 37
5. 'Reason of State' and *Machtstaat*   44
6. 'Class Struggle' and 'Governing *Élites*'   50
7. The Disruption of the Notion of the State in Modern Political
   Science   59

PART II. POWER

1. Government by Men and Government by Laws   69
2. State and Law: the Basic Notions   75
3. The Rule of Law   82
4. In Search of Sovereignty   89
5. The Birth of the Modern State   96
6. Leviathan Unfettered   104
7. The 'Mixed State' and the 'Division of Power'   114
8. The Plurality of Legal Systems   124
9. Church and State   132
10. Legality and Legitimacy   141

PART III. AUTHORITY

1. Law and Order   153
2. Nature and Convention   161
3. Country and Nation   170
4. Divine Right   182
5. Force and Consent   191
6. Negative Liberty   201
7. Positive Liberty   211
8. The Common Good   222

INDEX   231

INTRODUCTION

1. From the hour of birth to the hour of death our life is beset with innumerable forces which obstruct or protect its course and often determine its fate. Some of these forces are wholly outside our control—certain natural forces, for example. Others, on the contrary, are the result of circumstances created by ourselves or by others, sometimes intentionally, sometimes not. The most numerous of these circumstances—circumstances which at any time may require our doing certain things or prevent us from doing others —the most stringent, the most frequently experienced, are those which are commonly associated with the notion of a mysterious but omnipresent entity, of an indefinite but at the same time imperious and irresistible power: the notion of the State.

Suppose we put a question to the first man we meet in the street, and ask him if States 'exist'. He will look at us with surprise, wondering if we want to make a fool of him. But if we ask him to tell us what States 'are', unless he has been brought up on books and studies which provide him with a ready-made definition, he will find it difficult to explain briefly and clearly the meaning of the word, which is certainly one fairly familiar to him, and which he may come across or use every day, in talking, in business, in every kind of activity in which he may be engaged, both as a man and as a citizen.

2. Let us try to examine the meaning of the word as used in common parlance and known to us at first hand. A moment's thought will suggest the following outstanding points:

(*a*) The word 'State' is generally associated with the notion of a force outside the individual will, superior to it, and able not only to issue commands but to enforce them.

(*b*) The fact that the notion of the State is associated with that of an imperative and superior force, which is attached to its commands and not to others, does not imply that this force is inscrutable and arbitrary. On the contrary, the notion of the State is closely associated with that of a power exercised in accordance with definite procedure, with rules that are known, or at any rate knowable.

(*c*) The recognition of this power as exercised according to definite rules implies the recognition of an obligation to submit to these rules. The word 'State' in this sense provides a term of reference for these obligations. It refers not merely to a force which exists in actual fact, or to a power which makes itself felt in accordance with certain rules, but to an authority which is recognized as warranted and justified in practice.

3. These three points correspond to three different possible ways of approaching the problem of the State, and all three views have been put forward and upheld during the long process of reflecting upon the problem.

When we consider the existence of the State as a purely factual question, it is the importance of force that first attracts our exclusive attention. The State 'exists' in as far as a force exists which bears its name. The relations of the State with individuals as well as those between States are relations of force. The existence of the State is commonly and naïvely represented in the shape of the policeman and the tax-collector, who watch over and ensure the peaceful living together of men. It is also represented in the shape of big armies, of powerful guns, and fortresses, set up to protect and defend that coexistence against external dangers arising from the potential threat of the 'force' of other States.

4. On the other hand, when we consider the manner in which this force, which is taken to be essential to the State, is displayed; when we observe the peculiar and significant fact that this force, in order to be attributed to the State, can never, or ought never, to be arbitrary force; then the State tends to appear as a collection of rules and regulations which not only control the coexistence of individuals, but are the very condition of the existence of the State itself. Force is no longer mere force: it is a 'qualified' force, a force displayed in a regular and uniform manner. It is exercised 'in the name of' certain rules and regulations, of those very rules laid down by the State which constitute its special responsibility.

Thus the notion of law appears to be closely associated with that of the State; but the word 'law' is here used in a quite different sense from that in which it is used when we speak of physical laws, of the so-called 'laws of nature'. It is not a question of purely factual uniformities and regularities, independent of man's will. These 'laws' are made by men, and by men who established, and

INTRODUCTION 3

wished to establish, an 'order' in their relations with each other for the achievement of certain ends, first and foremost that peaceful coexistence which is needed to make further ends attainable.

5. The close association of State and law does not, however, exhaust the multiplicity of problems that the notion of the State has raised in the minds of those who, from the earliest times, have meditated on the subject.

The State is force, but qualified force: force exercised 'in the name of the law'. But the laws themselves, as we have seen, are created by men. They can remove the character of arbitrariness from force, but can themselves be arbitrary. What is it that can make them 'obligatory'? Merely the fact that they are imposed by the State? But if this were the case, we should again identify the State with force, whereas in reality the fact that we refer the laws to the State in order to justify their obligatory character means that we are adding a further qualification to the State's force: it is a force exercised in accordance with the law, and in accordance with a law that is obligatory because it is a law laid down by the State. We are in a vicious circle from which we cannot escape unless we admit that the force of the State in reality carries a twofold qualification: that it is qualified by the law and also by a 'value' which is inherent in the State and expressed in the law. Actually, some such value already exists, although unrecognized, in the minds of those who limit themselves to stating that force is necessary as a guarantee of the peaceful coexistence of men, or who underline the merits of force 'exercised in the name of the law' as a token of the regularity and uniformity of State action.

6. The same conclusions can be reached by a different method of reasoning. There is a noticeable difference in our way of speaking when we talk of the compulsion put upon us by a definite kind of force (the force of the 'State') and of the degree of regularity and uniformity with which this force is employed (according to 'laws'), and when we say that this force and these laws are obligatory. Two different kinds of proposition are involved here, the first descriptive, the second prescriptive. The mere statement of the existence of laws and of means to enforce them does not necessarily entail any pronouncement on the duty of obeying them. A pronouncement of this kind is additional to the statement of their existence. This addition may be implicit and is often unnoticed. But it

involves a substantial shift from description to prescription that radically alters the type of our discourse.

It is not difficult to notice this shift taking place in many of the discussions commonly held on the 'State'. Those, for example, who maintain that the obligatoriness of the State's commands is due to the fact that these commands can, if necessary, be imposed by force, are in fact doing nothing else than attributing to force itself a paramount value. If cornered, they will readily admit that force, being necessary, is in its own way a good thing. Similarly, those who insist that laws must be obeyed because they are laws (*Gesetz ist Gesetz*), are inserting a value-clause into what is otherwise purely and simply a tautology. In actual fact the most frequent explanation of the obligatory character of laws is that derived from the end they secure, the discipline of human relations without which human life would hardly be possible. But a no less plausible explanation may also be derived, and is often derived, from the claim that laws are the expression of a value called 'justice'. It is the presence of such value that makes obedience to the laws a duty.

No doubt it is perfectly possible to speak of the State in purely descriptive and factual terms: but only at the cost of neglecting an important aspect of the use made of the word 'State' in common speech, where the State is conceived as a force regulated by laws and worthy of respect and obedience.

7. Consider, on the other hand, how our mental picture of the State varies according to the point of view from which it is approached.

In the first case the State is force; it even has the monopoly of force. Indeed, in our modern world the force at the State's disposal is greater than the human imagination can conceive, and the mind almost shrinks from considering the consequences that could follow from its full employment. There are, on the one hand, psychological forces affecting everyone everywhere; these become more pervasive every day with the growing efficiency of techniques such as mass propaganda and hidden persuasion. On the other hand, there are, above all, new and unheard-of material forces, made available by the increasing perfection of scientific instruments, of weapons, of means of defence and offence. And yet these forces are in the hands of men, often of a few men. To be sure, from this point of view it is the executives, the 'bosses', the 'war-lords', who *are* the State: it is they who make decisions and give commands. They hold the fate of us all in their hands. We seem to be left with no choice but submission.

8. In the second case, the vision of the State is a wholly impersonal one. Men disappear behind the laws; or rather, if we look for the State, what we encounter are stern, solemn figures wearing gowns and uniforms: officials, magistrates, judges, all who are entrusted with the task of 'guarding' the law and administering it. But officials, magistrates, and judges are not the 'State'. The functions they carry out are established by the laws. Their 'competence', their 'powers', are conferred upon them by law. For the jurist the State can be nothing other than the body of laws in force at a given time and place. The State itself is created by the law. State and law coincide: the State *is* the legal system.

Nor does this state of affairs obtain only in internal relations. On the international level also the State is bound by laws which it must respect in order to exist and to achieve its purposes. These laws may be less precise and effective than those which govern the State's relations with its citizens. But they can certainly be assessed, and are recognized, if not always in codes and by law-courts, by the conscience of all civilized nations. Thus, even in the eyes of international law, the State is a legal structure. Outside the law, force, however thoroughly exercised, has a purely factual existence.

9. In the last case, the notion of the State grows into a wider but also a vaguer vision. On the one hand, there is the fact of social cohesion, of men living together and keeping the laws, often, if not always, of their own free will and with no need of compulsion. On the other hand, there are men whose words, opinions, and actions 'count': electors, whose votes decide a situation, party-leaders who outline the policies to be followed, public figures who have won the esteem and respect of their fellow citizens and in-fluence their behaviour. In both cases this behaviour appears to be due to a sense of obligation, to 'agreement' on the ends to be pur-sued in the common life, on the criteria which fix and condition obedience. This kind of 'agreement' is not merely an important element in the notion of the State; it is the very condition of its existence.

The 'tutelary genii of the city' preside over it: consciousness of a cohesive bond of unity, agreement on purpose, a civic sense, love of country, complete dedication to the common cause. These are goods which neither force alone, nor the impersonal voice of the laws, can succeed in securing. And the 'State' lives by them: the State is the sum of these goods, perhaps, indeed, one of the highest goods which men can hope to attain in their earthly pilgrimage.

10. I propose to distinguish the three approaches that I have outlined by three different names: 'might', 'power', 'authority'.

The State regarded as 'might' or mere force is the State as it is conceived by what is usually called 'political realism': a way of thinking of the State that has a long tradition behind it, and recently, perhaps owing to the circumstances of life today, this has seemed to be the only objective and plausible way of approaching the problem of politics. This traditional way of thinking, although closely bound up with the consideration of force relations existing at a particular moment in history, has contributed a large number of concepts both to the vocabulary and to the theory of politics. Actually, as we shall see, it was the 'realists' who first coined and popularized the word 'State', and who now, surprisingly enough, insist on its total irrelevance.

The State regarded as 'power' is the State of legal theorizing, where power means force qualified by the law, force with the sign 'plus' attached to it. It is not surprising that it was precisely this 'plus' sign that attracted the exclusive attention of the jurists, to whom we owe the refining and further elaboration of the concept of the State and the identification of its essential attributes, first and foremost among them the attribute of 'sovereignty'.

The State regarded as 'authority' is the State that requires a justification which is not, and cannot be, provided by mere force or by the sole exercise of power. The demand for some justification of this kind is a very old one, and one which has provided material for fierce controversy and deep speculation. These in turn have had a strong influence not only on the modern notion of the State, but even on its shape and its structure. If for no other reason than to enable us to understand this peculiar structure, political theory must in the end be guided by philosophical knowledge.

11. The words chosen to describe the three aspects of the problem of the State have the value that mere words have. Their meaning

in common use is far from unequivocal. It is worth remarking, however, that in most European languages various expressions and phrases are used when the State is under discussion, and when an attempt is made to describe the ways in which it manifests its presence and action. *Forza, potere, autorità*; *puissance, pouvoir, autorité*; *Macht, Gewalt, Herrschaft*; might, power, authority: these are all words to whose exact implications no great weight is attached in current speech; even the greatest thinkers sometimes use them at random. Yet it is fair to presume that they refer to different properties, and their meaning should therefore be carefully assessed and examined. Possibly it is only quite recently that the vocabulary of politics has begun to be explored from a strictly semantic standpoint; this kind of exploration has only just started, and may well lead to some interesting discoveries. Thus Weldon remarks that ' "Power" and "Authority" are clearly connected with one another closely. Much unnecessary difficulty has arisen because their logical grammar has been commonly misconstrued. We use them correctly only when we recognize that they are not the names of two different but related entities of which one somehow depends on the other.'[1] This is perfectly true, but Weldon fails to point out that the distinction and relation between *potestas* and *auctoritas* were long ago clearly laid down by no less an 'authority' than Cicero.[2] The correct use of these words is a question not only of logical grammar, but of historical perspective. The concept of power, as well as that of authority, has a long history behind it; in this history lawyers such as Cicero have played a leading part, perhaps an even more important one than that of political philosophers and theorists. It is to them that we must turn for further clarification of our notions about the State. Some of their arguments, indeed, provide illuminating commentaries on most of our problems.

12. Thus we find legal theorists sometimes making a subtle distinction between the 'efficacy', the 'validity', and the 'legitimacy' of the rules which they study—those rules which, taken together (as a system or 'order'), constitute for them the 'reality' of the State. This distinction, I believe, is of the utmost relevance for the theory of the State in general.

[1] T. D. Weldon, *The Vocabulary of Politics*, London, 1953, p. 50.
[2] *De Legibus*, III, 28: 'quum potestas in populo, auctoritas in senatu sit . . .'.

Political realism—the attitude described above, which in its essence consists in seeing the State as simply an expression of force —cannot logically, on its own assumption, consider any attribute important in defining the State except one concerned with its effectiveness or efficacy. States exist or not according as they have the force to impose their commands, both inside and outside their boundaries. Where might is lacking there is no State: there is nothing but chaos and anarchy.

The legal theory of the State, on the other hand, is chiefly concerned with the validity or 'legality' of commands. The power of the State is a legal power, conditioned by the existence and the observance of law, 'valid' only in so far as it is legally determined and appointed. Where law ends, power ends—even though the contrary may not be the case, i.e. there may be rules that are valid, as parts of a legal system (a 'State'), but are not (at any rate for the time being) efficacious. The task of the lawyer, the civil servant, the judge, is to defend legality: legality at all costs, whatever the hardships involved. Indeed, might controlled by bad laws may be better than might exempt from law altogether. The 'certainty' of law is preferable to the utter uncertainty of lawlessness. 'Fidelity to law' has rightly been described as the basic virtue of the legal profession.[1]

A view of this kind has its own dignity and grandeur. Where it errs, and is limited, is in its confusing 'legality' with 'legitimacy'. Perhaps 'confusing' is not the right word. It may well be a deliberate identification. To legalize force, if it means subjecting might to right, is a noble task, a token of humanity and progress. But it does not necessarily follow that all laws should be obeyed nor that all power should be accepted. Surely there is still room for a critical approach to what philosophers used to call the problem of political obligation. We should not assume that we have fully unravelled the notion of the State unless we are able to explain how force, first legalized as power, becomes in turn legitimate as authority.

13. The division here proposed between the three types of problem which can be raised about the 'State' makes no claim to originality. It roughly corresponds to the division most commonly adopted, on the Continent at least, by those who treat of the subject:

[1] L. L. Fuller, 'Positivism and Fidelity to Law—a Reply to Professor Hart', in *71 Harvard Law Review* (1958).

the division, that is, into the socio-political, the legal, and the philosophical concepts of the State.

But to distinguish and contrast the different concepts of the State may be highly misleading. It may be taken to imply that there must be in fact three different entities to which the name 'State' refers, each one with different attributes and functions. Actually, there may be no such 'entity', but only a peculiar and complex situation which calls for our attention. The word 'State' is not the name of a 'thing', says Weldon. But it certainly is a name for a state of affairs in which we are all involved and in which we cannot help being interested. The difference lies in the line of approach, in the image built up in our minds, not in our basic experience. And that experience is the one from which we started, viz. the fact that from the hour of birth to that of death our life is beset by the State's all-pervading and unmistakable presence.

'Man is born free and everywhere he is in chains', wrote Rousseau at the beginning of his famous book—perhaps the most important book ever written about the State in modern times. It may be, and has been, objected that man is not born free, and that it is untrue that he is everywhere in chains. Yet the fact remains that, as Cicero pointed out, man does not belong to a solitary race; that, as Aristotle said, man is a political animal, whose fate is closely dependent on his association with other men. None of us is free to do everything he wishes. Our possibilities are limited. Whether we like it or not, the State is one of the chief artificers of these limitations.

14. The awareness of human dependence thus lies at the root of all our reflections on the nature of the State. This dependence, we often hear it said, constitutes the basic assumption of politics, the essence of political relations. What matters is to keep in mind that dependence is not always, and not necessarily, a matter of force alone. Force, power, and authority are closely interwoven: none of them is easily to be found separated from the other two. The mistake of certain modern theorists is to believe that dependence can be treated as an empirical datum, as something that can be measured and studied without probing the reasons which motivate men's actions, or assessing the values which their choices may possibly indicate. Contemporary political science bears a striking resemblance to certain old notions of the State as merely a relation of force. One of its greatest shortcomings is to neglect

the importance of the legal structure in which the force of the State is contained and by means of which it is most commonly justified and accepted.

But if it is true that the force which belongs to and exists in the State is force qualified by law, it is equally true that the halo which surrounds power extends far beyond the precise limit of legality. Not even a legal notion of the State can solve the problem of the nature of its commands, nor can it provide an adequate reason for their obligatoriness. To explain the one and to account for the other we are forced to admit that the commands of the State are 'invested' with a value that force alone can never possess, and which law in the very act of invoking it recognizes as necessary.

This book proposes to investigate the long and often mysterious ascent that leads from force to authority. The 'investitures' of which I spoke were once displayed in strange and yet visible symbols—cloaks, sceptres, crowns, and diadems—which made them visible and fixed them firmly in men's hearts and imagination. In our days, even when they have not been deliberately abolished, such symbols have almost completely disappeared. But this does not make it any less necessary to try our hand again at answering the age-old and still recurring question: what is it that can transform force into law, fear into respect, coercion into consent—necessity into liberty?

NOTE

Some further explanation of my use of the words 'force' (or 'might'), 'power', and 'authority' may be added here. I have already pointed out that their meaning, even in what purports to be the technical language of modern political science, is far from unequivocal. In fact, the most popular of the three is certainly 'power', a word which is often used indifferently to cover all three of the notions I have tried to distinguish in this Introduction. This in turn makes it necessary to qualify the various types of power by means of further adjectives, such as 'naked', 'institutionalized', 'social', and 'political' power, etc. Strangely enough, 'force' is considered an objectionable word, and is almost unanimously shunned by modern political writers.

Much loose talk could have been avoided had Max Weber's precise definitions been kept in mind, and especially his distinction between *Macht* and *Herrschaft*.[1]

[1] The distinction is to be found in M. Weber's pioneer work, *Wirtschaft und Gesellschaft*, 2nd edn., 1925 (Eng. trans. by A. M. Henderson and T. Parsons, *The Theory of Social and Economic Organization*, London, 1947).

Macht (of which I assume the English word 'might' to be the direct equivalent) does not necessarily refer, according to Weber, merely to physical force, and even less to violence. It means, Weber says, 'the possibility of effecting one's will within a given social relationship', regardless of the means used and in spite of any kind of resistance. In fact, political writers of the past who conceived of the State in terms of pure might were perfectly clear that the dependence of one man upon another man's will may be the result of the most different factors. What matters, on the level of might or force, is that such will is carried out, that commands are obeyed. The emphasis is on effectiveness.

Herrschaft is contrasted with *Macht* primarily in view of the way in which the dependence of man on man is effected. What is relevant here, according to Weber, is that obedience is given to a 'particular command' issued 'by certain people'. As Carl Friedrich has rightly pointed out, 'rule' is the essential characteristic of *Herrschaft*.[1] But its proper equivalent is neither 'rule' nor 'imperative control': it is 'power', power in its strict legal sense, in the sense in which we speak of 'power-conferring rules', or say that public officials have 'powers'. The emphasis is on legality.

Lastly, as far as my approach to authority is concerned, I willingly admit its close relationship to Weber's notion of *legitime Herrschaft*. But I would like to emphasize that authority should be taken to indicate not a situation of fact, but one of obligation. As I see it, authority is not even necessarily linked to the existence of law, of institutionalized power; but it does provide (or should provide) the ultimate ground of its validity—where validity is taken not as a simple descriptive statement, but as a true ought-proposition.

One of the greatest merits (and one of the most surprising results) of modern political theory is, in my view, to have brought out again the importance of the problem of legitimacy in connexion with that of power. It remains to be seen whether this will in the end lead to a renewal of critical interest in the foundations of power—in a word, to a revival of political philosophy.

I shall make no attempt to discuss and evaluate the immense literature that has been poured out during the last decades, if not strictly on the subject of the 'State', at any rate on the subject of law, power, and authority.

Such works as are directly relevant to the points raised in this book will be mentioned in the course of each chapter.

[1] C. J. Friedrich, *Man and his Government*, New York, 1963, p. 180, note 1.

PART ONE

MIGHT

1

THE ARGUMENT OF
THRASYMACHUS

THE oldest expression of the argument of force, or, if not the oldest, the first to be set forth coherently in all its aspects and with all its consequences, is that which Plato puts into the mouth of Thrasymachus, one of the participants in the dialogue of the *Republic*.

The argument is presented by Plato in a dramatic and unforgettable manner. The sophist Thrasymachus, after listening with ill-concealed impatience to the calm discussion barely outlined by Socrates and Polemarchus of the essence of justice, springs at them 'like a wild beast on its prey'. A learned discussion on justice is silly. Justice is only a name for describing that which, in the 'city', the ruler wills and desires. He who commands is the master, and therefore 'sound reasoning gives the conclusion that the same thing is always just—namely what is advantageous to the stronger'.

The statement that force is the most important factor in human society is of course only the first among many controversial arguments put forward by Plato in his inquiry into the nature of justice. Socrates, as we know, has an easy time demolishing each in turn. To Thrasymachus he points out that the ruler may make mistakes as to what is to his advantage, and that mere submission is no final answer to the problem of political obligation. Our interest here is in the various stages by which Thrasymachus is compelled to modify his argument and to present it in different ways.

Replying to the objections of Socrates, Thrasymachus at first admits that there is more in the relation between ruler and ruled than appears at first sight. We must assume a particular knowledge on the part of the ruler, or recognize a particular quality in his will. 'A ruler, so far as he is a ruler, is infallible, and being infallible he prescribes what is best for himself, and this the subject must do.' In other words, Thrasymachus admits that obedience may be the result not only of physical force, but of the skill and ability of the ruler. Socrates pursues the point, observing that skill and ability, if really such, cannot fail to take into account the advantage of the ruled as well as that of the ruler. This Thrasymachus refuses to admit. The art of governing is to him nothing else than the art of imposing one's will, taking advantage if necessary of the innocence, the weakness, and the cowardice of men. What matters is that one will prevails, by whatever means. To talk about justice in relation to the State is therefore irrelevant. If one is determined to do so at any cost, one must recognize that 'injustice, when great enough, is mightier, freer, and more masterly than justice'.

We are here confronted with the most extreme position which 'political realism' can adopt, and has adopted, in the course of successive presentations. Political relations are relations of force. Any statement about them is a statement of fact—of the fact that some rule and others obey—not an assessment of means and of ends, nor a statement of value. The only valuation possible, from this point of view, is one concerning the efficiency of the rule itself, or the adequacy of the means to the ends. Such judgements have nothing to do, they are in fact most often in contrast, with those reached in the name of morality or justice. This is the view we shall see clearly set out by Machiavelli.

Plato's analysis of the argument, however, brings up a number of points which call for some further discussion.

Socrates has succeeded in making Thrasymachus admit that the force of the ruler is not pure physical force, but force accompanied by a particular ability and knowledge. This theme is taken up again in the course of the description of the ideal City, where the task of ruling is entrusted to the 'guardians'. These should be men who 'know' what is the City's good, and have been taught and trained in the art of governing. But, once again, physical force alone does not suffice for that purpose. There is need of a deep knowledge of the motives that lead men to act. Strength must be joined to wisdom. Men are not all capable of seeing the truth, nor is it always a good thing for them to know it. In order to prompt them to obey it is necessary to know how to stir their heart and their imagination much more than their intellect. The guardians may, therefore, when necessary, 'deceive either enemies or citizens for the City's welfare'. They may 'tell falsehoods', instilling beliefs which can arouse enthusiasm and end by being accepted as true. There are lies that are 'useful' or 'necessary' for political coexistence. There is even a magnificent, a 'noble', lie, which ought to convince not only the subjects but the rulers themselves, and which constitutes the cohesive element of the City, the pivot of the harmonious co-operation of the various classes—guardians, warriors, and people. This noble lie is described by Plato as a fable of Phoenician origin. It teaches that men, forged by the earth on which they dwell, must look on their land as their mother and nurse, and on themselves as all brothers; not, however, in the sense that they are all the same, but as formed of different metals: the guardians of gold, the warriors of silver, the farmers and other craftsmen of iron and copper. God himself 'put gold in those who are capable of ruling'. And 'there is an oracle that the City shall perish when it is guarded by iron or copper'.

Plato's theory of the noble lie sheds an interesting sidelight on the manifold aspects of political realism. Plato, it is true, is speaking of the ideal City. But the stress he lays on the importance for the rulers of securing obedience by means of widespread conviction is directly relevant to the analysis of rule itself in terms of effectiveness and efficiency. Persuasion too is an important factor in power. Even the staunchest supporters of force must make allowance for it. In times much nearer to our own the theory of the noble lie has reappeared under new and different labels. It is a favourite argument among writers who propound a factual approach to politics. The noble lie is now termed 'ideology', or 'myth', or 'political formula'. The name is of little importance. What matters is the recognition that force is a very complex phenomenon, and that it cannot and should not be reduced to mere physical compulsion.

Closely connected with the theory of the noble lie, and not unlike it in its relevance to the consideration of the problem of force, is a theory which plays an important part both in Plato and in Aristotle, and which has met with great and recurring success in the development of political thinking. This is the theory that compares the State to an organism—more specifically, to a 'body' or a 'person', where the head represents the ruling function, the limbs the various activities of the State, and single individuals are only the parts or 'organs' of a whole, the docile but necessary instruments for carrying out the orders given by the head.

Used merely as a metaphor, the organic theory—as it is usually called—provides a further illustration of the difficulty of describing political relations in terms of force pure and simple. Indeed, the limbs and the other parts of the body may be said to 'obey' or to 'submit' to the head; but they do so in a manner which is different from, and more complex than, that in which they might be said to submit if they were exposed merely to physical pressure. If anything, to compare the State to an organism means excluding the possibility of its being conceived as a mechanism. In fact the organic metaphor is intended to stress the point that the State cannot be reduced merely to 'force-relations' between individuals. The State is a living, articulate force, apparently different from that of the individuals who compose it. An organism cannot break up into parts without ceasing to be an organism. Its force is not the simple sum of the force of the parts; it is a new force, greater than that of all the parts put together. Above all, a harmonious co-operation between the parts is required in order that the organism may display its full vigour.

Undoubtedly the organic metaphor does suggest an important aspect of the particular kind of force which people have in mind when they think of the State. This explains its success, the recourse had to it by innumerable writers, and its tenacious survival in the vocabulary of politics. Even schoolboys know by heart the apologue of Menenius Agrippa. In this sense, and in this sense only—as a description of the particular kind of co-operation in which the force of the State consists—the metaphor stands up to criticism by un-prejudiced political realism. It does, in fact, provide an instrument for a better understanding of what actually takes place in political relations.

But the organic theory does not stop here, or at any rate it does not stop with a simple statement of fact on the part of some of the most famous authors who used it. The comparison of the State to an organism often turns into a 'personification' of the State, into the assertion that the State is a living social reality. One step further—and this step was certainly taken by Plato as well as by Aristotle—and the State takes on the value of an end with regard to the parts that compose it. To it all the parts 'belong'; from belonging to it, and only by doing so, they derive their true life and significance.

It is difficult to see how propositions of this kind can stand the test of empirical verification. Experience does indeed lead us to recognize the existence of complex social forces. But these forces are always exerted by men, not by abstract entities. On a purely factual plane, the State does not 'exist': it is nowhere to be found, a real person of flesh and blood. Only individuals can be found, whose decisions and actions are said to be the State's because of some peculiar qualification. This can only mean that, in order to 'personify' the State, a number of assumptions are needed. One such assumption, and perhaps the most important, is the existence of a legal system. Like all corporations, the State is said to have capacities and liabilities: but it is the law, and the law alone, which creates and determines them. Another assumption may be avowedly of a metaphysical kind: such is the one that is made when the State, or the 'Whole', or the 'General Will', is pronounced to be the highest value and the ultimate focus of duties. Such assumptions are entirely beyond the perspective of political realism. From a strictly realistic standpoint the State is nothing more than a system of force-relations between individuals. If we want at all costs to use the organic metaphor, we can do so only as Hobbes did, and say that the State is 'an artificial man', not a man in the ordinary sense in which we are men.

The view taken here has not only common sense, but a solid tradition behind it. Lawyers of the past, both Civilians and Canonists, carefully developed a theory of corporate personality, where corporations—and among them the 'State'—were conceived as *personae fictae*, fictitious legal beings. This view was challenged during the nineteenth century by a school of thought which called itself 'realistic', because it denied the fictitious character of corporate bodies, and maintained that groups have a 'real' existence, with a life and a will of their own, distinct from and superior to the parts that compose them. But the stir caused by this theory when it was first propounded in Germany has long since subsided. Legal theory does not seem to have derived much benefit from its unwarranted assertions. Neither has such a thing as 'group personality' ever been proved to exist by means of factual investigation. Looking at it in the perspective of time, it is not difficult to unmask the organic theory of the State as the ideology it certainly was: as one of the many ways in which, during the last hundred years, the attempt was made to belittle and to discredit the value of the individual in political life, thus paving the way for the tribalism which bore such bitter fruits for a later generation.

By exploding the fallacy of organicism, even at the cost of

reducing politics to mere individual force (as is the case with Machiavelli), true political realism can render great services to political philosophy. Its modern heir, political science, does not fail to give due attention to all 'social' manifestations of force (to mass-phenomena, to collective psychology, or whatever else they are called). But as a strictly empirical enterprise it can never admit that a personified abstraction of this force (the 'State' as much as any other 'institution' or corporation) should be assumed to be a reality distinct and different from those with whom force ultimately originates and to whom it applies, individual human beings.

REFERENCES

Plato, *Republic*, Book I, 336–44; II, 382; III, 389, 414–15; V, 459 (quot. from A. D. Lindsay's trans.); *Laws*, Book II, 661 ff. Aristotle, *Politics*, Book I, chs. i and ii (1252^a–1253^a) (quoted from Sir Ernest Barker's trans.); Hobbes, *Leviathan*, Introduction and ch. 16.

On the role of ideology in politics the outstanding work is still K. Mannheim, *Ideology and Utopia*, London, 1936. On Plato's theory of the 'noble lie' as an anticipation of the modern notion of ideological propaganda: K. R. Popper, *The Open Society and its Enemies*, 1st edn., London, 1945, vol. I, ch. 8, as well as R. H. S. Crossman, *Plato To-day*, London, 1937, p. 130. *Contra*, and in defence of Plato: J. Wild, *Plato's Modern Enemies and the Theory of Natural Law*, Chicago, 1953, ch. 2, sect. iv; and F. M. Cornford's Note on *Rep.* 414 in his recent translation of the dialogue, Oxford, 1941.

On the 'organic theory' in Germany the relevant information can be found in R. Emerson, *State and Sovereignty in Modern Germany*, New Haven, 1928; but the most brilliant assessment of its background and implications is still that made by Maitland long ago (in the Introduction to his translation of Gierke's *Political Theories of the Middle Age*, 1st edn., Cambridge, 1900) and later taken up and developed, still on the same lines, by E. Barker (in the Introduction to Gierke's *Natural Law and the Theory of Society*, Cambridge, 1934).

Two recent articles may be found very useful and stimulating: H. J. McCloskey, 'The State as an Organism, as a Person, and as an End in itself', in *The Philosophical Review*, 1963; and A. Ross, 'On the Concepts "State" and "State Organs" in Constitutional Law', in *Scandinavian Studies in Law*, 1961.

2

REALISM AND PESSIMISM

I have hitherto assumed that political realism is practically tantamount to a purely empirical approach to political matters. Its conclusions, it would seem, are warranted by factual verification. A realist is supposed to be a man who does not shun the truth, and the truth seems to be that force is the ultimate test of all States and governments. It may be objected that this is not really the case; that, in his quest for, and in his selection of, facts, the realist is not entirely unbiassed. His attitude is shaped, as it were, by a preconceived idea of how things happen in the world, and by a peculiar and by no means indisputable way of conceiving human nature. It is only because men are all thought of as wicked, or at least as possessed by an insatiable desire to impose their will upon others, that might, not right, is believed to determine their mutual relations. Only an incurable pessimist can take pleasure in tearing away the veil from power and authority in order to expose the sad or squalid reality hidden behind them. He alone can accept the judgement which the poet Manzoni puts in the mouth of his dying hero Adelchi: '. . . a cruel force possesses the world, and makes men call it justice.'

It is, of course, possible to reply to an objection of this kind that, where empirical verification is concerned, the question is one of fact, not of opinion. It is therefore for those who attack the realists for painting an unattractive picture of politics to prove that they are wrong: indeed, as we shall see, this is the only effective way of meeting the Machiavelli 'scandal'. In any case the objection does not affect the line of argument followed so far, since from the outset I have expressly underlined the view that there are different lines of approach to the problems of politics. But the fact remains that a realistic notion of the State does often correspond to a pessimistic conception of politics, and that pessimism in its turn is nearly always conducive to realism. Men who, for one reason or another, take a dim view of other men are bound to look at the State as essentially an organization of force. A case in point is that of St. Augustine in the *City of God*, a book which, strangely enough, affords a clear illustration of political realism long before Machiavelli.

St. Augustine certainly never intended in his most famous work to deal specifically with political matters. He is faced with the problem of the State within the framework of a grandiose interpretation of history. Moreover, the political problem arises in the *City of God* in connexion with the strictly apologetic purpose of the book, the purpose of refuting the accusation that Christianity was the cause of Rome's ruin. Last, but not least, St. Augustine, unlike Plato and Aristotle, starts from well-defined religious and theological premisses. The idea that human nature has been corrupted by sin and that ultimately all power comes from God are the basic assumptions of his approach both to history and to politics.

In point of fact, the problem of the State for St. Augustine is the problem of that particular State in which all the political experience of his time was summed up, the Roman Empire. If all power comes from God, there should be no doubt that the Empire was ordained by Him. The 'virtues' of the Romans were rewarded by 'the glory of the most excellent empire'. But what a price was paid for this glory! Wars, slaughter, wickedness of every kind. And how can the virtues which secured the greatness of Rome properly be called virtues, if true justice is to be found only in Christ and in the observance of His law? Judged by this absolute standard of justice, such virtues and such greatness can only be seen as illusions. Liberty, power, and glory of country should not lure man away from what alone matters, the salvation of his soul. 'As far indeed as this mortal life of ours is concerned, a life which is lived out in a few short days, what does it matter under whose government man lives, since he must die, provided that those who govern do not force him to do evil?' Let those who lust for power grasp it: politics is a sordid, wicked affair. The State is the faithful image of that wickedness: 'when justice is absent (*remota iustitia*), what else are kingdoms than large gangs of robbers? and what else indeed are such gangs than rudimentary kingdoms?'

Here, with this famous apostrophe, we seem to have reached the deepest pit in the depreciation of politics. But it is hardly necessary to point out that St. Augustine's meaning is far from being clear and unambiguous. His words may be taken to imply that there is only a difference of degree between the State and a criminal undertaking: both are organizations founded on force and devised to coerce men into doing what they would not otherwise do. If this were the case, then the State would in fact be nothing else than the visible embodiment of the Devil's city. Nothing good can come out of it. Better leave it to consume in its own flames, to run into self-destruction. But the sentence can also be given an entirely different meaning. It may be taken to imply that there is one way of redeeming the State from evil: that of making it an instrument of the City of God by making it subject to justice.

It is indeed hard to say which of the two is the correct interpretation. Ever since St. Augustine, Christian political thought seems to have oscillated between these two opposite poles. There is in fact a note of despair in St. Augustine's words which is in keeping with the pessimism of his approach to history and politics. And it is worth remarking that later writers who shared his pessimism were also emphatic in stressing that force, not justice, is the essence of the State. Take Luther, for example: to him politics is the rule of the sword. The Christian must take refuge in the inner world of his conscience; his only right is that of suffering and bearing his cross. Princes are the 'scourges', the 'executioners' of God, needed 'to tame evil-doers, and, by a reign of terror, to make external order and peace prevail in a world peopled by corrupt men'. The soldier and the hangman are the pillars of society. As an indication of God's wrath war itself is divine. Such views are by no means the exclusive monopoly of Protestants. A Catholic writer, de Maistre, shared them to the full. Pessimism seems to have brought these writers to take the most depressing, and yet the most realistic, view of the hardships of politics. Once again, it is for those who refuse to share that view to prove that these writers were wrong, to show that factual evidence does not justify such purely negative judgements.

If the *City of God* only provided an illustration of the close connexion between pessimism and realism, the importance of its contribution to the theory of the State could still be in doubt, and the work itself could be thought politically rather shallow. But it contains something more, something of remarkable importance. It contains one of the first strictly factual definitions of the State, where all consideration of values is left out and the attempt is made to determine the constituent elements of the State without any reference to its ends or to the 'goods' which it may or may not embody. In this sense, the realistic approach provides a startling anticipation of modern political science, where value-judgements are deliberately set aside or put within brackets. St. Augustine's definition of the State is, in the full sense of the phrase, an 'ethically neutral' definition.

Needless to say, the path by which that definition is reached is quite different from that which a modern political scientist would follow. We have seen how St. Augustine's pessimism led him to a drastic depreciation of the State, a depreciation reflected in his indifference to the purely earthly 'virtues' that ensure its greatness, and in his equation of the State—'in the absence of justice'—to a simple organization of force. In interpreting the political aspects of Roman history, St. Augustine finds a formidable polemical tool in a definition of the State taken from Cicero,[1] where justice is described as essential not only to the justification but to the very existence of the State. If justice, he points out, is a condition of the State's existence, then Rome ceased very early to be, perhaps cannot even claim ever to have been, a State. For even admitting that it was one in remote antiquity Cicero himself recognized that, once political life began to be corrupted, the very quality of the State was lost. 'Not by any accident, but because of our vices, though we retain the name of the State, we no longer are one.'

It is precisely this paradoxical and yet inescapable conclusion that leads St. Augustine to review the whole question of the definition of the State. The problem is, in fact, to decide whether it is possible to understand political reality independently of any moral or religious considerations, to define the State in such a way as to explain why Rome, even while practising injustice and ignoring all Christian standards, could nevertheless be considered and thought of as a State. On this point St. Augustine is quite categorical. 'According to more plausible definitions, Rome, in its own way, was a State: a State that was better administered by the ancient Romans than by the later ones.' He maintains that a definition

---

[1] 'Est igitur, inquit Africanus, res publica res populi: populus autem non omnis hominum coetus quoquo modo congregatus, sed coetus multitudinis iuris consensu et utilitatis communione sociatus.'

Commenting upon this definition, St. Augustine maintains that by *iuris consensus* Cicero must be taken to mean 'respect for justice' (*ubi ergo iustitia vera non est, nec ius potest esse*). But the phrase can also be translated more simply by 'consent to law', and in this case Cicero's definition takes on a quite different meaning. For a further discussion of this point see below, p. 75–77.

of this kind is not only possible but necessary. All that is needed is to focus attention on the fact of organization, on the bond that holds the State together and on which its force depends, rather than on the requirement of justice. This force is nothing else than that of human wills banded together in the pursuit of common aims. Such aims may vary greatly. Their goodness or badness is irrelevant.

This emphasis on the bond of cohesion which constitutes both the force and the condition of existence of the State is in fact already clearly evident in the development of the disconcerting simile drawn between the State and an association for criminal ends. In that earlier passage St. Augustine had described this similarity in further detail. Here is an assemblage of men governed by one head (*imperio principis regitur*), held together by mutual agreement (*pacto societatis adstringitur*), observing a law in the division of spoils (*placiti lege praeda dividitur*). It suffices that this band should grow strong enough to make itself master of a territory, and to establish itself there, for it to be perfectly entitled to be called a State (*evidentius regni nomen assumit*). St. Augustine recalls the answer made by the pirate captured by Alexander the Great, who asked him what right he had to infest the seas: 'the same right that you have to infest the world. But because I do it in a small boat I am called a robber, while because you do it with a large fleet you are called an emperor.' All this argument implies that, by respecting justice, the State itself can and will in the end be justified. In the absence of justice—*remota iustitia*—political association is worth little more than an association for crime. Nevertheless, by the very fact of its existence, it is already, it is still always, a State.

Compared with this striking and penetrating analysis of the different elements that form the structure of the State (government, agreement, and law), the definition St. Augustine proposes as more 'plausible' may sound disappointingly short. In fact, it is an exact counterpart to the one given by Cicero, where the bonds that unite a people into a State (*res publica* = *res populi*) were seen to consist in the respect for justice (*iuris consensus*) and in the existence of a common interest (*utilitatis communio*). For St. Augustine neither justice nor utility is what determines the existence of a 'people', and hence of a State. The simple conscious convergence of wills towards an end is enough. 'A people is an assemblage of rational beings linked together by shared convictions about the things they desire.'[1] A definition of this kind makes it possible to understand why 'the Roman people was a people and their State undoubtedly a State'. They were so always, even when they neither knew nor practised justice: the requisite of justice simply does not enter into the definition of the State. This certainly does not mean that St. Augustine belittles or denies the importance of justice—far from it. But structurally the State is there whenever there is an organization of rational beings for the pursuance of a common end. St. Augustine's definition may be critized as too concise to be adequate. It does not distinguish the State from other human associations. It does not account for the complex organization which the State requires. But it certainly remains a perfect example of a 'neutral' definition. The element of value is entirely absent.

The way in which St. Augustine presents his new definition in the *City of God*, where he goes to some length to prove its advantages, shows clearly that it does not represent a casual and isolated statement, but is the fruit of mature reflection on his part. This definition, he points out, not only enables us to recognize the existence of a 'people', and therefore of a 'State', even where the requirement of justice is lacking; it also allows us to estimate the quality of the State and its degree of goodness or badness. This is the point, we should say, where a judgement of value takes place. If the essence of the State lies in a shared conviction (*concors communio*) about the ends to be pursued, it is these ends that must be considered when the State is judged or is to be justified. 'Indeed, in order to appraise the character of a people, we must look at the things which it desires.' History provides us in Rome with an example of a State which, starting from a relatively high level of virtue, descended to the lowest depths of corruption without ceasing to be a State, until, owing to the wickedness of its citizens, the sharing of convictions, the *concordia* itself, disappeared. Then, and then only, can the Roman State be said to have vanished. And the same can be said, according to St. Augustine, of all the great empires known to history, the Greek, the Egyptian, and the Assyrian alike. They ceased to be 'States' when their rule ceased to be effective.

The neutral definition of the State which can be found in the

---

[1] 'Populus est coetus multitudinis rationalis rerum quas diligit concordi communione sociatus.'

City of God is a singular, isolated episode in the history of political thought. Its singularity emerges above all in the fact that the political writers who followed St. Augustine—at any rate the Christian political writers of the Middle Ages—seem to have ignored it almost deliberately. The reason for its lack of success, in contrast with the favourable acceptance of Cicero's definition, must be sought chiefly in the changed attitude to politics which characterizes medieval thought. The concept of the State and the Christian ideal of justice ceased to be contradictory from the moment when the State itself became christianized. Indeed, the very reason for a neutral definition disappeared at this stage. Possibly the full value of St. Augustine's account is only appreciated today in a political climate which in large measure resembles that in which he lived. This does not involve an unqualified acceptance of the doctrine of 'ethical neutrality' in the social and political field. What matters is to realize that the study of human behaviour is one thing, and the attempt to value and justify it another. Once the State is described as a complex of social forces, the problem remains of understanding how those forces can be legalized into power, and how power in its turn is accepted, not merely as a fact, but as a holder of authority and a source of obligation.

REFERENCES

Cicero, *De Re Publica*, I. 25, 39. St. Augustine, *De Civitate Dei*, II, 21; IV, 4; V, *passim*; XIX, 21–24. Luther, *Von weltlicher Obrigkeit*, 1523. J. de Maistre, *Considérations sur la France*, 1796, ch. iii; *Les Soirées de Saint-Pétersbourg*, 1821, I and VII.

For the contrasting interpretations of St. Augustine's political theory, cf. R. W. and A. J. Carlyle, *A History of Medieval Political Theory in the West*, vol. I, Edinburgh, 1903, part iii, ch. 14; J. N. Figgis, *The Political Aspects of St. Augustine's 'City of God'*, London, 1921; C. H. McIlwain, *The Growth of Political Thought in the West*, New York, 1932, pp. 154–60.

On St. Augustine's realistic approach to politics, R. Niebuhr, 'Augustine's Political Realism' in *Christian Realism and Political Problems*, London, 1954.

On the notion of 'ethical neutrality', as described above, see M. Weber, *The Methodology of the Social Sciences*, trans. and ed. by E. A. Shils and H. A. Finch, Glencoe, Ill., 1949.

3

THE STATE—A NEOLOGISM

I T may well seem that in the preceding pages I have been deliberately ambiguous in using a modern word, 'State', to describe a condition of affairs for which, to be precise, Plato, Aristotle, Cicero, and St. Augustine (to mention only the authors with whom we have dealt so far) have quite different names: *polis*, *res publica*, *civitas*, *regnum*. It is time now to ask whether these words describe something common to them all, and to examine the credentials of the modern word, which for the sake of convenience I have hitherto substituted for them without proper warrant.

First let us consider why the writers of antiquity, as well as those of the Middle Ages, used different words for 'State' when dealing with political matters. There are two main reasons for this. The first is that the situation to which they referred was different in each case, or at any rate for each of the periods in which they were active. Greek political experience, at least in the classic age, was summed up in the *polis*, the city-state, a small and exclusive concern, which both Plato and Aristotle assumed to be the highest expression of the common good, that is, the embodiment of a moral value. In modern language the *polis* can only be described as both a 'State' and a 'Church'. The whole destiny of man was involved in the State. We are apt to forget this, when in present-day speech we use a Greek word, 'Politics', to indicate merely the science and art of government.

The Roman horizon was much wider and more complex than the Greek—not only because it broadened out from the restricted vision of the City-state to that of the universal framework of the Empire, but because it introduced into the notion of the State an element which had remained at least partially unknown to Greek thought—the legal element. From this point of view Cicero's definition of *res publica* is particularly significant. The accent is here shifted from the goal to the structure of the State; *ius* is the distinguishing feature of political associations.

As far as St. Augustine is concerned, his choice of words is sometimes perplexing. He does in fact use different terms such as *res publica, civitas, regnum* in referring to political matters; but the definitions he gives of each of them in turn are almost identical. These are, indeed, precisely the terms which recur most often in medieval political writings, but with different meanings according to the different circumstances to which they apply, to the great variety of forms or types of human association. In medieval political language *civitas* usually referred to the city-state which flourished in various parts of Europe, and more particularly in Italy. *Regnum* was used to describe the territorial monarchies in process of formation from the time of the high Middle Ages onwards. *Respublica* was reserved in most cases for describing a wider community, the *respublica christiana* which united all believers in one sheepfold. The angle of vision determined whether that community was the Church or the Empire.

Down to a certain date the word 'State' is missing altogether. It was missing—and this is the second reason why other words were used in its stead—because it had not yet been coined, or, more exactly, because it had not yet acquired a definite, precise meaning. In its modern acceptation the word 'State' is a new word, found in the various European languages only in a period relatively near our own. Its acceptance was linked with certain factual circumstances, with the fact above all that it referred to a new state of affairs, one that differed in many respects from that which was visible to the eyes and imagination of the political writers of antiquity and of the Middle Ages.

But if medieval political writers did not as yet recognize either in name or substance the 'State' in its modern acceptation, it is all the more interesting to see the effort they made to grasp the essence of the new political reality which was beginning to take shape during the last centuries of the Middle Ages. Many of the characteristics we now associate with the State were undoubtedly there, and did not escape their notice. The expedient to which they generally had recourse was to extend the Aristotelian notion of the *polis* to include the city-state and the territorial kingdom in a single category. Significantly enough, *polis* is usually translated in medieval texts by *civitas vel regnum*. But by the very act of extending the Aristotelian notion to cover a new experience, that experience came, so to speak, to be seen and interpreted in an entirely new light: the Greek political ideal made its mark on medieval political reality. From the day—about the middle of the thirteenth century—when Aristotle's *Politics* began once more to be read and studied, a startling change took place in political thought. Emphasis and interest shifted from the unity of the Christian community to the plurality of separate communities into which that unity had split or was in the process of splitting: the *civitates* and the *regna*. To each of them individually was ascribed that character of a perfect, self-sufficing community which Aristotle had reserved for the *polis*. The phrase *communitas perfecta et sibi sufficiens* is the description which in medieval political theory most nearly approaches the modern notion of the State. Not, however, until the heyday of the Renaissance would the word finally be found to provide a new conceptual framework for the new situation.

There is a widely held opinion that the chief merit for having definitely fixed and popularized the modern meaning of the term 'State' belongs to Niccolò Machiavelli. This opinion is certainly in great measure justified, but it should not be accepted without reservations. In fact, the word 'State' seems to have entered the vocabulary of politics before Machiavelli. And by Machiavelli himself the word was at times used indiscriminately, with different meanings which can be traced to preceding linguistic usage. I shall make no attempt to describe in detail how these meanings gradually evolved and finally settled down to that particular sense in which the word 'State' is now accepted in all civilized languages. Here are a few relevant points which can be gleaned from those authors who have made a special study of the subject.

All philologists agree that the remote origin of the word 'State' is the Latin word *status*, a neutral word meaning condition or way of existence. The first indication of its use in a political sense is usually traced to low and medieval Latin, where instances can be found of *status* as equivalent to prosperity, well-being, sound order of a particular community—Church, Empire, or Kingdom. The most often quoted example of this use is a well-known text of the Emperor Justinian, *statum reipublicae sustentamus*. But countless instances could be drawn, if necessary, from medieval sources, such as *precari pro statu ecclesiae* or *regni, tractare de statu ecclesiae* or *populi christiani*, etc.

Over and above this still very vague and general meaning, two further and more precise qualifications are relevant. The first is the one that appears with the use of the word *status* to describe a particular social or economic condition, and hence a particular category or class of people. This is one of the meanings the word *état* (originally *estat*) takes and keeps for a long time in French (*États généraux*, *Tiers État*), while in other languages other words are used to express it (e.g. the German *Stand*). In English, of course, both *status* and *estate* still convey this original meaning.

But another and, for our purposes, much more important qualification of *status* is that revealed by its use to describe the particular legal structure of a given community, what we should nowadays call its constitutional components. This meaning may well have been inspired, as some authors maintain, by a famous text in the *Digest*, where 'public law' (*ius publicum*) is defined as *quod ad statum rei romanae spectat*.[1] Whatever its source, the point is that the Latin *status* and the Italian *stato* are increasingly used in this sense in later medieval sources: thus Dante, for example, in *Inferno* xxvii, 54 contrasts a 'free state' with a tyranny. The gradual fining down of the term 'State' to the sense in which it is used today is here clearly apparent. The fact, however, that the word was still used indiscriminately to indicate the actual exercise of power or government, and the people or territory on which a particular power or government is exerted (e.g. the 'State' of the Church, the 'mainland State' of Venice, etc.) shows that we are still considerably remote from a precise use of it.

If we keep all these different usages in mind, we are not surprised that Machiavelli should not always be coherent in his use of the word 'State'. All the different meanings we have listed so far can be traced in his works, sometimes even within the same context. According to some very authoritative scholars, Machiavelli's language and style are more plain and direct in *The Prince*, less hampered by literary tradition, than in any other of his writings. It is certainly there that we find the most decisive evidence of a new meaning of 'State', hardly ever noticeable in earlier sources. In fact, from the very first sentence of *The Prince* the term 'State' appears to be used to indicate a collective unit whose shape and form of government may vary, but which, in one essential feature,

[1] This sentence, as well as that of Justinian quoted above, are further discussed on p. 80–81.

remains the same throughout and is the proper object of politics. 'All States, all Dominions that have had, or now have rule over men, have been, and are, either Republiques or Principalities.' It looks as if Machiavelli was deliberately using here a new word to describe a new state of affairs, that of the contemporary world with its two types of 'State', republics and monarchies. Many further examples could be gleaned from *The Prince* to illustrate this entirely new and modern use of the word: for instance where Machiavelli contrasts the 'new' States with the old ones, or where he describes Italy as divided into 'several States', or where he praises the Italians for their knowledge of 'matters of State', that very knowledge which—in a celebrated letter to his friend Vettori —he boasts of having acquired in his long service of the Florentine republic.

It would of course be absurd to expect a full-blown definition of the State at this stage and from such an unsystematic writer as Machiavelli. But it seems fair to say that we certainly find in his work the word 'State' used in connexion with what will, after him, be recognized as the basic and essential feature of the State, viz., that of being an organization endowed with the capacity of exerting and controlling the use of force over certain people and within a given territory. We should also not be too wide of the mark in supposing that it may well have been due to the extraordinarily wide diffusion of Machiavelli's work that the word finally came to acquire its recognized special meaning in the political vocabulary of all modern nations. As far as Italy at any rate is concerned, this is undoubtedly the case; while in other European countries the final acceptance of the word seems to have been slower and to have met with some opposition.

In these other countries, in fact, the word 'State' had to compete with other terms derived from earlier usage or transferred to the vernacular from Latin. Thus, for example, Bodin, a French author of capital importance in the development of the modern theory of the State, still entitles his work *De la République* (1576) and describes the State by this name. In spite of some interesting indications to the contrary, the word *état* retains in his work its narrower meaning of condition or order (e.g. *estat d'une république, l'estat de la France*). Similarly, English writers of this period normally describe the State (and it is certainly already possible to speak of the State in its modern sense in the England of that time) with

expressions such as 'realm', 'body politic', or 'commonwealth'—
the latter being a very exact translation of the Latin *res publica*.
Although the word 'State' is already beginning to gain wide cur-
rency in international relations, it is only with Hobbes that we find
the words *civitas*, 'commonwealth', 'State', purposely and expressly
equated (*Leviathan*, Introduction). After Hobbes, with Pufendorf
and his translator Barbeyrac, the word 'State' (*status = état*)
becomes definitely part of political theory; while, owing probably
to Montesquieu's great authority (*Esprit des Lois*, 1748, Book II),
the use of the word 'republic' is now restricted, as Machiavelli
had already restricted it, to indicating a particular type of State,
different from, and opposed to, monarchy.

Perhaps even more significant is the fact that in England the
name of 'commonwealth' should have been officially adopted after
the fall of the monarchy. Consequently, this particular word was
bound to fall into disrepute after the Restoration. Not so seriously,
however, as to deter Locke from continuing to use it, albeit with
a clear note of apology.

By commonwealth, [he writes in the *Second Treatise of Government*,
1690 (§ 133)], I must be understood all along to mean, not a democracy,
or any form of government, but any independent community which the
Latins signified by the word *civitas*, to which the word which best
answers in our language is commonwealth, and most properly expresses
a society of men, which community or city in English does not, for there
may be subordinate communities in a government. . . . And therefore to
avoid ambiguity I crave leave to use the word commonwealth in that
sense, in which I find it used by King James the First, and I take it to
be its genuine signification; which if anybody dislike, I consent with
him to change it for a better.

As a matter of fact, the word 'State' does not seem to have
fared as well in England and in English-speaking countries as it
did on the Continent. A foreign observer is apt to be struck even
today by the extraordinary circumlocutions resorted to in English
to indicate what in his own language would be called 'the State'
without any doubt or equivocation. There may be deep-rooted
traditions for this, as well as an inclination to use plain and simple
speech whenever possible. As far as technical language is concerned, Maitland pointed out long ago that the word State 'was
slow to find a home in English law-books'. Indeed, a Statute of

1887 actually had to explain that phrases such as 'Service of the Crown', 'Service of Her Majesty', and 'Service of the State', all had the same meaning. Americans, on the other hand, call 'Federal Government' what Continentals would call the 'State', and 'States' what certainly do not deserve that name, at any rate in international usage. In common speech both Americans and Englishmen, unlike the Latin races, hardly ever mention the State: they prefer to talk about the government, or the people, or the nation, or the country. Nevertheless, the word is to be found, and is given an honourable place, in the *Oxford Dictionary*.

So then the question remains, as I put it at the beginning of this chapter: how far can the use of the word 'State' in current phrases like 'the notion', or 'the theory of the State', be justified, especially in dealing with periods when it was not yet known, let alone accepted? Let us admit at once that, if the use of this modern word should lead us to ignore the substantial differences which exist between the political structures of those periods and our own, then to speak of the 'State' in referring to the Greek *polis*, or to the *res romana*, or to the medieval *communitas perfecta*, would have to be condemned out of hand as an abuse of language. But this abuse vanishes, or is at least greatly diminished, when the word 'State' is accepted as a brief, almost a shorthand, indication of what is common to these different experiences. This common element is the basic fact of organized force, in the precise sense constantly underlined by those writers whom, for convenience sake, I have called political realists. In order to understand the differences between, say, the Greek *polis* and the modern State we must forsake the level of political realism altogether. These differences may be of a legal kind, of structure and distribution of power. They may be differences of values and ends, such as are of interest to political philosophers. But the first step in political theory is and remains the recognition of the fact that, in order to achieve those ends, in order to set up those structures, force has to be resorted to, and must be effective. The notion of the State, however different its versions, always comes back ultimately to the successful carrying through of man's will, to a relation of command and obedience in a social context.

Such considerations, or others of a similar kind, are the necessary introduction to reading Machiavelli, the consummate theorist of political realism. They also explain why the notion of the State, conceived in terms of pure force, plays such a capital role in his whole *Weltanschauung*. What is new in Machiavelli is not in fact his way of looking at political experience. The recognition that, in a specific situation, force can be, and is, the *ultima ratio* is not new. Thrasymachus and St. Augustine had both placed force at the core of political matters, though each had done so in a very different spirit. Nor was the method of 'effectual truth', which Machiavelli proclaimed as his own, entirely unknown before him, although no one had ever applied it so ruthlessly and so thoroughly. What was new was the state of affairs which Machiavelli described and from which he drew his conclusions. What was new was, in fact, the 'modern State'—the 'new principality' as he called it, in which, to use his own words, 'the difficulties consist': a situation where, for the first time, politics were approached, practised, and analysed, without any concern other than that of effectiveness. Which amounts to saying (and it has been said many times!) that Machiavelli was a product of his age, and also that, of his age, he is the supreme interpreter.

REFERENCES

The brief sketch traced in this chapter is based on the work of a number of authors to whom I gratefully acknowledge my indebtedness.

Among older authors, the following must especially be mentioned: O. Gierke, *Political Theories of the Middle Age*, trans. by F. W. Maitland, Cambridge, 1900/22; F. W. Maitland, 'The Crown as Corporation', in *Collected Papers*, vol. III, Cambridge, 1911; J. N. Figgis, 'Respublica Christiana', Appendix I to *Churches in the Modern State*, 2nd edn., London, 1914; H. C. Dowdall, 'The Word "State" ' in *39 Law Quarterly Review*, no. 153, Jan. 1923; F. Ercole, 'Lo Stato nel pensiero del Machiavelli' in *La Politica di Machiavelli*, Rome, 1926.

Among more recent works the following are particularly helpful: R. Derathé, 'État, souveraineté, gouvernement', Appendix I to *J. J. Rousseau et la science politique de son temps*, Paris, 1950; R. T. Marshall, 'Studies in the Political and Socio-religious Terminology of the *De Civitate Dei*', in *Patristic Studies*, LXXXVI, 1952; F. Chiappelli, *Studi sul linguaggio del Machiavelli*, Florence, 1952; F. Crosara, 'Respublica e Respublicae. Cenni terminologici dall'età romana all'XI secolo', in *Atti del Congresso Internazionale di Diritto Romano e di Storia del Diritto*, vol. IV, 1953; F. Chabod, 'Stato, nazione, patria nel linguaggio del Cinquecento', in Appendix to *L'idea di Nazione*, Bari, 1961; M. Isnardi, 'Appunti per la storia di État, République, Stato', in *Rivista Storica Italiana*, vol. LXXIV, 1962; Gaines Post, *Studies in Medieval Legal Thought. Public Law and the State, 1100–1322*, Princeton, 1964, part ii, chs. v–x.

Quotations from Machiavelli's *Prince* (and *Discourses*) are, and will be, given, whenever possible, in Edward Dacres's translation (1636–40).

4

THE 'NEW PRINCIPALITY' AND THE METHOD OF 'EFFECTUAL TRUTH'

THE 'new principality' was not, of course, the modern State. It was not even the only type of State with which Machiavelli was concerned and which he submitted to analysis. But among the various kinds of monarchy it is the one which illustrates most vividly and emphatically the problem of force, which for Machiavelli was the central problem of politics. Almost the whole of the small treatise, which in spite of its brevity, or perhaps because of it, has contributed more than anything else to the posthumous fame of the Florentine Secretary, is devoted to the new principality.

It would indeed be hard to deny that Machiavelli put the idea of force at the centre of his political vision. For him force is not only the condition of existence of the State. It is its peculiar countersign, almost its constituent element. In fact, Machiavelli comes very near to distinguishing clearly between 'force' and 'power', as, for example, when he says 'He who acquires dominion (*imperio*) but lacks strength (*forze*) is doomed to ruin.' The reason is that the State is force before it is power. Defence and offence abroad, obedience and discipline at home, are decisive factors in its life and survival. The statesman who neglects force 'sins' against the State, as those cowardly princes sinned against Italy when they allowed foreigners to invade their country and to 'conquer it with chalk'. Let the reader turn to Chapter 12 of *The Prince* or to the closing lines of *The Art of War* if he cares to know how strongly Machiavelli felt on this point. For my part, among the countless other quotations which come to mind, there is one in *The Prince* which I find particularly significant. For in it Machiavelli sums up the basic theme which he had already developed years before in a short political memorandum. At that time it had been a question of persuading his reluctant fellow citizens to do their duty for the defence of the Florentine Republic. Now, in the terse language of the political treatise, the same argument was hammered out again for the benefit of the new principality. But, almost word for word, the lesson is the same: the State must be strong if it is to face the many odds that oppose it. 'A prince ought to have two feares, the one from within, in regard of his subjects, the other from abroad, in regard of his mighty neighbours; from these he defends himself by good armes and good friends, and always he shall have good friends if he have good armes; and all things shall always stand sure at home, when those abroad are firme.' In a world dominated by the iron law of force, and therefore constantly threatened with anarchy, the State represents the only element of cohesion, order, and safety.

But Machiavelli was well aware that the force which holds the State together and assures its safety is not a purely material force. 'A long experience of moderne affaires, and a continual reading of those of the Ancients' had taught him that there were innumerable types of State where might (*potenzia*) and safety (*securtà*) were assured not only by 'good weapons' (*buone armi*) but by 'virtuous traditions' (*virtuose successioni*). Not all principalities were 'wholly new'; in 'those which are hereditary and accustomed to the family of their prince', in addition to the force of traditional loyalties, there can exist 'an infinite number of good institutions' (as in the case of the French monarchy), which are 'the reason of the safety of the King and the Kingdom'. In republics, where 'the name of liberty is powerful', the very love of liberty is the chief reason of their 'greater vitality' and therefore of their indomitable force, as was clearly shown by Sparta, Rome, and the 'rough' but 'very free' cities of Switzerland. It was only in the new principality that the possession of material force and its exercise by one man over others were seen to constitute the decisive factor. 'States that suddenly fall into a mans hand, as all other things in nature that spring and grow quickly, cannot well have taken roots, nor have made their correspondencys so firm, but that the first storme that takes them, ruines them.' But even in the case of the new principality, material force was only an instrument of which the prince would make more or less adequate use in accordance with his own statesmanship (*virtù*). In spite of his metaphor taken from nature, the State was not for Machiavelli a 'reality' of the same order as the reality of nature. It was a creation of man's, a 'work of art', according to Burckhardt's classical definition: a creation limited and conditioned by the very same factual elements with which and on which man works, just as the *virtù* of the prince, however outstanding, was conditioned by the favour or hostility of mysterious *fortuna*.

Certainly the 'new principality' is not the modern State. On the contrary, it was a typical product of the Italy in which Machiavelli lived and worked. The intrinsic weakness of Machiavelli's thought lies in the exclusive stress laid on the creative and governing skill, on the *virtù* of the prince, just as it was the weakness of the Italian political creations of his time, fated to crumble as soon as they clashed with other States more firmly rooted in their foundations and traditions. But, as Professor Chabod pointed out with great penetration in one of his admirable studies of Machiavelli, 'in creating *The Prince* in order to satisfy a passionate desire and to fulfil an immediate purpose, Machiavelli cannot have suspected that he was thus handing over to Europe the blueprint of two hundred years of her history'. The States that were to dominate Western history in the centuries following Machiavelli were not exclusive creations of one man. They were slowly produced by historical evolution. They had 'roots and correspondencys' in their native soil which were to enable them to stand up like solid oaks to new unexpected storms. And yet the princes who ruled them were all in their own way, to a greater or lesser extent, 'new princes'—just as Machiavelli had given the title of 'new prince' to Ferdinand of Aragon. They were masters of the use of force both 'at home' and 'abroad', and of the introduction of 'new regulations and methods', 'for securing their own and their State's safety'. Above all, they were masters at handling, even while pretending to condemn it, the new 'political art' which Machiavelli had dreamed of teaching to an Italian prince for the defence and liberation of Italy from the assault of foreign 'barbarians'.

Political art, I said, not political science. This is not merely because Machiavelli himself speaks of an 'art', not of a 'science', of the State, and because it is quite impossible to reduce his thought to a system without using arbitrary pressure. It is also and above all because the perplexing ambiguity in his actual teaching must not be glossed over. Machiavelli seems indeed constantly to switch from the analysis of a fact to the formulation of a 'general rule', from a descriptive to a prescriptive type of discourse. It is this ambiguity that has led to so much controversy, and is the final reason for the 'scandal' caused by his teaching, a scandal which, despite some of our pundits, has never been, and never

can be, allayed. The accusation of 'immorality' which has pursued
Machiavelli throughout the centuries is not one to be treated
lightly. It is a fact that he does not hesitate to advise the statesman
'to learn how to be not good'; 'not to mind being called miserly'
or 'the reproach of cruelty'; to take small account of 'keeping his
words'; in short, 'to know how to make use of the evill upon
necessity'. Certainly we can and must stress, as Meinecke does,
the key-word 'necessity', and point out that all Machiavelli's
teaching, including his notion of *virtù*, is conditioned by it. Or we
can agree with Croce that Machiavelli seems to be 'divided in
mind and spirit where political matters are concerned. For politics
seem to him at times to involve the sad necessity of soiling one's
hands because of having to deal with wicked people, while at other
times they almost seem to amount to a sublime task, that of founding and upholding the State, that greatest of all institutions.'
Indeed, however carefully we read Machiavelli, we never seem to
be certain whether in his heart he condemns 'those cruel practices,
hostile not only to Christian but to all human life', or whether he
is not in fact announcing a kind of new gospel, a new morality
where the good of the State is the ultimate value. 'Let a Prince
therefore take the surest courses he can to secure victory and to
maintaine the State: the means shall alwaies be thought honorable,
and commended by everyone.' Does this merely indicate that,
when political goals are in view, means must be weighed and
measured accordingly; or does it suggest that the goal which the
statesman pursues is so high that all discussion of means is irrelevant? There is no denying that we are here faced with an ambiguity.
It is only if we look at the matter more closely that we come to
realize that this ambiguity is wholly confined to the normative
sphere, that it is closely linked with the prescriptive character of
Machiavelli's teaching. We too shall be divided in mind and spirit
unless we are able to determine exactly the nature and impact of
his precepts.

On the other hand, as far as the descriptive side of his argument
is concerned, Machiavelli leaves us in no kind of doubt about what
he intends. Political reality is what it is, and as such it must be
accepted and studied. Here the method of 'effectual truth', as it
is set forth in the challenging paragraph of the fifteenth chapter of
Machiavelli's political treatise, is in complete control. Translated
into modern language, that paragraph amounts to a profession of

strict 'ethical neutrality' in the study of politics. What Machiavelli deliberately proposes is an approach to political matters in
purely factual terms; an inquiry into 'how we live', not 'how we
ought to live'; a study of the State as a problem of force, not of
power nor authority. The praise bestowed on Machiavelli's teaching by Bacon is particularly significant on this score: 'We are much
beholden to Machiavell and others, that write what men doe, and
not what they ought to do. For it is not possible to joyn serpentine
wisedom with Columbine Innocency, except men know exactly
all the conditions of the Serpent; his basenesse and going upon his
bellie, his volubility and lubricity, his envy and sting.' The only
way of taking Machiavelli to task, if we really want to do so, is to
question the accuracy of his description. Why should the world of
politics be comparable only to a ditch full of snakes? Certainly
Machiavelli's view of 'effectual truth' is, if not biassed throughout,
at least thoroughly pessimistic. The old idea of the fundamental
corruption of human nature reappears in him with a vengeance.
But unlike Augustine's or Luther's, Machiavelli's pessimism has
no theological roots. It is a psychological pessimism. It is inspired
by a sombre view of his country and his times, which appear to
him 'bespotted with all manner of filthiness'. Men, as seen by
Machiavelli, are wily and evil (*tristi*). They are possessed by an
inextinguishable thirst for dominion and wealth ('it is a thing
indeed very naturall and ordinary, to desire to be of the getting
hand'!). Indeed, in order to understand politics properly, 'it is
necessary to assume that all men are potential criminals, and always
ready to realize their evil intentions whenever they are free to do
so'. If anything, statements of this kind need to be refuted rather
than made the subject of scandal. Nor are arguments for refuting
them lacking in Machiavelli's own writings, as, for instance, when
he speaks of the 'virtues' of the ancient Romans or of those simple
and uncouth communities which have not yet been touched
by corrupt civilization. 'If any one in these days would frame
a Republique he should find it easier to deale with rude
mountainers'!

The fact remains that this particular interpretation of 'effectual
truth' is the premiss of much that is 'invidious' in Machiavelli's
teaching. For it is out of it that he constructs a political theory
couched, oddly enough, in an almost endless series of precepts,
of 'general rules'. But surely there is no need to drag in the

'autonomy of politics', or the notion of politics as something 'beyond good and evil', as modern Italian critics fondly do, in order to understand the true character of these rules. They are, as it were, Machiavelli's own way of conveying the conclusions he has reached on the ground of his own peculiar reading of the 'truth of the matter'. In fact, for the most part these rules are not 'imperatives' at all, or at most, as Cassirer pointed out, they are 'hypothetical imperatives', 'technical' rules, intended to describe appropriate behaviour in a given situation with a particular end in view, the conduct which the statesman must follow if he wishes to lead the State successfully. Only in a very few cases—but they are important ones—the particular end envisaged by these rules (the security of the State, the safety of the country) is clearly set forth as the supreme end, as an absolute good: with the result that the hypothetical imperative, 'if you want to save the State you must act thus and thus', becomes a categorical imperative, 'to save the State is man's highest duty'.

Shall we then discard once and for all the view that seeks at all costs to see in Machiavelli the founder of modern political science? His was an 'art of the State': the words are his, and there is no reason why we should not leave him the title he chose to take a pride in. But the rules of this art he emphatically claimed to have discovered owing to his knowledge of 'effectual truth', and in his method at least he did indeed anticipate the kind of work which is done nowadays by the 'scientists'. The fact that his conclusions were set forth in a prescriptive language should not deceive us. For it is the easiest thing in the world to turn these prescriptions into actual descriptions, just as it is easy to turn the rule, 'if you want to be healthy be moderate in the use of tobacco' into the statement that 'the abuse of tobacco is dangerous to health'. Thus it can well be said that Machiavelli's 'art of the State' was, in its own way, a science. Modern upholders of a political science strictly confined to empirical research can well claim, if they like, kinship with Machiavelli. There is only one difference, but it is one that matters. Political scientists of our day carefully avoid formulating their conclusions in the preceptive mood used by Machiavelli. Who can say whether, if they ventured to do so, their precepts might not appear even more scandalous than those of 'old Nick', their beloved ancestor?

REFERENCES

Machiavelli, *Parole da dirle sopra la provisione del danaio* (1503); *Il Principe*, Dedication and chs. 1–3, 5–7, 10, 12, 15–19, 21; *Discorsi*, I, chs. 3, 11, 26; II, Preamble and ch. 19; III, ch. 41; *Istorie Fiorentine*, ii, 34. Bacon, *Advancement of Learning*, 1629 edn., II, xxi, § 9.

The works referred to in this chapter are the following, in order of reference:

F. Chabod, *Machiavelli and the Renaissance* (a collection of essays trans. by D. Moore, London, 1958); F. Meinecke, *Die Idee der Staatsräson in der neueren Geschichte*, Munich, 1924 (Engl. trans. by D. Scott, *Machiavellism*, London, 1957), part i, ch. 1; B. Croce, *Elementi di politica*, II, 1: 'Machiavelli e Vico. La politica e l'etica', now published in the vol. *Etica e Politica*, 4th edn., Bari, 1956; E. Cassirer, *The Myth of the State*, London, 1946, part ii, chs. x–xii.

5

'REASON OF STATE' AND
MACHTSTAAT

A THEORY which belongs to the same kind of political art or preceptive political theory as that which we have considered in Machiavelli contributed largely to the spread of his teaching under a borrowed name in the late sixteenth and early seventeenth centuries. This is the theory of the 'reason of State', a theory which inspired a large number of works that now lie dusty and forgotten on our bookshelves, in spite of the fact that distinguished scholars like Croce, Meinecke, and others have taken them down and dusted them in an attempt to show that they made a positive contribution to modern political thought.

The success achieved in Italy by the theory of the 'reason of State' throws light on one of the saddest periods of our history. This was the time when in other parts of Europe the modern theory of the State was taking shape, with a new approach to the problem of power; when the notion of sovereignty, which was to play such an important part both in legal and in political theory, was first hatched or at least given a clear definition. It was also the time when the problem of authority was passionately debated from a new standpoint, and theories of all kinds, often flatly contradictory, were being produced to explain political obligation. Meantime in Italy we were toying with interminable discussions on whether it is possible to govern States 'in accordance with the dictates of conscience', on how far it is permissible for a statesman to break the moral law in the interest of the State, on how to set about constructing a science or 'reason' of State as the knowledge of 'what has to be done in conformity with the essence or form of that State which we plan to maintain or establish'.

And yet such discussions were not wholly without significance or value. They do more than reveal the discomfort of a reawakened moral sensitiveness in face of the 'iniquitous maxims' of Machiavelli. In its own way the theory of the reason of State, with its distinction between the factual demands of a given situation and the moral judgement which can and must be passed on them, implies a clear recognition of the different angles from which the problem of politics can be approached. These different angles, as we have seen, throw light on the different aspects under which the State is bound to appear, depending on whether we are concerned with understanding its mechanism or with putting a value on its deeds. The desperate attempt to find some way of reconciling what Machiavelli had so sharply divided accounts for the suspicion of hypocrisy we feel in reading 'the pedantic, despised and abused Italian writers on the reason of the State' (the words are Croce's!): as though they wished to find excuses for the political art of which they proclaimed themselves to be teachers, and to justify with suitable caution the maxims which their great fellow countryman had ventured to formulate about it. But what after all is hypocrisy, according to a famous definition, but the homage rendered to virtue by vice? Here again there is no need to refer to the pretended discovery and 'autonomy' of pure politics in order to understand what the theorists of the reason of State were saying or what they were worth.

What they were saying—if their 'prescriptions' are translated as 'descriptions'—was substantially what Machiavelli had already said: that politics is a world dominated by force, and that consequently it is necessary to reckon with force if one wishes to found and establish a State and to make it prosper. And as for their worth—if we compare these writers with their contemporaries in other European countries, with political thinkers of the calibre of Bodin, Hooker, or Grotius—we must admit that it amounts to very little. Their thought was as feeble as their moral fibre was feeble, when it allowed them to feel gratified with the role of counsellor to princes, and to accept without misgivings a state of affairs little better morally, in fact still more depressing in some respects, than that which Machiavelli had visualized and dissected. They, too, in their own way, were teachers of political realism, but not in the bitter and yet generous sense of Machiavelli, whose mind was set on awakening his fellow countrymen and on freeing Italy from the 'barbarians'. Their teaching was narrow and stale, as the horizon of Italian political life was narrow during this period, and the people's sense of duty stale—a people which submitted wearily to the formal security of princely government and kept aloof from

the proud disputes and the fierce discussions that shook the other
nations of Europe.

To say, as one of them does, that the reason of State 'takes as
much account of things ugly as of things honourable, and concerns itself with injustice no less than with justice', can mean that
political reality must be considered as existing factually and in the
play of forces which determines its existence. But it can also, and
did in fact, mean indifference to the way in which these forces
converge, to the form which the State assumes, and to the principles
that inspire its conduct. The theorists of the reason of State were
wrong, not in having concentrated their attention on the purely
descriptive plane, but in having stopped there, as if the ultimate
secret of the State were to be found there alone. They were wrong
in accepting as final the political state of affairs existing at one
given moment; in taking no account of its rapid evolution, of the
emergence not only of new forces but of new forms, which were to
make the 'new principality' of the Italian type one ingredient, but
not the sole or exclusive one, in the modern State—as Machiavelli
had clearly foreseen.

Even if this vast literature made no lasting contribution to the
modern theory of the State, it bears eloquent witness to the shattering effect of Machiavelli's teaching on European thought. 'Machiavelli's theory', wrote Meinecke, 'was a sword which was plunged
into the flank of the body politic of western humanity, causing it
to shriek and rear up.' The principle of force revealed in all its
nakedness by Machiavelli, and, above all, the rules he had laid
down with lucid and pitiless severity for its use and manipulation,
so obviously challenged the traditional views, not only of the
Christian conscience but of humanistic culture, that an effort had
to be made to find a rational explanation for them and to preserve
the truth they contained. It was precisely this effort that was made
by those theorists, who ended by making many of the invidious
truths mercilessly expounded by Machiavelli acceptable under
cover of 'reason of State'. They showed that politics had its own
laws, often opposed to moral laws, and that these laws must be
known and borne in mind by all statesmen. Force is here thought
of as an instrument, not as an end; and this indeed is not widely
different from Machiavelli's way of thinking of it in most cases.
The State is force, but this force lies in men's hands to make good
or bad use of it 'according to necessity'.

But there is another aspect of Machiavelli's teaching referred to only in passing when I said that in his writings the good of the State seems sometimes to be regarded as the supreme good, and that his 'hypothetical' imperatives seem at times to sound like categorical ones. In all such cases force ceases to be simply a means and becomes an end. The State, the supreme expression of force, is therefore itself an incarnation of the highest value. It pursues its own ends, creates its own law, and is not subject to current judgements of morality. The timorous theorists of the reason of State were certainly far removed from this kind of personification and glorification of the State; and in my view Machiavelli, with his freedom from all prejudice, never really indulged in it to the full. But others have seen in him the discoverer of the 'daemonic force of power' and the founder of a 'realistic' conception of the State, which according to Ritter (one of the authors referred to) was to predominate on the Continent of Europe, in contrast with the 'legalistic' and 'moralistic' conception that, for different reasons and because of various influences, prevailed in England and in the English-speaking countries generally. This glorification of the State *qua* force (*Machtstaat*) was to be fully developed in Germany by the historians, philosophers, and politicians of the nineteenth century, 'from Fichte and Hegel, through Ranke and his school, down to Heinrich von Treitschke'. It was in fact in Germany that 'something quite new and extraordinary occurred': Machiavellism ceased to be an 'art', a set of precepts for rulers, and took on the appearance of a new ethic. Reason of State ended its wretched, precarious existence in the shadow of Council rooms, and came out into the open to be hailed as the very 'soul of the State'.

Something infinitely more serious and momentous than what Meinecke rather euphemistically described as the 'legitimization of a bastard' was at stake. What happened was a complete reversal of the traditional standpoint of political realism. Thrasymachus, Augustine, Machiavelli himself, all who had borne witness to the paramount importance of force in politics, had never dreamed of confounding force with justice, efficiency with justification, facts with values. In fact, no one distinguished the *is* from the *ought* more clearly than Machiavelli: his is the crude recognition of the great distance that lies between 'how one lives' and 'how one ought to live', between 'the road of good' and that of evil. Indeed, one is almost tempted at times to think that there might be some truth in a view that has cropped up time and again ever since the publication of *The Prince*. According to this view, which was held by Rousseau, Alfieri, and Foscolo, Machiavelli's message was a coded message. It can be read equally well as an instruction to the prince and as a warning to all other readers. Indeed, warnings of a kind are not lacking in many of Machiavelli's writings. In the *Discourses*, for example, he frankly admits that the demands of politics may be so frightful and excruciating that the life of a private citizen might be preferable to that of a statesman. In a different and more humorous vein he once described in a letter to Guicciardini his idea of a good preacher as one who should teach men 'the true way to Paradise' by picturing the way to Hell, so that they might avoid it.

But now that very evil which statesmen must 'know how to make use of upon necessity' became the way to Paradise. Machiavelli, wrote Hegel in a youthful work, spoke the truth and spoke in earnest. His *Prince* embodied a supreme imperative: to make Italy a State. There is nothing more absurd than to judge statecraft by the standards of private morals. 'The greatest, indeed the only crime against the State is anarchy. . . . The chief duty of the State is to maintain itself and to destroy anyone who dares to threaten its existence.' Treitschke, the most thorough-going upholder of the theory of the *Machtstaat*, paid a similar tribute. 'It will be to Machiavelli's abiding honour that he set the State upon its own feet . . ., that he was the first to declare distinctly that the State is power. . . . The consequences of this thought are far-reaching. It is the truth, and those who dare not face it had better leave politics alone. We must never forget our debt to Machiavelli for this.'

In this entirely new perspective the whole relationship between morals and politics, which had so deeply worried the theorists of the reason of State, was radically altered. Nowhere does this appear more clearly than in a famous passage in Hegel. 'Where politics is alleged to clash with morals and to be always wrong, the doctrine propounded rests on superficial ideas of morality, the nature of the State, and the State's relation to the moral point of view.' What Hegel's 'deeper ideas' about morality and the nature of the State actually were is not our concern here; they were certainly not Machiavelli's. Machiavelli and his earlier interpreters would probably hardly have understood what Hegel meant by defining the State as the 'actuality of the ethical ideal', 'the actualization of freedom', or 'the march of God in the world'. Their notion of the State as grounded on force was entirely matter of fact, there was nothing metaphysical about it. They were not concerned with right, but with might: they were perfectly clear that one does not necessarily entail the other. But to those who extolled the *Machtstaat* might *was* the ultimate source of right: their claims far exceeded the boundaries of political realism. Theirs was a theory of authority; their bloodthirsty God was an ultimate value. In so far as their problem is not one with which we are concerned here, we can clear them out of our road without much regret, at any rate for the time being.

REFERENCES

Giovanni Botero, *Della Ragion di Stato*, 1589 (Eng. trans. by P. I. and D. P. Waley, New Haven, 1956), Dedication and Book II, §§ 6 and 15. Ludovico Zuccolo, *Della Ragion di Stato*, 1621 (ed. by B. Croce and S. Caramella, Bari, 1930). Hegel, *Die Verfassung Deutschlands*, 1802 (ed. by G. Lasson), § 9 (Eng. trans. by T. M. Knox in *Hegel's Political Writings*, ed. by T. M. Knox and Z. A. Pelczynski, Oxford, 1964, p. 221); *Grundlinien der Philosophie des Rechts*, 1821 (Eng. trans. by T. M. Knox, Oxford, 1942), §§ 257–8 and additions 152–3, § 337. H. von Treitschke, *Politik*, Leipzig, 1897–8 (Eng. trans. by B. Dugdale and T. de Bille, 1916, repub. by H. Kohn, New York, 1963), Book I, ch. 3.

On the doctrine of the 'reason of State' the two pioneer books are those of B. Croce, *Storia dell'età barocca in Italia*, Bari, 1926, I, § 2; and of F. Meinecke, *Die Idee der Staatsräson in der neueren Geschichte*, Munich, 1924 (Eng. trans. by D. Scott, *Machiavellism. The Doctrine of Raison d'État and its Place in Modern History*, London, 1957).

For the interpretation of the doctrine of the *Machtstaat* referred to in this chapter see G. Ritter, *Die Dämonie der Macht*, Munich, 1948 (Eng. trans. by F. W. Pick, *The Corrupting Influence of Power*, Hadleigh, 1952).

For the medieval precedents of the doctrine of 'reason of State' see the excellent study by Gaines Post, '*Ratio Publicae Utilitatis, Ratio Status*, and "Reason of State", 1100–1300', now in the volume *Studies in Medieval Legal Thought*, Princeton, 1964, ch. v.

6

'CLASS STRUGGLE' AND 'GOVERNING *ÉLITES*'

THE Marxist notion of the State is not entirely free from meta-physical assumptions. It certainly is permeated throughout by a deep commitment to values. Yet, in its conclusions at any rate, it bears the unmistakable mark of a realistic appraisal of political issues. The greatest emphasis is laid on force as the decisive factor in human relations. Hegel's dialectic, 'turned upside down', pro-vided Marx and Engels with their basic interpretation of the historic process. That interpretation in turn constituted the frame-work within which the problem of the State could be clearly seen. The crude facts of politics seem to fit most appropriately within that framework. The antagonisms and clashes of social life, the fierce conflicts which characterize man's dominion over man, could easily be presented as the outcome of the dialectic of history. The State was to the Marxist the result of historical conflict. 'The history of all human society, past and present, has been the history of class struggle.' 'Strictly speaking, political power is the organized use of force by one class in order to bring another into subjection.' 'The modern state authority is nothing more than a committee for the administration of the consolidated affairs of the bourgeois class as a whole.' These are the words of the *Communist Manifesto* of 1848. But already, a few years earlier, Marx and Engels had argued that 'the State . . . is nothing more than the form of organization which the bourgeois necessarily adopt both for internal and exter-nal purposes, for the mutual guarantee of their property and interests. . . . The State is the form in which the individuals of a ruling class assert their common interests.'

Up to this point we seem to be faced merely with a factual account of the force relations existing between men, the same sort of account which is characteristic of political realism in all its manifold versions. The move towards a different level of argument —a level where it is no longer facts, but values, which are at issue—

is, however, soon apparent. Strangely enough, it was effected by means of an appeal to the immanent process of history. From the recognition of the existence of a conflict of forces we are led to a 'dialectical interpretation' of that conflict, and hence to the prediction that it will be superseded in the future society, where all contrasts and oppression will come to an end. An interpretation and a prophecy of this kind are already outlined in the *Manifesto*. They reappear and are further developed in the works which expound Marxist doctrine in its mature form. The State, Engels wrote, is an historical product, 'a product of society at a certain stage of evolution'. But it is also, and at the same time, a proof of the dialectic inherent in history, inasmuch as it is 'the confession that this society has become hopelessly divided against itself, has entangled itself in irreconcilable contradictions which it is powerless to banish'. The solution of this contradiction is to be found in the conquest of power by the proletariat and in the transfer of all means of production to society itself. Only by this conquest of power and transfer of ownership can class differences and class antagonism be got rid of; and 'as soon as there is no longer any social class to be held in subjection, as soon as class rule and the individual struggle for existence based upon our present anarchy in production . . . are removed, nothing more remains to be repressed, and a special repressive force, a State, is no longer necessary'. Indeed, the State will not be 'abolished'. It will 'wither away', and with it all the instruments of oppression which have so far characterized its rule. For the first time in history men will be fully masters of their destiny, and 'the ascent of man from the kingdom of necessity to the kingdom of freedom' will take place.

Clearly we are here very far from a purely descriptive approach to the problem of politics. Diagnosis has led the way to therapy, and therapy in turn to the promise of a complete recovery. Superimposed on the prophecy that the coming of a classless society is the logical result of historical development is the imperative to bring that society into being. 'To accomplish this act of universal emancipation is the historical mission of the modern proletariat.' The ultimate value attributed to the attainment of liberty gives this imperative an absolute, categorical meaning. This does not, however, rule out the fact that the reign of liberty is far off, and that social relations as they exist today are determined by other, different laws, by other, different imperatives. The reign of necessity is the reign of force. For this reason the State as the outcome of class struggle and the instrument of man's oppression amounts to nothing else than the monopoly of power in a given society. On this point, at any rate, the Marxist vision of politics does not differ substantially from that of Machiavelli.

The return of the keyword 'necessity' has a particular significance in this context. Still more significant for Italians is the tribute paid to Machiavelli by one of their greatest Marxist interpreters, Antonio Gramsci. In his 'Prison Note-books' Gramsci has some curious and revealing remarks on what he called the 'myth' of *The Prince*. That myth, he believed, consisted in Machiavelli's 'plastic' and 'anthropomorphic' presentation of 'the process of formation of a definite collective will pursuing a definite political end'. According to Gramsci, that myth could be applied to the present-day political situation, no longer embodied in a particular individual, but in the action of men united to attain a particular end—the ultimate political end of the conquest of power. In writing these words, Gramsci was obviously thinking of the action of those to whom he assigned the task of carrying through the liberating revolution, of 'founding a new type of State'. He was thinking of the proletariat organized in the Communist Party. All the principles laid down by Machiavelli in his time for his prince would hold good for the 'new Prince': the same indiscriminate use of good and bad means 'according to necessity'; the same possibility of justifying those means 'with a view to the end', i.e. to the attainment of power. The knowledge of 'effectual truth' would thus find expression in a new set of rules for political action, capable in its turn of being transfigured and canonized as a new code of ethics.

Here then is a neat modern version of the doctrine of might, a parallel to the old arguments of Thrasymachus and Machiavelli. But the Marxists are not alone in possessing the merit or the blame of stripping off all illusions about the State and of presenting the realist case in a new and forcible manner. At the opposite pole is a group of writers who, in the modern world, have taken a no less realistic view of political affairs and have therefore quite aptly been described as the 'new Machiavellians'. The arguments they use are the familiar ones of the theorists of might; but the conclusions they reach are exactly the reverse of those of the Marxists. Their pessimism is not relieved by any expectation of an impending catharsis. I am referring to the theory of the 'ruling class' or the 'governing *élite*', a theory first formulated by two Italian writers, Mosca and Pareto, and now very popular with modern political scientists. This theory is put forward as being exquisitely 'realistic', in that it purports to be a purely descriptive analysis of political facts and of existing situations of power. It affirms, in Mosca's words, that

among the constant facts and tendencies that are to be found in all political organisms, one is so obvious that it is apparent to the most casual eye. In all societies . . . two classes of people appear—a class that rules and a class that is ruled. The first class, always the less numerous, performs all political functions, monopolizes power, and enjoys the advantages that power brings; whereas the second, the more numerous class, is directed and controlled by the first, in a manner that is now more or less legal, now more or less arbitrary and violent.

Pareto puts the case in almost identical language. 'The least we can do is to divide society into two strata: a higher stratum, which usually contains the rulers, and a lower stratum, which usually contains the ruled. The fact is so obvious that it has always forced itself upon the notice of even the most casual observer.'

It would be easy to point out that if the state of affairs described by Mosca and Pareto is as obvious as they say, we should have to ask ourselves where lies the novelty of their doctrine, so highly praised by contemporary students. The novelty, if it be a novelty at all, lies in the emphasis they lay on the role of force in bringing about this state of affairs, and in their use of this argument in favour of conservatism and against social change and innovation. In Pareto's words,

We need not linger on the fiction of 'popular representation'—poppycock grinds no flour. Let us go on and see what substance underlies the various forms of power in the governing classes. Ignoring exceptions, which are few in number and short in duration, one finds everywhere a governing class of relatively few individuals that keeps itself in power partly by force and partly by the consent of the subject class, which is much more numerous. The differences lie principally, as regards substance, in the relative proportions of force and consent; and as regards form, in the manner in which force is used and consent obtained.

Clearly, consent is merely the aftermath of force, and force in turn does not necessarily imply the use of physical force, but may well consist in the possession of particular skills on the part of the rulers. The only point that matters, in the study of politics, is the basic fact of subjection of man to man. Like other conservative writers before them (I have already mentioned de Maistre), Mosca and Pareto relish describing and stressing the inevitable hardships of politics. 'States are not ruled with prayer-books', but with ruthless discipline.

Indeed, the conservative bent of Mosca's and Pareto's views is most apparent when we compare them with those of the Marxists. Their basic assumption bears an undeniable resemblance to that of Marx and of Engels. Both Mosca and Pareto believe that the existence of political power depends on the struggle between rival, antagonistic classes, and therefore that the State is only the more or less stable and lasting monopoly of the instruments of power by one particular class, always restricted in numbers. According to Mosca, 'the whole history of civilized mankind comes down to a conflict between the tendency of dominant elements to monopolize political power . . . and the tendency towards a dislocation of old forces and an insurgence of new forces'. Pareto in turn writes: 'Aristocracies do not last. Whatever the causes, it is an incontestable fact that after a certain length of time they pass away. History is a graveyard of aristocracies.' And further: 'Revolutions come about through accumulations in the higher strata of society . . . of decadent elements no longer possessing the qualities [literally, 'residues'] suitable for keeping them in power, who shrink from the use of force; while meantime in the lower strata of society elements of superior quality are coming to the fore, possessing qualities suitable for exercising the functions of government and willing enough to use force.' An echo of Marxist ideas is clearly audible in these pronouncements of Mosca and Pareto. But there is an obvious difference. There is no mention here of a possible escape or liberation from the struggle, the antagonism, the 'contradiction'. Social reality has always been and always will be the oppression and exploitation of one group of men by another.

The 'lesson of facts' in the theory of *élites* emerges clearly: so much so that a recent student has correctly defined it as a theory of 'bourgeois defence', and one which might even be called a breviary on the preservation of the established order. The 'ruling classes' must be on their guard. They should treasure the teaching of history. They should learn the art of founding power on consent as well as on force, as is always possible by having recourse to a suitable ideological equipment (the 'political formula' of Mosca, the 'derivations' of Pareto: how do they differ from Plato's 'noble lie'?). Above all, they should always be on the watch and ready to defend themselves with all available means, making use of force and cunning, 'of the fox and the lion', as Machiavelli had said long before! Once again the reference to Machiavelli is significant. The picture of 'foxes' and 'lions' is Pareto's; indeed, the doctrine of force takes a much cruder shape with him than with Mosca, whose vision of politics is much more complex and whose notion of the State is still influenced by the feeling for legality and justice. Both of them, however, are tireless in denouncing the perils of 'humanitarianism', which spreads a veil over effectual truth, and only helps to reduce the energy of the ruling classes by making them 'lose the habit of dealing with people of the lower classes and commanding them directly' (Mosca), or by weakening the 'resistance on the part of people in power, so clearing the ground for violence on the part of the governed' (Pareto).

I have called this a theory of conservative defence; but hitherto the more provocative assertions of the new Machiavellians could still be interpreted as simply constituting a set of technical prescriptions, as merely laying down a number of practical formulae on the pattern: 'given that politics is what it is, the ruling class must act in such and such a way in order to retain its power.' In fact Mosca and Pareto also suggest something quite different. They too slide more or less deliberately from the descriptive plane to one of values. They are not only ready with a theory of force, but with its justification. This shift of ground is nowhere more clearly apparent than in the ambiguous use of such words as 'the best' or 'the *élite*', which makes it possible to assert in one breath the dominant position of one group or class that retains power, and the 'legitimacy' of this retention. Thus, according to Mosca, the ruling classes govern because they possess certain qualities: 'the fact that they are ruling classes shows that at a given time, in a given country, they contain the individuals who are best fitted to govern.' According to Pareto, the *élites* are by definition the class 'of people who have the highest indices in their branch of activity'. Statements of this kind entail an appreciation of values notwithstanding their factual tone, and regardless of the possibility, which is still left open, of acknowledging a discrepancy between the *élites* that are such 'by merit' and those that are such 'in fact'.

The talk is no longer, or not only, about what is, but about what ought to be: or, more precisely, what is is taken to correspond to, or to be a token of, what ought to be. To put it metaphorically, the 'bosses' are the only true 'tutelary genii of the city' and deserve to be revered as such: what other protectors can we invoke in a world where force is the *ultima ratio*? In the name of 'effectual truth' Mosca and Pareto were not waging war on 'humanitarian dreams' only, but on equality, on popular sovereignty, on democratic principles, on the whole political ideology of their times, all of which, like so many other new Machiavellians of our age, they intended to undermine and to challenge. The history of the last half-century bears witness to the great success of their endeavour.

These strictures, if strictures they may be called, on the theory of the ruling class and the governing *élite* are not impaired, I believe, by the detailed and fruitful controversy which has taken place in recent years about the correct interpretation and use of that theory. There has been of late, and there still is, much discussion on the validity, that is on the correspondence to fact, of the '*élite* model'. This is an issue which concerns the political scientist rather than the political philosopher. The question whether political power is in the hands of the few or the many, and whether its actual distribution in a given society follows the pattern of oligarchy rather than that of democracy, is a question which can only be decided in the field, by a careful assessment of evidence. But there has also been much discussion as to whether and how the *élite* doctrine can be reconciled with democratic ideals, i.e. with the entire set of values currently accepted in the West, those very ideals for which Mosca, at any rate in his youth, and Pareto, throughout his life, had nothing but contempt and derision. An elaborate effort has been made to show that the notion of a political *élite* is not necessarily incompatible with the working of a healthy democracy, at any rate if *élites* are conceived as 'open *élites*', or if the presence of a plurality of competing *élites* is secured, or, finally, if that process of the 'circulation of *élites*', which Pareto himself had envisaged, is accelerated to the point of ensuring a constant renewal and control of the governing class, as well as a free and deliberate acceptance of the structure of power on the part of the whole community. Clearly, by doing so the modern democratic defenders of the 'élitist' doctrine are casting it in an entirely new mould, and so turning it into a very different theory from that which Mosca and Pareto propounded. Whether by stressing the equality of opportunity existing in modern societies they succeed in taking away the sting of anti-egalitarianism, which was so pronounced in the early 'élitist' doctrine, remains to be seen: the question is also whether that equality really obtains in our present societies, or is made a mockery of by prevailing conditions of wealth, class, or education. But by stressing the necessity of consent in order to legitimize the rule of the *élite* they certainly break away from what was Mosca's and Pareto's main contention: that force, not consent, is the determining factor in the relationship of man to man, the basic element of politics. In fact, they introduce a consideration of value into a doctrine which, at the outset at least, purported to be entirely value-free, the true heir to old-time political realism. To this particular value we shall return in due course, when we are no longer talking of a realistic approach, but of a critical assessment of the foundations of the State and of the essence of politics.

REFERENCES

Marx and Engels, *Manifesto of the Communist Party*, 1848 (Eng. trans. by Eden and Cedar Paul, *The Communist Manifesto of Karl Marx and Friedrich Engels*, London, 1930), §§ i and ii; *The German Ideology*, 1845–6, ed. by R. Pascal, New York, 1947–60, ch. i, § 2. F. Engels, *Anti-Dühring*, 1878 (Eng. trans., *Socialism, Utopian and Scientific*, Marxist Library, vol. II, New York, 1935), part iii; *The Origin of the Family, Private Property and the State*, 1884 (Eng. trans., Chicago, 1902), ch. ix. A. Gramsci, *Opere*, vol. v, *Note sul Machiavelli*, Turin, 1949. G. Mosca, *Elementi di Scienza politica*, vol. I, Rome, 1896, vol. II, 1923 (Eng. trans., *The Ruling Class*, New York and London, 1939, ch. ii, §§ 1 and 8; ch. iii, § 1; ch. iv, § 6; ch. xvi, § 4). V. Pareto, *Trattato di sociologia generale*, Florence, 1916 (Eng. trans., *The Mind and Society*, New York, 1935), §§ 2031, 2047, 2053, 2057, 2174, 2178, 2185, 2227, 2244.

For an excellent appraisal of the doctrine of the ruling class, and of its historical background and implications, see J. H. Meisel, *The Myth of the Ruling Class. Gaetano Mosca and the Élite*, Ann Arbor, 1958.

For a survey of the vicissitudes and reformulations of the theory of the *élite* in Italy see N. Bobbio, 'Teorie politiche e ideologie nell'Italia contemporanea', in the volume *La filosofia contemporanea in Italia*, vol. II, Asti, 1958; and in the world at large, T. B. Bottomore, *Élites and Society*, London, 1964.

For the 'critique of the ruling *élite* model' see the homonymous article by R. A. Dahl in 52 *American Political Science Review*, 1958, 2; and the symposium *Le élites politiche* (IV World Congress of Sociology, 1959), Bari, 1961.

The phrase 'the new Machiavellians' is borrowed from J. Burnham's well-known essay, *The Machiavellians: Defenders of Freedom*, London, 1943, and has become very popular.

THE DISRUPTION OF THE NOTION OF THE STATE IN MODERN POLITICAL SCIENCE

I HAVE so far made only passing reference to modern political science. Such reference as I have made should, however, prove sufficient to give some indication of what this 'new science' purports to do; more important still, of what it purports to be. Its very claim to scientific dignity is based on a strictly empirical approach to political facts and on a strict adherence to ethical neutrality. In view of such assumptions, the purpose and aims which modern political science sets out to achieve may seem to be not substantially different from those that Machiavelli and the political realists of the past had in mind: the purpose of pursuing the 'truth of the matter', the aim of providing accounts and explanations of political phenomena which should be thoroughly uncommitted as far as 'values' or preferences are concerned.

There are, however, two important differences that distinguish the modern 'scientist' from the older 'political realist'. The first is, that the former's vast output of writing carefully avoids (or pretends to avoid) any kind of didactic or normative discourse, shunning, whenever possible, the enunciation of rules—of even such 'technical' rules as the old political realists never tired of laying down in their endeavour to discover and to teach the 'art of governing'. The primary concern of the modern political scientist is no longer to 'instruct', but to probe and to explain. He leaves it to others—to the statesman, to the politician, and in the end to each one of us—to draw the practical inferences from his discoveries, from the factual data which he assembles and arranges in a system. The second and no less important difference is one that completely alters the perspective of traditional political thought. Modern political science tends to dissociate the study of political phenomena from an exclusive concentration on the problem of the State. Being concerned in general with the force

relations existing in any social context, it can afford to take little
notice of the specific label or 'name' which happens to be applied
to organized force at a particular moment in a particular society.

The disruption of the notion of the State in modern political
science is such a challenging and portentous event that it is surprising no detailed study should yet have been made to account
for it and to explain it. In this chapter I can only try to illustrate it briefly by referring to the teaching which comes to us
from the United States, the country where the new science has
the greatest influence. In fact, most of the themes that have been
developed and emphasized by American political scientists in
recent years can be found much earlier in Arthur F. Bentley's
book—a pioneer work published in 1908—and there is no need to
look much further in order to grasp the true nature of the challenge. The very title of Bentley's book—*The Process of Government*
—is revealing. It is almost impossible to translate this title adequately into a Latin language. From the start, Bentley's approach
sounds totally alien to traditional Continental ways of thought about
the State and politics.

Bentley's thesis, in a nutshell, is as follows. 'Government' (what
we, using the old language, should probably still continue to call
by the name of 'politics') is 'first, last, and always activity, action,
"something doing" '; and this *doing* is 'the shunting by some men
of other men's conduct along changed lines, the gathering of forces
to overcome resistance to such alterations, or the dispersal of one
grouping of forces by another grouping'. Here and nowhere else
is 'the raw material for the study of government'. It consists in 'the
action of men with or upon each other'. We have it before us 'in
the form of purposive action, valued in terms of other purposive
action'; in the shape of a 'process', not of 'ideas' or 'institutions'.

The first and inevitable outcome of thus reducing political
experience to a process is to belittle, if not actually to deny, the
importance of whatever represents an arrest or a crystallization in
its flow. According to Bentley, the true nature of politics cannot be
inferred from lawbooks, 'which merely state the method by which
certain participants in government proceed', nor even from 'the
"law" behind the lawbooks, except as this is taken to mean the
actual functioning of the people'. It is not revealed 'in the pro-
ceedings of constitutional conventions', nor 'in essays, addresses,
appeals, and diatribes on tyranny and democracy'. It must not be

sought 'in the "character of the people", in their specific "feelings" or "thoughts", in their "hearts" or "minds" '. The raw material of government 'can be found only in the actually performed legislating-administering-adjudicating activities of the nation and in the streams and currents of activity that gather among the people and rush into their spheres'.

Having defined the nature of politics, Bentley outlines its study as follows. The task of political science, as of the social sciences in general, lies in singling out the purposes or 'interests' which determine men's actions and which link them together in an infinite variety of relations or 'groups'. In fact, it is impossible to separate the notion of group from that of interest. They are not separate. They are closely intertwined. 'There is no group without its interest', and 'an interest . . . is the equivalent of a group.' Bentley, however, is anxious to explain that the notion of interest must be understood in a broader sense than that of mere economic profit. On closer inspection an interest turns out to be nothing else than the cohesive principle of a particular group. Any such principle can be the object of study. We must study it 'as impassively as we would the habits or the organic functions of birds, bees or fishes'.

But political phenomena do not consist only in activities that embody an interest. They are further characterized by the presence of an element which equally calls for attention. They are 'from start to finish phenomena of force'. But 'force' is an 'objectionable word'. An imprecise term even in the natural sciences, it is 'too closely identified with so-called "physical force" and too apt to be understood as in opposition to non-force factors of a sympathetic or moral or ideal nature'. Bentley therefore proposes to use the word 'pressure' in its place, because of the advantage of concentrating attention 'upon the groups themselves, instead of upon any mystical "realities" assumed to be underneath and supporting them', and also because 'its connotation is not limited to the narrowly "physical" '. 'Pressure, as we shall use it, is always a group phenomenon. It indicates the push and resistance between groups. The balance of the group pressures *is* the existing state of society.'

It is precisely at this point that Bentley comes out into the open with his attack on the notion of the State. He finds it difficult enough to define the term 'government' and to justify its use. The term does not coincide exactly with what is meant by political

phenomena in general. It is both narrower and broader, and all
that can be said is that in its most common use it indicates some
kind of 'differentiated' activities by means of which the adjustment
or balance of interests in a given society is achieved. But there is no
point whatever in complicating matters further by using the word
'State' to describe such activities, thus putting them 'in a class
all by themselves with sanctions peculiar and distinct from those
of other forms of social organization'. The distinction is purely
'artificial', and can only lead to a 'barren formalism' that will make
us lose sight of what matters exclusively, the process of government itself. The 'idea of the State', which 'has been very prominent,
no doubt, among the intellectual amusements of the past', may
have served 'at particular places and times . . . to help give coherent and pretentious expression to some particular group's
activity'. But its claims are based on 'too minute a factor' to deserve
a special place in political inquiry. In dealing with administration,
legislation, or even with jurisdiction or the constitution, political
science must 'go behind' the 'formal element' to find 'what are the
real interests that are playing on each other through this agency'.
Ultimately, there is nothing left except the bare fact that some
people succeed in carrying out their will by determining the
behaviour of others.

Such were the views Bentley put forward more than fifty years
ago, and it would no doubt be of much interest to explore in greater
detail their background and sources. It is not too difficult to trace
in them the clear influence of Pragmatism, as well as a possible
reflection of the lack in American linguistic usage (already noted)
of a precise connotation for the word 'State'.[1] Having regard more
particularly to the notion of the State, we could draw a fascinating analogy between Bentley's strictures and the disruption of the
formal concept of law at the hands of the American Legal realists.
Both may well stem from a common root: the behaviourist approach, which is a characteristic feature of American social sciences.
However that may be, the point that matters is that Bentley's
arguments are still echoed by contemporary writers over half a
century after the appearance of his work.

Thus we find David B. Truman, in a book which acknowledges
even in its title (*The Governmental Process*, 1951) a direct indebtedness to Bentley, frankly admitting that the 'group interpretation

[1] See above, p. 34.

of the political process . . . inevitably must ignore some greater unity designated as society or the State', and concluding that 'the institutions of government' are nothing else than 'centers of interest-based power'. Messrs. Lasswell and Kaplan, on the other hand, in another much-quoted and most influential work (*Power and Society*, 1950) set out to analyse 'such political abstractions as "State" and "sovereignty" in terms of concrete interpersonal relationship of influence and control', and concede that we may, if we like, still speak of a group as a 'State', 'whenever a certain pattern of identifications, demands, and expectations with regard to power exceeds some selected frequency in the group'. But perhaps the most devastating attack on the notion of the State is that contained in David Easton's book, *The Political System* (1953), a book that is considered in the U.S.A. practically a must for college and graduate students in political science. In a detailed chapter Easton maintains that in view of the confusion and variety of its meanings the very word 'State' should be avoided scrupulously by the political scientist: nothing fruitful can be expected from it for empirical work. Political science is concerned not with particular kinds of institutions or organizations, but with 'a kind of activity', the activity involved 'in the formulation and execution of social policy, in what has come to be called elliptically . . . the policy-making process'. In order to achieve a 'minimal homogeneity and cohesion', political science should focus attention on 'the authoritative allocation of values for a given society as influenced by the use and distribution of power'. Behind this strange and highly sophisticated language, what we hear once again is the call of the political realist to tear away the veil of verbal illusions and to look at the facts.

Indeed, with the final disruption of the notion of the State at the hands of the modern empiricists, one conclusion seems to stand out as the inevitable outcome of any approach to the problem of politics in strict realistic terms. This conclusion can only be that, from a purely empirical standpoint, the State does 'exist' only as a kind of force-relation among men—however much disguised the ultimate datum of force may be by such broader and milder expressions as 'pressure', 'influence', 'control', and so forth, expressions preferred by modern writers to the crude old language of might, the language of Thrasymachus and Machiavelli. The mistake—or it may be more appropriate to say the limitation—of the realistic approach is in not seeing that force, by the very fact of being qualified, ceases to be force, or, more exactly, admits of a qualitative, and not only a quantitative differentiation. It is precisely this qualitative difference which may possibly give some sense to the notion of the State which has fared so badly in contemporary political theory. No doubt the political realist is perfectly justified in maintaining that the State, looked at empirically, is nothing more than one group among other groups, one system of force (or pressure, or influence, or control) among others. But to maintain, as modern political scientists also do, that the notion of the State is an 'abstract' or 'formal' concept is to concede that the notion represents a conceptual elaboration of the empirical datum of force, a particular way of experiencing and framing certain facts which enables the student to single them out among the infinite complexity of the force-relations existing in the social context. What matters is that force is used and exercised in a certain manner, that the influence exerted by a certain group is qualitatively different from that exerted by others—in the same way that the order given by the policeman is different from that given by a gunman, and the rule of law is different from the pressure or the control exercised by a powerful lobby.

Now it seems difficult to deny that among the various possible qualifications of force the first and most characteristic is the legal one. It is a qualification which can be defined as follows: 'Force is exerted with a certain uniformity and regularity in accordance with certain known rules.' Expressed in such terms, the legal qualification is nothing more than a description of something that actually takes place—a purely descriptive proposition. It is possible of course to think of other and different qualifications of force, such as 'a just force', 'force exercised for the common good' or for some 'moral' purpose. Such qualifications do not merely describe; they imply a judgement of value. They refer to a state of affairs which may or may not exist, but is considered desirable. Indeed, it may well be that, in order to understand the 'prescriptive' character of law, we shall have to devote some attention to the nature of such value-judgements. But let us, for the time being, be content to explore the legal qualification of force in purely descriptive terms, as an empirical or, to be more precise, as an historical datum. Surely it is the case that in modern societies force has been channelled, harnessed, controlled—in one word (a word which political scientists themselves freely and frequently use), 'institutionalized' in a legal system. I believe that some knowledge of the law is an indispensable condition for the understanding of the notion of the State. It is, to put it mildly, rather strange that political theory should not take greater stock of the age-long effort to conceive of the State as a 'legal fiction'.

REFERENCES

A. F. Bentley, *The Process of Government: A Study of Social Pressures*, Chicago, 1908, repr. 1948, part I, ch. iv; part II, chs. vi; vii, x, xii. D. B. Truman, *The Governmental Process: Political Interests and Public Opinion*, New York, 1951, 6th repr. 1959, part i, ch. 3, 1 and part iv, ch. 16, 1. H. D. Lasswell and A. Kaplan, *Power and Society: A Framework for Political Inquiry*, New Haven, 1950, 5th repr. 1963, Introduction and Part III, ch. viii, § 8, i. D. Easton, *The Political System: An Inquiry into the State of Political Science*, New York 1953, 3rd repr. 1963, ch. iv, 4; ch. v, 2–4.

For a general appraisal of the views discussed in this chapter: Dwight Waldo, *Political Science in the United States of America*, Unesco, Paris, 1956; B. Crick, *The American Science of Politics*, London, 1959; H. Eulau, *The Behavioral Persuasion in Politics*, New York, 1963.

An interesting and striking parallel to what I have called the 'disruption of the notion of the State' in modern political science is provided by the very similar conclusions which, starting from quite different premises, the Italian philosopher Benedetto Croce reached with regard to the State.

To Croce the State was 'nothing else than a process of utilitarian activities by a group of individuals or among the components of that group'. The very word 'State' was misleading and should be shunned by the student of politics. It was coined by the Italian writers of the Renaissance, and sounds almost like a paradox, 'because it recalls the notion of something "static" in a field like political life which, like life in general, is something essentially dynamic, or, more exactly, spiritually dialectical'. These views were fully developed in Croce's *Elementi di Politica*, first published in 1925, and now edited, together with other essays, in the volume *Etica e Politica*, 4th edn., Bari, 1956.

PART TWO

POWER

1

GOVERNMENT BY MEN AND GOVERNMENT BY LAWS

To conceive of the State in legal terms or, which is the same thing, to define power as force exercised according to, and in the name of, law, does not necessarily imply that we are expressing a value judgement on what the State ought to be, nor on the ends to be aimed at in the exercise of power. This definition simply takes account of the fact that the State cannot be conceived in terms of force alone, and that in order to understand its nature we must turn from the easy and obvious statement that there do exist relations of command and obedience between men, to an analysis of the command itself, and of the manner in which it is expressed and carried out in the social context. Returning to our original definitions, we must consider the grounds which make it possible for a particular will to impose itself on others in a certain way and under certain conditions. We must know the particular circumstances and qualifications of the man or group of men from whom the command stems, as well as of those on whom it is laid and who may, if necessary, be compelled by force to observe it.

This proviso is of capital importance. It is the only way of avoiding a possible ambiguity that lies hidden in the contrast drawn between 'government by men' and 'government by laws'—a contrast employed since ancient times to express a meaning distinctly favourable to 'government by laws' as being a better government than 'government by men', just as the contrast between the 'rule of force' and the 'rule of law' is generally understood to imply that the latter is superior and preferable.

The indication of a preference of this kind is itself an expression of a value judgement. It has nothing to do with the conceptual analysis of the relation between 'laws' and 'government', or, in modern language, of the relation between State and law which is our concern for the time being. I certainly do not intend to exclude the possibility of a judgement of that kind, i.e. of a justification of the State *because* it represents a control of force, *because* it ensures law and order. But our present problem is a different one. We have to decide whether and in what sense 'power' can be distinguished from 'force', to ascertain how the fact of using force according to law changes the quality of force itself and presents us with an entirely different picture of human relations. We must, in other words, prove convincingly that the very notion of the State is intimately bound up with the notion of law, not only in the sense that might and right are closely associated in everything that concerns the State, but in the sense that a coherent conceptual construction of the State can only be reached within the legal framework.

As is well known, the contrast between 'government by men' and 'government by laws' played a very large part in Greek political thought. The divergent views of Plato and Aristotle on this point provide a dramatic illustration of a conflict of ideas which reappears throughout the long development of Western political theory.

Plato's ideal in the *Republic* was of a State governed by wise, superior men, by 'philosopher-kings', that is by men who 'know' what is good, and cannot therefore be subject to any control over their commands and decisions. The bonds that hold the State together are not the impersonal rules of law, but the particular gifts of the rulers on the one hand, and the education (today we should say the proper conditioning) of the citizens on the other. As Professor Sabine rightly remarked in his *History of Political Theory*, what chiefly strikes the modern reader in Plato's *Republic* is the 'omission of law'. In view of Plato's premisses, this is a perfectly logical and coherent omission, but it is one which makes the *Republic* of little interest to legal theory.

Plato seems to depart from this decided preference for 'government by men' in his other and later works, the *Statesman* and the *Laws*. In them he stressed the merits of 'government by laws', possibly because he was turning from the ideal to practical realities. In the *Laws* he described the 'common law of the State' as 'the golden, . . . the sacred thread', 'which each of us must follow and never abandon'. In the *Statesman* the rule of law provides the basis of the distinction between 'good' and 'corrupt' kinds of government. The worst of all is tyranny, arbitrary government by one man alone. But for Plato these kinds of 'legal' governments were always dictated by necessity. The ideal remains that of a government founded not on the law but on a rational knowledge of the good. To pursue the good, not merely to establish the rule of law, is the reason for the State's existence.

In open disagreement with Plato, Aristotle emphatically maintained that 'government by laws' was superior to any 'government by men'. 'He who commands that law should rule may . . . be regarded as commanding that God and reason alone should rule; he who commands that a man should rule adds the character of the beast. Appetite has that character; and high spirit, too, perverts the holders of office, even when they are the best of men. Law [as the pure voice of God and reason] may thus be defined as "Reason free from all passion".' 'That from which the element of passion is wholly absent is better than that to which such an element clings. Law contains no element of passion; but such an element must always be present in the human mind.' It is unnecessary to point out that the Aristotelian doctrine of the supremacy of law is much more complex than these short quotations can indicate. If the laws are to be supreme, they must be wisely drawn up and 'just'. Even so, they cannot foresee every eventuality. It is therefore necessary that government by laws should be implemented by government by men (either by a single person or a body of persons) in every case where the law, because of its general character, cannot lay down precise rules. Finally, Aristotle made one important reservation in regard to the supremacy of law—the possible appearance of exceptional individuals, of men whose quality and merits are 'so outstanding as to surpass those of all the rest'. Such men cannot be subjected to what applies to the average. 'They are a law in themselves', and it is right that they should be given unlimited power and be obeyed.

If one conclusion can be drawn from this brief summary of the chief passages in which Plato and Aristotle expound their views on the relationship between law and government, it seems to be this. However different their preferences, their purpose was the same. They were not concerned with assessing the 'nature' of government or power, but with determining the manner in which it is best exercised. They did not stress that law is an essential attribute of the State, but rather that it is an instrument more or less necessary for carrying out the State's activities and for attaining its ends. If this be the case, not even Aristotle's notion of the State, in spite of all the emphasis laid on the need to have a government of laws rather than a government of men, can properly be described as 'juridical' or 'legal'.

Aristotle came much closer to such a notion at the beginning of the *Politics*, where he examined the differences between political association and other forms of social life, such as the household and the village. He pointed out that these differences are not only quantitative but qualitative, and that the power of the statesman differs in kind from the power of the head of a family or of a master of slaves. The most important of these differences lies in the attainment of justice, which in its turn cannot exist apart from law. 'Justice belongs to the *polis*; for justice, which is the determination of what is just, is an ordering of the political association.' The same idea was expressed even more forcibly in the *Ethics*: 'Justice exists only as between men whose relations to one another are governed by a system of law.' A closer examination, however, shows that, even so, the law, the 'ordering', was only one aspect, not the essence, of the State. The ultimate purpose of the State was moral, not strictly juridical. 'It is . . . for the sake of good actions, and not for the sake of social life, that political associations must be considered to exist.' As Sir Ernest Barker has pointed out, the kind of justice that was realized in the State was not merely justice in a 'particular' or formal sense: the kind of justice which consists in respecting the rules and in giving to each one his due. It was justice in a 'general' or substantive sense, a 'good' achieved not only through the outward ordering of rules, but by laws 'intended to make the citizens good', in a constitution ensuring a certain 'way of life'; and above all by means of a system of education directed to prepare, through a process of habituation, the ground for conscious goodness. Such views alone would suffice to distinguish the Aristotelian notion of the State from all that we moderns associate with the strictly legal, as opposed to the 'ethical', notion of the State: the idea that the State is first and foremost concerned with guaranteeing the law, not with promoting the moral life of its citizens.

Possibly Aristotle approached the modern notions of law and State most nearly in a different definition of the constitution, which he put forward in another part of the *Politics*. Here the moral viewpoint, according to which the constitution is defined as 'a way of life', was replaced by a quite different line of approach. 'A constitution (or polity) may be defined as "the organization of a *polis*, in respect of its offices generally, but especially in respect of that particular office which is sovereign in all issues".' A little further on Aristotle indicated his meaning more fully and more precisely: 'A constitution may be defined as "an organization of offices in a state, by which the method of their distribution is fixed, the sovereign authority is determined, and the nature of the end to be pursued by the association and all its members is prescribed". Laws, as distinct from the frame of the constitution, are the rules by which the magistrates should exercise their powers, and should watch and check transgressors.'

As is well known, the first of these two definitions provided the basis of Aristotle's famous classification of political forms, perhaps one of the most popular doctrines of the *Politics*, though it is not without precedent in Greek political thought. The standard adopted here is indeed strictly 'juridical', i.e. formal and technical. It refers to the structure rather than to the ends of the State: more precisely, to the organization and distribution of power. According to whether the ultimate, the 'sovereign', power is in the hands of 'either One, or Few, or Many', three typical forms of government emerge, bearing names which are still used even in our present-day language. Let us not forget, however, that alongside the purely formal, 'juridical', standard, Aristotle resorted to a moral one, which led to a wider classification. Constitutions do not fall only into three subdivisions on the basis of number. They fall into three further subdivisions in accordance with the end pursued by States, in accordance with the just or unjust, good or bad, exercise of power. There thus emerge not three but six typical forms of government: three directed to the common good (Monarchy, Aristocracy, and 'Polity'), three to individual interests (Tyranny, Oligarchy, Democracy). This classification, which welds together both moral and legal, substantive and formal criteria, was destined to become the stock-in-trade of later political theory. Only Machiavelli and Montesquieu dared to make a radical departure from it, as we shall presently discover.

With this definition of the constitution in strictly technical terms, and, perhaps more important still, with this precise assessment of the role of law in the exercise of power, Aristotle does indeed bring us within sight of the answer to the question: what exactly is the relation between State and law, what is it that distinguishes the mere use of force from the exercise of power? We have been told that the *polis* cannot exist without a constitution, that is, without a distribution of power; in turn, that the holders of power are such because of laws that determine their office and duties. This can only mean that the State is a complex of relations between man and man according to rules which can be known and assessed—that the State is a 'legal system'. Clearly, we should not hesitate in attributing to Aristotle the merit of having first grasped the importance of law for the notion of the State, of having paved the way for construing the State as a legal concept. But perhaps in saying this we are belittling the wide scope of Aristotelian political thought, which has been valued historically not so much for its juridical relevance as for its philosophical and ethical significance. For the moment, then, let us be content to remember that the problem of the relation between State and law was far from being unknown to the Greeks. The clear and final interpretation of this relation remains, however, the imperishable glory of Roman legal theory.

REFERENCES

Plato, *The Laws*, Book I, 645; *The Statesman*, XXX–XLI, esp. 293–6. Aristotle, *Politics*, Book I, ch. ii; Book III, chs. i, vi, vii, xi, xiii, xv–xvii; Book IV, chs. i, xi; Book VII, ch. i; and, more especially, 1253^a, 1274^b, 1278^b, 1281^a, 1282^b, 1284^a, 1286^a, 1287^a, 1288^a, 1289^a, 1295^a, 1323^a; *Nicom. Ethics*, Book V, ch. vi, 1413^a.

The passages from Aristotle's *Politics* are given in Sir Ernest Barker's translation. His Introduction, Notes, and Appendixes have provided invaluable help for this chapter.

2

STATE AND LAW:
THE BASIC NOTIONS

THE basic notions to which we still resort in discussing both law and State are, for the greater part, Roman in origin.

This is markedly the case whenever a precise definition of the State is attempted. The definition which Cicero puts into Scipio's mouth in the first book of the *Republic* is of particular importance in this respect.[1] Whatever interpretation is to be given to the deceptively simple phrase, *res publica res populi*, with which that definition opens, the statement which follows is absolutely clear and free from any ambiguity: the State is not based on interest alone, but on law; it is intimately linked to legal experience. 'A commonwealth is the weal of the people; but a people is not any and every sort of human association brought together in any fashion whatever, but an association of many united in partnership by consent to law and by sharing of interests.'[2]

In assessing the grounds of political association Cicero, as can be seen, did not ignore the utilitarian motive—what today we should probably call the State's 'economic' or 'sociological' basis. But alongside of interest Cicero sets the *consensus iuris*, the setting up of laws, as the distinctive mark of the State; 'for indeed', he adds in another passage, 'I cannot conceive of a people unless held together by consent to law'. Like Aristotle, Cicero saw the State as a product of human nature: 'the prime cause of this coming together is not so much man's weakness as a kind of natural human gregariousness.' But, unlike Aristotle, Cicero laid stress not so much on the purpose of political association, on the 'good deeds', on the 'good life' it fosters, but rather on the structure of

[1] Cicero's definition has already been mentioned. The Latin text is given on p. 24.

[2] Like many and better scholars before me, I have tried my hand at giving a new rendering of this difficult passage, though drawing much from McIlwain's and Barker's translations. As I have already pointed out (p. 33), I believe that the old English word *commonwealth* comes very close to the Latin *respublica*, both literally and in meaning.

the State, on the 'plan' (*consilium*) which governs it, on the normalization of human relations it ensures. 'Every people, which is
such an association of many as I have described, every city (*civitas*),
which is an ordering of the people (*constitutio populi*), every
commonwealth, which, as I said, is the weal of the people, must,
if it is to last, be governed according to some plan (*consilio quodam
regenda est*). And this plan must first and always be referred to the
cause which brought the city into being.' Now the forms of political
association may vary according as power is in the hands of one,
few, or all. Discussion as to whether one form is better than another
is possible and profitable. But all political organizations alike have
one thing in common. They must use force in the name, or on the
basis, of a rule, of a binding standard of regular procedure: for a
government is acceptable only 'if it secures the bond which first
joined men together in the partnership of the commonwealth'.
That bond is the bond of the law, for it is law that holds society
together (*lex* [*est*] *civilis societatis vinculum*).

These well-known passages from Cicero's *Republic* would alone
suffice to show how closely connected for the Romans were the
idea of law and the notion of the State. It is, however, important
to notice that Cicero's definition of the State may well not be a
strictly 'juridical' definition. In stressing the acceptance of law
as a requisite of the State, as a condition of the State's existence,
Cicero very probably did not have in mind the acceptance of any
law, whatever its content.[1] *Ius* and *iustitia* are inseparable, and
just as unjust laws are not laws, so a State cannot be a State without
justice. This at any rate, as we know, was the interpretation which,
according to St. Augustine, Cicero himself, through the mouth-
piece of Scipio, gave of his definition of the State as based on the
consensus iuris. Clearly, if this interpretation is accepted, the State
is defined not only in legal, but in moral terms: the requisite of
law leads straight on to a moral evaluation. It was precisely in
view of the paradoxical consequences of such an interpretation

---

[1] I have translated both *ius* and *lex* by 'law', and my reason for doing so is
that *ius*, in the 'objective' sense (i.e. as a *norma agendi*), is in fact equivalent to
lex in Latin usage. As is well known, however, *ius* (like its Continental equiva-
lents *droit*, *diritto*, *Recht*) has a wider meaning than *lex*; it can be taken in a
'subjective' sense (as a *facultas agendi*), and is then better translated by 'right'.
Finally, in its etymologic roots, *ius* is closely connected with the notion of
righteousness (*iustitia*), and, not unlike the English word 'right', admits of
markedly moral connotations.

that St. Augustine, as will be remembered, pleaded for a new definition of the State where moral evaluation is left out, a definition which is thoroughly 'neutral'.

No doubt Cicero's *consensus iuris* can be taken to mean both 'respect for justice' and 'consent to law', and in the former case his definition must be understood as a request for a further justification of the State in terms of justice or natural law, of that 'true law' which he himself described as 'right reason conformable to nature, universally diffused, unchanging and eternal'. Yet in terms of pure definition it is the emphasis on the element of law, not on the quality of the law itself, that particularly matters. In this more restricted sense, the importance of Cicero's definition can be said to lie in the fact that it definitely inserted the idea of law in the notion of the State—from which it was not to be dissociated again, at any rate for many centuries. And it is precisely in this sense that that definition may be said to be still present in the minds of all those who refuse to reduce the State to a pure phenomenon of force, but conceive of it as a power exercised within the framework of legality.

But there are in the passages just quoted two further notions which call for consideration. The first is the notion that there exists in any given political community a supreme power (*summa rerum, summa potestas*) from which the law emanates; and that this, according to where it resides, determines not only the form of government, but the very structure of the State (*status reipublicae*). In the traditional Roman view this supreme power resided in the people, and laws, accordingly, were the expression of the people's will. Gaius, one of the greatest jurists of the classical period, stated this principle very forcibly in a famous dictum: 'Law is what the people orders and establishes';[1] and Papinian, a jurist of the following generation, repeated the same notion in different words: 'Law is the general pronouncement of the community.'[2] As such, statute law (*lex*) is the basic source of law: and it is significant that an earlier writer, Julian, in order to account for the validity of custom (*consuetudo*), had found no better argument than placing it on a level with *lex*: for, he said, it makes no difference whether the people expresses its will deliberately (*suffragio*) or tacitly (*rebus ipsis et factis*).[3]

This principle, that all power derives from the original *potestas*

[1] 'Lex est quod populus iubet atque constituit' (Gai. *Inst.* 1, 2–7).
[2] 'Lex est . . . communis reipublicae sponsio' (*Dig.* 1, 3, 1).   [3] *Dig.* 1, 3, 32.

of the people (*potestas* as distinguished from *imperium*, the power which belongs specifically to individual magistrates), does not interest us for the moment as a political principle, as implying a preference for what today would be called a 'democratic' régime, founded on popular sovereignty. In the *Republic*, Cicero attributed a preference of this kind to the extreme popular faction, where, he adds, it was supported with the characteristic argument that 'in no other city except in one where the people has the supreme power, can liberty find its abode: liberty, than which without doubt nothing can be sweeter'.[1] Cicero's own preferences, as we shall see, were for a 'mixed' régime, about which we shall have more to say later.

Among Roman lawyers, on the other hand, the principle of the derivation of power from the people has a markedly 'juridical' or legal, not a political, meaning. That principle enabled them to present all the various sources of law as stemming from a common root, as we saw was the case with statute law and custom. They held to it faithfully, even after all the sources of law had dried up during the later Empire, when the Imperial 'constitution' came to be the sole expression of positive law. They held to it by construing the power of the prince as being an emanation from, and a conferment of, the original power of the Roman people, in the manner that is described in a famous passage attributed to Ulpian in the *Digest*: 'What the prince has decided has the force of law, inasmuch as by a special enactment (*lex regia*) concerning his government the people has conferred to him and upon him the whole of its government and power.'[2]

In this passage, which was to cause much heated discussion in centuries nearer our own, attention should not be focused solely on the tribute paid to the principle that all power derives from the people. The important point is the notion that there is in the State a power which, whether held by the people or by the prince, is the source of the law, and for this very reason (as is said in another passage from Ulpian, also transmitted to us in the *Digest*) higher than law itself, i.e. *legibus solutus*.[3] This notion cannot be properly

---

[1] 'Nulla alia in civitate, nisi in qua populi potestas summa est, ullum domicilium libertas habet: qua quidem certe nihil potest esse dulcius.' (*De Re Publica*, I. 31).

[2] 'Quod principi placuit legis habet vigorem: utpote cum lege regia, quae de imperio eius lata est, populus ei et in eum omne suum imperium et potestatem conferat' (*Dig.* I, 4, 1). [3] *Dig.* I, 3, 31.

understood except in terms of law itself—as a legal, not as a political, principle. It must not be interpreted as affirming an arbitrary power in the State in the sense that at a certain point, beyond and above the law, the ultimate decision is a matter of force alone, naked and unbridled. Rather, it should be taken as a recognition that the relation between power and law must necessarily appear in a different light when it is considered from the angle of those over whom power is lawfully exerted, or, on the other hand, from the angle of the actual holder of power. In both cases power is conditioned by law: in the case of the holder of power, it may be 'absolute', but it cannot, by definition, be arbitrary. This is the only way to understand how, in the Roman doctrine, power was conceived as force controlled by and subject to law, and yet as the source of law, and thus superior to the law which is its own creation. Indeed, this is the only possible way of giving a plausible interpretation of a celebrated text concerning the relationship between power and law which dates from a period when the Imperial power, having absorbed the whole process of legislation, had become, in the full sense of the word, *legibus solutus*.

The passage occurs in a Constitution of the Emperors Theodosius and Valentinian, set down in the Code, and it solemnly asserts not only that the prince should profess himself bound by the law, but that his very authority depends on it.[1] Clearly, the fact that the lawgiver was the creator of the law did not mean that he was, because of this, 'lawless'. The 'State' remained throughout, in the Roman view, a 'legal structure': and that this was the case is still more apparent if we compare the view, held by Plato and Aristotle and by Greek thought generally, of the exceptional man who may be superior to the law, and indeed be 'a law in himself', with the view presented in a Byzantine text, of the Emperor as *nomos empsychos* or *lex animata*.[2] Whilst in the first case it was the personal qualities of an individual which made the bondage of the laws superfluous, in the second case it was the office which conferred a particular position on the lawgiver in respect of the law, regardless of his personal qualifications. But the 'office' itself was created by the law: *de auctoritate iuris nostra pendet auctoritas*. In

---

[1] 'Digna vox maiestate regnantis legibus alligatum se principem profiteri: adeo de auctoritate iuris nostra pendet auctoritas. Et re vera maius imperio est submittere legibus principatum. Et oraculo praesentis edicti quod nobis licere non patimur indicamus' (Const. 'Digna Vox', *Cod.* I, 14).

[2] *Nov.* CV, 4.

a theory of this kind, power appears as something completely impersonal. This too is a consequence, and, as we shall see, a consequence of no little importance, of the legal approach to the State, of the notion of power as force lawfully exerted.

The last point mentioned—the 'depersonalization' of power— leads us back to a notion already contained in the passages I referred to in Cicero: the notion of the *status reipublicae* as a particular structure, as the particular mode of being, of the community. I have already drawn attention in the first part of this book (Ch. 3) to the importance of this phrase in the formation of our political vocabulary. What should interest us now is the use made by the Roman lawyers of the notion of the *status reipublicae* in order to single out, among the innumerable rules that determine human behaviour, those particular rules which define the distribution and the control of power in the community, and thus to present them in one single category as the very texture, as the essence, of the State. What they did was to distinguish the 'public' from the 'private' concern, and the rules relating to the one from the rules relating to the other: thus positing a distinction which, at any rate in Continental legal theory, still plays a capital role in drawing the dividing line between the sphere of the State and that of all other relations existing in a social context.

This distinction, which has a long history behind it, is summarized in another well-known passage attributed to Ulpian at the beginning of the *Digest*. Legal rules are divided into two main categories, those which affect the interests of private citizens and those which affect the *status reipublicae*, the organization of the State: 'public law is what pertains to the state of the Roman commonwealth; private law, what pertains to the well-being of single individuals.'[1] The 'public', that is the impersonal, character of everything pertaining to the State emerges clearly in this definition: law is said to be public law when it affects the State, and the State, as an abstract entity, is distinguished from, and contrasted with, living, single individuals. In fact the Roman jurists appear to hesitate between this broader conception of public law as consisting of the rules which determine the structure and the organization of the State, and a more restricted view of it as law laid down by the *populus* through the *lex* and other sources regarded

---

[1] 'publicum ius est quod ad statum rei romanae spectat, privatum quod ad singulorum utilitatem' (*Dig.* I, 1, 1).

as equivalent to the *lex*. But it is quite clear that they were deeply aware that not every kind of 'will' could produce rules of a 'public' character,[1] but only a will possessed of certain characteristics and assigned to a particular office: a will which was indeed endowed with force, but was authorized by the law and directed to its maintenance. Power, in other words, is the exclusive attribute of the State and of its officials; it exists for the sake of, and is conditioned by the respect for, the legal order.

On this point the list which Justinian himself gives us of the duties adhering to Imperial power is particularly revealing. In the account which is made of these duties in the Constitution *Deo Auctore*, the Constitution which prefaces his great compilation, the Emperor is quite explicit in saying that they do not end with 'governing the Empire', or in 'bringing wars to a happy conclusion', or in 'ennobling peace'. They reach their highest culmination in guaranteeing the legal order of the State: *statum reipublicae sustentamus*. In the perspective which I have tried to outline this solemn pronouncement may perhaps be taken to sum up, better than any further comment, the lasting contribution of the Roman conception of State and law to political theory.

REFERENCES

Cicero, *De Re Publica*, Book I, §§ 25 and 26, 31 and 32; Book III, §§ 22 and 33, and, in addition, the 'Argumentum Augustini' in *De Civitate Dei*, II, 21 and XIX, 21. (The translations of these passages which I have particularly kept in mind are those given by C. H. McIlwain in *The Growth of Political Thought in the West*, New York, 1932, and by Sir Ernest Barker in *From Alexander to Constantine: Passages and Documents, etc.*, 2nd edn., Oxford, 1959. Mr. C. W. Keyes's translation in Loeb's Classic Library is far from satisfactory.) As a matter of convenience, I have given the references to Justinian's *Corpus Iuris* (viz. the *Digest*, the *Code*, and the *Novellae*) in the footnotes.

I should like to acknowledge my indebtedness, for the analysis of the Roman notions given in this chapter, to the work and to the advice of my colleagues in the University of Turin, Professors G. Grosso, S. Romano, and P. Catalano.

On the distinction between *ius publicum* and *ius privatum* there is a large literature: the most recent work is that of H. Müllejans, *Publicus und Privatus im römischen Recht und im älteren kanonischen Recht*, Munich, 1961.

---

[1] 'ius publicum privatorum pactis mutari non potest' (*Dig.* II. 14. 38).

3

THE RULE OF LAW

THE theory which conceives of the State in terms of law implies, as we saw, a conception of power as the lawful exercise of force. It entails the recognition of a system of human relations clearly set out and ascertained within the framework of legality. But the meaning of 'legality' itself is in turn strictly dependent on the meaning attached to 'law', and accordingly allows of quite different interpretations. The best illustration of this interdependence can be found in medieval political theory. If anything can be taken as its distinguishing mark, it is the emphasis on the paramount role of legality. Indeed, the 'Rule of Law' is the basic assumption of the medieval approach to the problem of power.

At first sight it is difficult to appreciate how the view that law should rule, and not men, differs from that taken by Aristotle in his discussion of the best type of government. The same view was emphatically set forth by Cicero in certain famous passages where he discussed the relation between law and power. Speaking, in the *De Officiis*, of the 'duties of magistrates', he described them as follows: 'The proper task of the magistrate is to be aware that he represents the State and that he must uphold its dignity and honour, respect the laws, define rights, and constantly bear in mind the things that are placed in his trust.'[1] This view is further developed in a passage from the *De Legibus*: 'Here you can see what is the power of the magistrate: he must lead, and command what is right, useful, and in accordance with the laws. For in the same way as the laws are superior to the magistrates, so are the magistrates superior to the people, and it may truly be said that the magistrate is a speaking law, whilst the law is a dumb magistrate'.[2] A correct interpretation of these passages would certainly

[1] 'Est igitur proprium munus magistratus intellegere se gerere personam civitatis debereque eius dignitatem et decus sustinere, servare leges, iura discribere, ea fidei suae commissa meminisse' (*De Officiis*, I, 34, 124).
[2] 'Videtis igitur magistratus hanc esse vim, ut praesit praescribatque recta et utilia et coniuncta cum legibus. Ut enim magistratibus leges, ita populo

require some further explanation of the notion of 'magistracy' in republican Rome, for it is this that Cicero obviously had in mind. Disregarding the historical aspect, however, the point which we need to stress is that Cicero is not here discussing the power *of* the State, but the position of the powers *within* the State. This is a problem altogether different from that of the relation between State and law that we considered in the preceding chapter and which is, for the time being, our proper concern.

Now the medieval conception of the Rule of Law affected not only the exercise of power, but the notion of power itself. The very relation between State and law, indeed the whole notion of the State, was thereby involved. Gierke's admirable description of the case is still worth quoting, for it has never been surpassed in accuracy and breadth:

Medieval doctrine, while it was truly medieval, never surrendered the thought that Law is by its origin of equal rank with the State and does not depend upon the State for its existence. To base the State upon some ground of Law, to make it the outcome of a legal act, the medieval Publicist felt himself absolutely bound. Also his doctrine was permeated by the conviction that the State stood charged with a mission to realize the idea of Law: an idea which was given to man before the establishment of any earthly Power, and which no such Power could destroy. It was never doubtful that the highest Might, were it spiritual or were it temporal, was confined by truly legal limitations.

This is a very different attitude to the State from any we have hitherto examined. The Romans too, as we saw, had conceived of the State in terms of law. Indeed, law and State were to them correlative notions. They could in no way be dissociated the one from the other. Exactly the opposite was the case with medieval writers. They began by separating what the Romans had bound up together. Law and State, though clearly connected, are two different things. In order to provide the basis of the State, law must be conceived as prior to the State, as not depending on it for its existence.

This result was arrived at in two different ways. First and foremost, by setting up natural law over and against all other laws of purely human origin. But it was also arrived at by a peculiar way of conceiving the nature of law which is characteristic of the Middle

praesunt magistratus, vereque dici potest magistratum legem esse loquentem, legem autem mutum magistratum' (*De Legibus*, III, 1, 2).

Ages, at any rate of the earlier centuries. The theory of natural law was an inheritance from classical thought. The Christian writers of the Middle Ages developed it into a complete system. The theory certainly contained precise indications of the nature of law, but it was chiefly concerned to establish a standard of valuation according to which the 'goodness' or 'justice' of the laws could be determined. If anything, the theory of natural law was an answer to the question: how can power be legitimized? rather than to the question: how can force be made lawful? We must therefore focus our attention on the notion of positive law if we wish to understand what the Rule of Law meant to the Middle Ages. Here, and here alone, lies the reason of that difference, so strongly stressed by Gierke, between the medieval and the Roman world as regards law and State, and, more generally, as regards the approach to the problem of power.

To open a medieval law-book is enough to make us realize this difference. In the Introduction to the *Decretum Gratiani*, the great twelfth-century compilation of Canon Law, some very interesting definitions can be found, which in turn go back to earlier sources. According to the first of these definitions, 'Mankind is ruled in two ways, by natural law and by customs (*mores*)'.[1] The distinction between natural and positive law is here presented as a distinction between rules that are universally and absolutely binding, and rules that are peculiar to a given human society. These last, which are human laws in the strict sense, consist in customary practices and habits; and the fact that these practices and habits differ among different peoples is the reason why human laws are manifold and at times even contradictory.[2] In a further paragraph, however, we read that human law consists not only of customs but of 'laws' (*leges*); and that a law, in the strict sense, is a 'written statute' (*constitutio scripta*). Nevertheless, in its deeper essence, human law is primarily custom, and positive legislation is only a way of drawing up custom for some special purpose. 'The point is, that customary law (*consuetudo*) is partly redacted into writing, partly left merely to the practice of those who observe it.

---

[1] 'Humanum genus duobus regitur, naturali videlicet iure et moribus' (*Decr. Grat.*, Dist. 1a).

[2] 'Humanae [leges] moribus constant, ideoque hae discrepant, quoniam aliae aliis gentibus placent' (*ibid.*, Dist. 1, c. i). This definition is taken from Isidore of Seville, a seventh-century writer.

That part of it which is redacted into writing, is called statute or law. That which is not is called by a general name, custom.'[1]

Better than any commentary these definitions bring out the essential character of the early medieval approach to the problem of law, the peculiar concept of law which is the starting-point of medieval political theory. This concept in its turn is crucial for the correct understanding of the particular way in which the relationship between State and law was conceived throughout the Middle Ages. The starting-point was exactly the opposite of the Roman view that law is the creation of the conscious, deliberate will of a legislator, whether it be the will of a whole community or of a single ruler. Law does not owe its existence to a creative act of the will, but is regarded as being one aspect of the collective life, as a set of practices, habits, or customs. The legislative act is depicted not as a manifestation of the will to make rules, but simply as a compilation or written recognition of what already exists as a body of tacitly accepted rules in a given society.

This is no place to examine the difficult and complicated question of the origin and source of such notions. They are usually related to the conception of law held by primitive peoples, and some scholars have not hesitated to see in them the most important contribution made by the barbaric races to medieval political theory. All that needs to be emphasized here is that such notions clearly corresponded to an extremely simplified and archaic view of social institutions, a view that can be found only among primitive peoples, where customs and immemorial traditions are surrounded, as it were, by a religious halo, and are the object of veneration and of respect bordering on fear. Such notions were further characterized by a markedly static conception of social life, in consequence of which law, instead of being regarded as an instrument placed at man's disposal for betterment and change, appeared rather as a limit imposed by a mysterious and transcendent force on the expression of their preferences and on the choices dictated by their needs. The Romans, in the full maturity of their legal awareness, had openly proclaimed the superiority of statutes over custom: the conscious, express will of the legislator can and

---

[1] 'Apparet, quod consuetudo est partim redacta in scriptis, partim moribus tantum utentium est reservata. Quae in scriptis redacta est, constitutio, sive ius vocatur; quae vero in scriptis redacta non est, generali nomine, consuetudo videlicet, appellatur' (*Decr. Grat.*, Dist. 1, c. v).

must always prevail, for it is the true, the ultimate, source of the law. This relation was reversed in the Middle Ages: positive legislation was no more than the recognition, the sanctioning, of law which already existed, *more approbata utentium*. This supreme, impersonal rule was the source, and at the same time the limit, of all political power.

Understood in this sense, the principle of the Rule of Law is the basic principle to be kept in mind in assessing the medieval notion of the State. But, as I have already pointed out elsewhere,[1] the question may well be raised, whether the use of the word 'State' is at all appropriate at this stage. And a further reason for doubt emerges from one other consideration. For indeed, at any rate in early medieval theory, the notion of the 'impersonal' rule of law is met by an equally marked view of the 'personal' character of power. The 'State' is not mentioned anywhere: it is always the 'ruler' who is spoken of, the ruler who is bound by the law and whose power is strictly conditioned. Bracton's famous dictum deserves special mention at this point: 'The King shall not be subject to men, but to God and to Law: since Law makes the King—*Lex facit regem*.' I propose to devote the last part of this chapter to a brief sketch of the more important consequences which derived, in medieval political theory, from this strange combination of the impersonality of law and the personality of power.

The first and perhaps the most important consequence was that power could be conceived only as limited and responsible. It was limited because the ruler was merely the executor of the law. His task was restricted to what we should nowadays call the judiciary and the executive. It was responsible, because law expressed and represented the bond of mutual obligation which united ruler and ruled. This contractual notion of power must not, however, be confused with the abstract constructions of the later theory of the social contract. Its roots lay deep in a constitutional reality, in the typical feudal concept of a bond between ruler and ruled, between lord and vassal. This bond gained recognition and sanction in the oath, which the medieval ruler was expected to take, to maintain the 'old laws', to respect them himself, and to enforce their observance. The State, if by it we understand the exercise of power, rested on the solid rock of the Rule of Law.

[1] Part I, ch. 3, above, esp. p. 29.

A second, and no less interesting, feature of early medieval political thought was the lack of a clear distinction between the 'private' and the 'public' exercise of power. This confusion is usually, and rightly, interpreted as a reflection of feudalism. Just as the bonds between vassal and lord, between subject and king, were personal bonds, so was the relation of command and obedience between men a private matter. The power of the lord or of the king was not different in substance from that of the master of an estate or the father of a family. Aristotle's painstaking analysis of the difference between political power and all other types of power was totally forgotten. But the confusion may not have been entirely due to the appearance of a particular type of social organization based on personal allegiance. It may also, and without undue strain, be seen as the inevitable consequence of the lack of a clear determination of the ultimate source of law: there was no 'State' to which certain particular rules—the rules of law—could be related or attributed.

Parallel, in a certain way, to this lack of distinction between the private and the public sphere was the confusion which occurred between matters religious and political. This is a third and decisive point which must be kept in mind when one talks about the Rule of Law in the Middle Ages. I have already pointed out the important qualification which the word *respublica* receives in the medieval vocabulary. If there was a 'State' in the Middle Ages, it was a Christian state, a *respublica christiana*. But the *respublica christiana*, as Figgis has so well shown, had the features of both a State and a Church—at any rate of what we call 'State' and 'Church' in our modern vocabulary. It was the 'community of the faithful', consisting of many different 'nations', but constituting one single 'mystical body' under the supreme guidance of the Pope and the Emperor. In this mystical body, 'temporal' or secular relations and interests were not clearly distinguished from 'spiritual' or religious ones; in every case the first were subordinate to the second. It is therefore not surprising if the 'law', which rulers were called upon to respect and put into effect, was not an exclusively secular law. Nor is it surprising that, in the absence of a precise notion of the nature of 'public' power, there was also an absence of any clear distinction between the religious and the political sphere. The features proper to the State were not yet recognized as those of a well-defined and wholly independent set of human relations.

The points I have rapidly sketched are, however, only starting-points. Medieval thought soon left them behind, spurred on by practical needs and by ideological factors of great importance. But it is only by starting from them that it is possible to know where to look for the first appearance of new, revivifying ideas which, without altogether destroying some characteristic views that have remained a precious inheritance of Western political thought, were to open the way to that particular legal construction of the State which we may with some reason call modern.

REFERENCES

As mentioned in the text, the brief outline presented in this chapter is based mainly—except for a few variations—on certain well-known works on medieval political theory which can well be considered 'classical'.

These works are: O. von Gierke, *Political Theories of the Middle Age*, trans., with an Introduction, by F. W. Maitland, Cambridge, 1900–22; R. W. and A. J. Carlyle, *A History of Medieval Political Theory in the West*, Edinburgh, vol. 1, 1903; J. N. Figgis, 'Respublica Christiana', in *Churches in the Modern State*, 2nd edn., London, 1914; F. Kern, *Kingship and Law in the Middle Ages*, trans. by S. B. Chrimes, Oxford, 1939; C. H. McIlwain, *The Growth of Political Thought in the West*, New York, 1932.

A translation of the passages from the *Decretum Gratiani*, together with a useful introduction to the subject, can be found in Ewart Lewis, *Medieval Political Ideas*, vol. 1, London, 1954, ch. i, 'The Idea of Law'.

4

IN SEARCH OF SOVEREIGNTY

DURING the centuries of its finest flowering, medieval political theory can be seen moving, slowly at first and then steadily more rapidly, along certain lines of development, in their turn determined by pressing historical needs. The first and most compelling necessity was to substitute for an essentially simple and static conception of society a view better suited to a greater complexity of human intercourse. Second, but no less important, came the need to assess the proper seat of power, and to define its nature in such a way as to differentiate the State from other social institutions with which, as we have seen, it had for some time been confused. These lines of development can be traced back to one central, inspiring motif, to a notion that emerges only gradually and for which political writers long sought a name in vain. For that name —'sovereignty'—was to be 'invented' only after the period usually called the Middle Ages had drawn to its close.

To begin with, provision had to be made for the needs of a rapidly developing society, such as that of the last centuries of the Middle Ages. The primitive, archaic conception of law examined in the preceding chapter—the view that law is essentially custom, that it is 'found', not 'made'—could not but appear inadequate in this new context. It is characteristic of medieval thought that it did not simply abandon the old ideal of the Rule of Law, but held fast to it, transforming it, as it were, from inside. The 'ruler' continued for long to be regarded as bound and conditioned by law in the exercise of his power. But the very concept of law underwent a substantial change. From being conceived as the expression of immemorial use and custom, law came gradually to be viewed as the expression of a consciously planned legislative act, adaptable to new situations and supplying them with suitable rules. This change was above all made easier by a clearer notion of the conditions which confirmed customary rules. These, as we saw, were held to be valid because, and in as far as, they were tacitly

approved by their 'users', that is, by the community in which they
occurred. The community itself should therefore be able to establish new rules as occasion required, and legislation should not be
limited any longer solely to the 'redaction in writing' of those that
already existed by tradition and custom. What mattered was that
the new rules should fulfil the same requirement as did the old
rules, or at least a similar one: that they should be confirmed by
the approval and the sanction of those to whom they would apply.
In the words of a famous maxim, which has a curious history
behind it, a rule that affects all must be accepted by all: *quod omnes
tangit ab omnibus approbetur*.

Without unduly simplifying what is and remains a very complex
historical issue, we can perhaps find here the seeds of two institutions which were to play an important role in later theories
about the State. The first of these is representation, in so far as it
arose from the need to find a constitutional device by means of
which the 'approval' of the community, required to make law
valid, could find clear and positive expression. Authoritative
scholars have recognized one of the most important contributions
made by the medieval theory of corporations in this 'fiction' of
representation, that is in the idea that the will of the individual
components of a community can be indirectly expressed through
delegates appointed *ad hoc*. This idea was worked out and perfected in the definition of the function and duties of collegiate
deliberative bodies, both ecclesiastical and secular. What we call
representative or parliamentary institutions were certainly born in
the Middle Ages: their bitter enemy, Rousseau, made no mistake
when he saw in them a survival of 'feudal' times.[1] They can be
found in almost every European country; but their uninterrupted
and in a sense model development can be most easily followed in
England. There the maxim *quod omnes tangit ab omnibus approbetur* was solemnly invoked at the famous Summons of the Clergy
to Parliament in 1295. There too the notion that 'Parliament
embodies the whole Community of the Realm' was first clearly
proclaimed. Both principles, however differently expressed, have
remained the pillars of the modern notion of the constitutional
State.

A much more complicated and arguable question is whether the
division of powers, or at least a distinction between legislative and

[1] Rousseau, *Social Contract*, III, ch. 15.

executive power, can also be traced back to the later development of the medieval notion of the Rule of Law. A distinction of this kind is in a sense implicit in the notion of power as conditioned by, and limited to, the safeguarding and application of law. It might seem to be logically completed by the recognition of the existence of a power parallel with, and in some sense superior to, that of the ruler, a power able to establish laws, and one to whose discipline everyone, including the ruler, must be subject. Nevertheless, medieval views on this point were on the whole quite different from our modern ones. A precise demarcation, let alone a deliberate contrast between the legislative and the executive, is nowhere to be found in medieval sources. We should look in vain for any abstract definition or vindication of the characteristic constitutional model which we associate with Montesquieu and his school. Professor McIlwain's opinion on this point is decisive: 'There is no medieval doctrine of the separation of powers, though there is a very definite doctrine of the limitation of powers.' No doubt the medieval notion of the Rule of Law provided one of the main foundations of modern constitutional theory. But a very different interpretation of that notion was bound to emerge from the great constitutional struggles of seventeenth-century England. In the hands of Sir Edward Coke, Bracton's dictum *Lex facit regem* takes on a completely new meaning. Only after the question 'who sets the law?' had been settled, could the boundary between laying down the law and bringing it into effect be finally drawn, and serious practical consequences attached to that demarcation. As we shall see in more detail later on, the modern doctrine of the separation of powers was much more than merely a constitutional theory about the structure of power in the State. It was a recommendation about the scope and uses of State-power, a political theory heavily loaded with ideological elements which would have appeared entirely unintelligible to the medieval mind.

However, even while the medieval notion of the Rule of Law was in process of adjustment to the needs of a more intense legislative activity, there can also be noticed a parallel endeavour to assess more precisely the nature of that activity, the kind of power which it both presupposes and entails. Once again, the notion of power appears to be closely linked to the notion of the State. If the existence of the State is conditioned by the existence of a legal system, the existence of a legal system is in turn an indication of the existence of a State. This was the capital discovery which imposed itself on the minds of medieval lawyers and political thinkers the moment they set out to analyse from the legal angle the new institutions which had been gradually overshadowing and superseding the old *respublica christiana*, with its claim to unity and to universal rule. Surely an important step in that direction had already been taken as soon as a device had been found for completing, and if necessary supplanting, the 'good old laws' of a static society, as soon as the source of 'new laws' had been identified in the will, or at any rate in the consent, of a single community. But medieval political theory would never have arrived at an exact determination of the ultimate seat of power, and of the characteristics proper to its exercise, without the help of the clear-cut notions deriving from the renewed study of Roman law.

I have analysed these notions in an earlier chapter. Their influence, when in the eleventh century they spread from Bologna to the rest of Europe, was so great and decisive that it can be said without fear of overstatement that but for them there would have been no modern theory of the modern State. For the philosopher of history that influence may provide a refutation of historical materialism, and a striking illustration of the impact of 'ideas' on social and economic 'facts'. For historians of political theory that influence is a bone of contention: indeed, opinions are still divided on the interpretation, and even more on the evaluation, of the impact of Roman law on Western life and thought. There will always be scholars ready to speak of a *damnosa hereditas*, and to regard Roman law as the chief contributor to the rise of Absolutism in the West. There will always be others ready to trace back to Roman sources the doctrine of popular sovereignty, which is the foundation of the modern democratic State. Whatever exaggeration there may be in such views, it is worth noticing that opinions started differing sharply at a very early stage, since even the first commentators were divided in their interpretation of the Roman texts. In the famous passage from Ulpian, *Quod principi placuit etc.*, some of them read an assertion of a complete and final 'alienation' of the power that had originally belonged to the people, while others saw in it merely the mention of a delegation or 'concession', which left the power of the people practically intact.

But the decisive contribution of Roman law to political theory must be sought elsewhere. It does not consist in the attribution of power to a particular holder. Clearly, the Roman notion of the *populus* as the original source of power could easily be combined with the concept, current in the Middle Ages, of the consent of the community as the source of the validity of law. In this sense it might be correct to say that the rediscovery of the Roman doctrine was an important factor in the rise of democratic thought. But the choice between the alternatives of attributing the ultimate power to the people or to the prince was, at bottom, a matter either of expediency or of party-politics. It did not affect the real substance of the Roman doctrine, the basic assumption that lay behind the two alternatives on which opinions diverged. This basic assumption is that there is somewhere in the community, whether in the people or in the prince, or in both the prince and the people united in one body, a *summa potestas*, a power which is the very essence of the State. The decisive contribution of the Roman doctrine was the new conception of law as an expression of this power, as an instrument which could be used and adapted in accordance with the changing needs of society, as a system of rules that were valid and effective as long as there existed behind them the control of a supreme will: a will which, in virtue of its supremacy, was *legibus solutus*, because it was not accountable to any but itself.

This was the doctrine which, to quote Gierke again, brought about a real revolution in the world of archaic ideas with which medieval thought had so far struggled in vain. By laying stress on the element of law as the cohesive factor in political association it provided an unparalleled tool for the analysis of political experience. Again, by focusing attention on the source of the law, it clearly indicated the way for determining the existence of a legal system, of a 'body politic' as distinguished from all other types of human association. Henceforth it would be a question of finding the 'will which legally commands and is not commanded by others'. All sorts of periphrases were used for lack of an appropriate word in the medieval political vocabulary. But the search for the *summa potestas* as the fundamental attribute of the body politic was none other than the search for what would one day be called sovereignty. A doctrine of this kind was bound to end in the final disruption of the ideal of the *respublica christiana*. A plurality of 'sovereigns' was substituted not only in fact but in law for the sole, exclusive holders of the *summa potestas*, the Pope and the Emperor. This was the unexpected and unpredictable result of the return of Roman ideas.

But the influence of these ideas went still deeper. A clearer grasp of the nature of political power and of its distinguishing features was to bear fruit in other fields as well. These distinguishing features had been neglected or overlooked by earlier medieval thought: hence its 'personal' concept of power and its confusion between the private and the public sphere. The clear definitions of the *Digest* contributed more than anything else to the distinction of these spheres. A 'de-personalization' of power set in that completely altered the perspectives with which men had been familiar until then. Ulpian's distinction between private and public law led to a more precise notion of the difference which existed not only between what pertained to public and private advantage, but between the situations (*res*) and the subjects (*personae*) to which legal rules applied. The rules which related to the *status reipublicae* were those that determined the structure of power, and power, whoever held it, implied a particular kind of relationship, intrinsically different from any other relation existing between men. The very means needed in the exercise of power were attributes of the office, not of the person exercising it: the 'Fisc' or treasury, for example, now ceased to be the private patrimony of the ruler and became a public concern. In short, power now emerged as something which could neither be 'sold' nor 'transferred', because it was inherent in the very structure of the community, in the *status reipublicae*: because without it—without 'sovereignty'—there would be no 'State'. Certainly, this State was not yet 'the State'. It was still a 'condition', a 'way of being' of the community, not an abstract entity, distinct and personified.

But what matters is not the absence of a clear notion of the State in medieval thought. It is this gradually growing awareness of the difference between one kind of human association and others, together with the attempt to establish that difference, to analyse it in legal terms: in terms of a 'sovereign' power which governs, makes laws, judges, and raises taxes, not in virtue of simply possessing material force nor of the personal gifts of a leader, but in the name of a system of rules which, because they pertain to the *status reipublicae*, are rules of public, not of private, law. What matters is not so much the endless discussion on who should be the actual holder of power, but the clarification, which lay behind that discussion, of the nature of power itself: for this alone would in turn enable the political theorist to determine the particular quality of that particular society of which sovereignty is the peculiar and exclusive attribute. In the end the *respublica christiana*, the single universal society, at one and the same time religious and secular, which to medieval eyes had represented the highest form of human association, would be replaced by a new type of organization, increasingly secular, narrower but much more clearly defined. The concept of sovereignty was paving the way for the coming of the modern State.

REFERENCES

Once again I have drawn heavily on many authorities for a quick summary, which, because of its brevity, will necessarily appear sketchy and arguable to a competent eye. For the older authorities the reader is referred to those listed at the end of the preceding chapter, with the addition of such excellent informative books as A. F. Pollard, *The Evolution of Parliament*, 2nd edn., London, 1929; Sir P. Vinogradoff, *Roman Law in Medieval Europe*, 2nd edn., Oxford, 1929; and C. H. McIlwain, *Constitutionalism Ancient and Modern*, Ithaca, N.Y., 1940.

Much recent work could and should be added, but I shall limit myself to mentioning (they both provide detailed bibliographies) two comprehensive and stimulating books: E. H. Kantorowicz, *The King's Two Bodies*, Princeton, 1957; and G. Post, *Studies in Medieval Legal Thought. Public Law and the State, 1100–1322*, Princeton, 1964. This last volume is a collection of essays, exhibiting admirable competence and clarity, and dealing with practically every point cursorily touched upon in my sketch.

Finally, I would like to acknowledge a special indebtedness to a short essay by F. Calasso, ' "Ius publicum" e "ius privatum" nel diritto comune classico', in *Studi in Memoria di F. Ferrara*, vol. I, Milan, 1943, which I have found particularly valuable for my treatment of the problem of private and public law.

These pages were already in the press when Mr. F. H. Hinsley's recent book on *Sovereignty* was published in the 'New Thinker's Library'. I can only express my regret at not having been able to avail myself of it in revising this and the following chapters, the more so since Mr. Hinsley's views on the history and nature of sovereignty seem to differ in many ways from the ones which are presented here, where sovereignty is interpreted as essentially a legal issue.

5

THE BIRTH OF THE MODERN STATE

Is it possible to state precisely when the modern State was born? Even to ask this kind of question sounds so presumptuous, and at the same time so challenging, that there is no need to be a scholar to realize the difficulties it involves. To ask when and how the modern State came into being means nothing unless a definition has first been arrived at as to what is meant by 'the modern State', or at least until a decision has been reached as to which particular attribute definitely establishes its existence: territorial unity, racial or national homogeneity, the monopoly of force, or any other traits that in turn, singly or together, characterize the complex experience of modern State life. The question takes on a more precise meaning only when the State is considered from the viewpoint of law. The modern State is a legal system. The power it exercises is not mere force, but force applied in the name of, and in accordance with, a body of rules, from which in fact we infer that a State 'exists'. The original question is therefore changed into another: how and in what way did the notion arise, the 'modern' notion, of a supreme, exclusive power, grounded on law and yet at the same time the creator of the law, and therefore not subject to other powers, at least not in the way in which the powers over which it has control are subject to it? Put in this way the problem of the birth of the modern State is no other than the problem of the rise and final acceptance of the concept of sovereignty.

In order fully to appreciate the impact of the concept of sovereignty on legal and political theory, it is best to consider separately the two different sets of relations where its influence is more clearly distinguishable: first, the relations of power *within* a given community—in the 'internal' sphere, as it were; second, the relations of power *between* several communities on the 'international' level.

As regards the relations of power which determine the structure of the community itself, it is one of the paradoxes of history that

it was not in support of the State, but of the Church, that the concept of sovereignty was first coherently worked out and its logical
consequences drawn. Long before the secular lawyers had fully
grasped its meaning and value, the lawyers of the Church, some of
whom reached the highest pinnacles of the ecclesiastical hierarchy,
had set out to assess the formal aspects of the organization of the
Church in terms of power and law, and to define the position of
its Head as the holder of sovereignty. The concept of sovereignty
was at once the pillar and the corner-stone of what is usually
called the 'theocratic doctrine', the doctrine which claimed for
the Roman Pontiff the supreme authority on earth—the *plenitudo
potestatis*. This phrase is certainly that which approaches, more
closely than any other used in medieval sources, the modern concept of sovereignty. The 'fullness of power' ascribed to the Pope
was first and foremost a legal attribute. It implied the full control
of the law: 'the Roman Pontiff is considered to hold all the laws
encompassed in his bosom.'[1] But it was also, and at the same time,
a political programme, for it entailed a complete recasting of the
traditional structure of the *respublica christiana*. Its full implications can be seen in the ambitious claim of Boniface VIII to
universal lordship and in the argument on which he and his supporters attempted to base that claim. The argument had a logic
of its own, which was precisely the logic of sovereignty. For—so
the argument ran—there can and must be in any community only
one supreme holder of power, only one ultimate focus of allegiance. Hence the age-old notion of the dual guidance of the world
should be rejected as absurd and obsolete. As Boniface VIII forcibly put it, in words that strangely anticipate Hobbes and Rousseau, a two-headed body is an unworkable 'monster'.[2]

But the concept of sovereignty was not an exclusive monopoly
of Church theory during the late Middle Ages. It can be seen
at work in the secular field as well, though less clearly and less
effectively. The transformation of the old social structures in
accordance with a new pattern of unified rule was a slow and
gradual process: on the Continent of Europe it was not fully
achieved until the French Revolution. The significant point is that
this process was very soon understood in terms which clearly

---

[1] 'Romanus Pontifex . . . iura omnia in scrinio pectoris sui censetur habere.'
[2] Bull *Unam Sanctam*, 1302. On Rousseau's use of the same argument, see
below, p. 112.

indicate a growing awareness of what I have called the logic of sovereignty. It was a logic of this kind which inspired the claim, on the part of individual rulers as well as of ruling assemblies, to *all* the power that, from their reading of Roman law, medieval writers had come to know as belonging to the 'majesty' of the Roman emperor or of the Roman people. Early in the thirteenth century one writer could already remark that 'what is true of the Emperor can equally be held true of all independent rulers. Each one has within his own realm as many rights as the Emperor has within the Empire.'[1] It is as if the rulers of the new communities were vying with each other for a share of the Imperial purple. The internal and external aspects of sovereignty are so closely inter-twined in late medieval literature that it is almost impossible to separate one from the other.

Nowhere in fact was the explosive force of the concept of sovereignty more apparent than on the international level. It was a matter here too of logical consequences. But these logical con-sequences were admirably suited both to explain and to foster what had already been at work for some time in the different corners of Europe: the break-up of the *respublica christiana* into a number of separate, individual, and independent States. Sove-reignty on the international level was felt to be the necessary con-dition of sovereignty in internal matters. In order to be truly 'sovereign', the power which is the supreme source of law within the State must prove not to be dependent on any higher power. It is precisely during this period that such formulae as *Rex in regno suo est imperator* ('a king is an emperor in his kingdom') and *Civitas superiorem non recognoscens est sibi princeps* ('an independent city is its own master') begin to appear and to spread widely. They express in conventional language the claim to sovereignty of the individual States, whether they are City-states still governed at least to some extent democratically, or territorial States ruled by ambitious monarchies.

The origin of these formulae has recently been the subject of much research and controversy. The statement *Rex in regno suo est imperator* used to be traced back to French sources, giving France the dubious honour of having first proclaimed its independence—

---

[1] 'Et quod dictum est de imperatore, dictum habeatur de quolibet rege vel principe, qui nulli subest. Unusquisque enim tantum iuris habet in regno suo, quantum imperator in imperio' (Alanus 'Anglicus', or 'ab Insulis', *ca.* 1207–10).

de iure as well as *de facto*—from the Empire. But some scholars have cast doubts on the exclusive responsibility of what already in the Middle Ages used to be called the national pride of the French (*superbia gallicana*) in bringing about the momentous break. They have pointed out that similar statements were made at the time, not in France only but also in other parts of Europe. Still other scholars in their turn have noted the fact that 'the earliest and most ardent statements of the theory of the *de iure* as well as the *de facto* independence of kingdoms come from canonists and theologians'. Finally, there have been some who have even gone so far as to see behind the spread of the formulae *rex imperator* and *civitas sibi princeps* a deliberate attempt on the part of the Church to undermine the unity of the Empire. The 'modern idea of the State', as one of these writers actually puts it, might thus have been a clerical invention—and a sinister one at that! One thing, at any rate, is certain. Whether its origin was lay or clerical, and its birth-place France or England, Italy or Spain, the notion of the full independence of individual States was almost universally accepted by the end of the Middle Ages. Behind it lay the recognition of the existence, in each independent community, of a single, supreme power, representing the source of the law and the cohesive element of the whole social structure. There lacked only a name to indicate clearly this conjunction of territorial and national independence with supreme legal power. The merit of having coined that name belongs to Jean Bodin, a French writer of the second half of the sixteenth century, who was both a politician and a lawyer.

'A Commonweale is a lawful government of many families, and of that which unto them in common belongeth, with a puissant sovereignty.' In this definition, with which Bodin's great work opens, sovereignty appears for the first time as the distinctive attribute of the State. Bodin boasted that he had discovered sovereignty. He was not entirely wrong in so boasting. In order to appreciate his originality, even before considering the meaning of sovereignty, it is enough to list some of the questions that Bodin set out to unravel with the help of his concept, displaying an ingenuity which distinguishes him sharply from all political writers before him.

Take the definition of the State. According to Bodin, the existence of sovereignty is what distinguishes the State from any other kind of human association. This means that a family (*mesnage*), however large, will never be a State, whereas a State, however small, remains a State as long as it is sovereign: 'a little King is as well a Sovereign as the greatest Monarch in the world.'

Next, take Bodin's definition of a citizen. The important point here is the impersonal relation of subjection. Whatever the differences in social standing, sovereignty entails a formal equality in those who are subject to it. Hence, however powerful an individual may be within his own circle of dependents, in his capacity as a citizen he 'loseth the title of master, head, and lord', yielding submission to a rule which is general and common to all.

Finally, consider the distinction which Bodin draws between 'State' and 'government'. In his view, this too is a 'rule of pollicy . . . not before touched by any man'. The type of State is determined by the seat of sovereignty; the type of government by the way in which power is exercised. The point made here involves a very fine legal distinction. Its importance was to be grasped only gradually by later political thought.

Let us turn now to the various aspects of sovereignty, and first to the short and concise definition Bodin gives of it. 'Majesty or Sovereignty is the most high, absolute, and perpetual power over the citizens and subjects in a Commonweale.' Several points call for attention here.

First, the cogency with which Bodin brings out what we have called the intrinsic logic of sovereignty. The two essential characteristics of sovereignty—perpetuity and absoluteness—which he singles out in his definition, afford a clear illustration of that logic. Sovereignty is 'perpetual' for the very simple reason that it is the basic attribute and the very foundation of the State. Without sovereignty there is no power; and without power the State ceases to exist. Power is here considered in its entirety: as such, it can be neither split nor divided. It can be 'transferred', but not 'conceded', for a limited concession implies that he who concedes, and not he to whom the concession is made, is the true holder of power, i.e. the real sovereign. Sovereignty is 'absolute', not only in the etymological sense of not being bound by law, but also in the sense already suggested that, being indivisible, it tolerates no restrictions or conditions. As medieval theorists had already found out to their cost, sovereignty is indissolubly associated with unity: *amat enim unitatem summa potestas*. Both perpetuity and absoluteness, with their corollaries of unity and indivisibility, would, however, be meaningless unless one further condition were satisfied for power to be truly sovereign: it must be 'highest' or ultimate, i.e. not derived from any superior power. In this sense sovereignty means full independence in the international sphere: 'there is none but he an absolute sovereign, which holdeth nothing of another man.'

Second, the particular feature of power which Bodin considers distinctive of sovereignty. That feature consists in what we should nowadays call the legislative function. 'Wherefore let this be the first and chief mark of a sovereign prince, to be of power to give laws to all his subjects in general, and to every one of them in particular.' 'Under this same sovereignty of power for the giving and abrogating of the law, are comprised all the other rights and marks of sovereignty: so that (to speak properly) a man may say, that there is but this only mark of sovereign power considering that all other rights thereof are contained in this.' It has been pointed out that Bodin's teaching here differs considerably from that of other writers of his time, for whom the chief attribute of sovereignty was not legislation but jurisdiction. The difference is of capital importance. Bodin's view exercised a decisive influence on the manner in which the respective roles of the various State "powers" were conceived in later days. We shall be better able to appreciate its farreaching consequences in the further course of this book.

Last, but not least important, the field in which sovereignty bears sway. This is the field of law proper, of positive law: for law is to Bodin the command of the sovereign, and it is through the channel of law that sovereignty makes itself known and felt. From the point of view of positive legislation, the sovereign is thus technically *legibus solutus*; but this does not mean that his power is arbitrary and lawless, since this would be a contradiction in terms. In point of fact, Bodin's sovereign is tied by a number of fetters: he is subject to the laws of God and of nature; he must respect property and private conventions; he cannot alter or abrogate the *leges imperii*, the basic constitutional provisions which, like the Salic law, establish the line of succession and thus lay down the very conditions that legitimate sovereignty itself.

The points which I have briefly summarized should suffice to indicate how essentially abstract and detached is Bodin's approach to the problem of sovereignty. He was not so much set upon propounding a political programme as on analysing the nature of power, on laying down the conditions which apply to all States. To him, a sixteenth century Frenchman, the ultimate holder of power, the 'sovereign', was the king. His theory of sovereignty had a direct and obvious bearing upon the predicament of the French monarchy of his days. But, on Bodin's own directives, it was perfectly possible to trace the presence of sovereignty in any other form of political organization, such as those where the whole community or a restricted number of individuals were the holders of power: sovereignty there must be if there is to be a State. Thus, in Bodin's hands, the concept of sovereignty somehow appears like a model specially constructed for the purpose of interpreting the system of power which had emerged at the close of the Middle Ages and was henceforth to characterize the modern age. Machiavelli, it could be further suggested, had described that system in terms of force as the 'new principality'. Bodin described it in terms of law and power as the 'sovereign State'. The word sovereignty provided a name for something that was new and unheard-of, and yet had its roots in experience and was the product of a slow and gradual growth.

Once again, what was needed was a neologism. With Bodin the word 'sovereignty' entered the vocabulary of law and politics as the word 'State' had done with Machiavelli. But its acceptance was not completely unchallenged. A French term, even if it came from Latin, the word 'sovereignty' was only slowly incorporated in other European languages. Its exact equivalent in Latin was for a long time doubtful, and Latin continued for more than a century to be the official language of writers on politics and law. Bodin, in his own Latin translation of the earlier French version of the *République*, used the word *maiestas*, but also at times the phrase *summa potestas*, to render the meaning of *souveraineté*. Grotius used *summa potestas* and *summum imperium* indifferently in the *De iure belli ac pacis* (1625) wherever sovereignty is mentioned. Hobbes treated these last two phrases as equivalent in the *De Cive* (1642), where he even listed them in the same context: *summa potestas sive summum imperium sive dominium*. But in the *Leviathan* (1651) he condensed all these various expressions into one: sovereignty. No wonder it is to Hobbes that our thoughts readily turn when we think of the full implications of sovereignty. The myth he created was so forceful and challenging that it still haunts our minds and our hearts. If anything marks, once and for ever, the birth of the modern State, it is the myth of Leviathan. Let us take a closer look at Leviathan itself, even if only to realize the menace it contained.

REFERENCES

Jean Bodin, *Les Six Livres de la République* (1st edn., 1576), Book I, chs. 1–2, 6, 8–10; Book II, chs. 1–2. Quotations (spelling modernized) are given from Richard Knolles's translation, *The Six Bookes of a Commonweale*, 1606 (facsimile reprint, ed. by K. D. McRae, Harvard Univ. Press, 1962).

On the growth of the notion of sovereignty in both ecclesiastical and secular literature during the last centuries of the Middle Ages the most recent and important works to be consulted in English are the following: B. Tierney, *Foundations of the Conciliar Theory*, Cambridge, 1955; W. Ullmann, *Principles of Government and Politics in the Middle Ages*, London, 1961; M. Wilks, *The Problem of Sovereignty in the Later Middle Ages*, Cambridge, 1963; G. Post, *Studies in Medieval Legal Thought*, Princeton, 1964. But among older works there are two which still deserve particular mention: J. N. Figgis, *From Gerson to Grotius*, Cambridge, 1907 (now available in Harper's paper-backs); and C. N. S. Woolf, *Bartolus of Sassoferrato*, Cambridge, 1913.

Among the many foreign books dealing with the problems discussed in this chapter I should like to acknowledge a special debt to the following: F. Ercole, *Da Bartolo all 'Althusio*, Florence, 1932; F. Calasso, *I Glossatori e la teoria della sovranità*, Milan, 1945 (3rd edn., 1957); S. Mochi-Onory, *Fonti canonistiche dell'idea moderna dello Stato (imperium spirituale—iurisdictio divisa—sovranità)*, Milan, 1951; G. de Lagarde, *La naissance de l'esprit laïque au déclin du Moyen Age*, vol. I, 3rd edn., Louvain, 1956, vol. II, 2nd edn., Louvain, 1958; P. Mesnard, *L'essor de la philosophie politique au XVIe siècle*, Paris, 1936; F. A. von der Heydte, *Die Geburtsstunde des souveränen Staates*, Regensburg, 1952.

6

LEVIATHAN UNFETTERED

HOWEVER well he may have been acquainted with law, Hobbes was a philosopher, and a very great one, before he was a jurist. As a philosopher he was bound to see the State in terms of authority rather than in terms of might or of power. His concern was not with factual description; it was to account for the existence of the State on rational grounds. He was perfectly well aware that relations of command and obedience can be set up on the ground of force alone, and that the patterns of regularity in men's behaviour and mutual intercourse do not necessarily depend on their scope and rationality. But considerations of this kind were to him nothing more than the introduction to the proper understanding of politics. Its ultimate secrets, he believed, could not be unravelled unless political obligation itself was explained. The search for such an explanation is something quite different from that which moves the jurist or the political realist in his inquiry regarding the State. The explanation which Hobbes offers is an extraordinarily compact, complete, and coherent one. The most extreme consequences follow with impeccable logic from a few basic premisses concerning the nature of man and his capacity for thought and action. Both in its object and in its method Hobbes's theory of the State is a philosophical, not a legal or a political, theory. With this theory I am not concerned at this stage. To defend or refute it implies accepting or rejecting a particular view of human affairs, a particular kind of justification of authority which Hobbes believed that he had found once and for all.

But the greatness of the political philosopher has for long hidden another element of greatness in Hobbes. He was not only the philosopher of authority. He was also an extraordinarily lucid analyst of power—of power in the sense in which I am taking the word here, that is of institutionalized force, or force channelled by law. He was concerned not only with justifying the State, but with assessing its nature. His inquiry into the concept of sovereignty stands out as a milestone in modern political thought. Indeed, it is only comparatively recently that this special value of Hobbes's teaching has been fully realized. When once old enmities had subsided, and the question of the 'atheism' and 'immorality' of the philosopher of Malmesbury had ceased to be an issue, Hobbes's political theory appeared in a totally different light, and could be hailed as what it certainly is, 'the first modern theory of the modern State'. The very fact that this theory was worked out as it were in a test-tube, with no direct reference to this or that particular experience, gives it a significance that may well be described as unique. As Hobbes himself put it, in that startling language of his, which is by turns imaginative, ironic, and sharp: 'I speak not of the men, but, in the abstract, of the seat of power, (like to those simple and unpartial creatures in the Roman Capitol, that with their noise defended those within it, not because they were they, but there).' As a theorist of power, Hobbes was not defending a cause. He simply analysed a situation, taking stock of what was the case in his days. To undertake this kind of analysis meant coming to grips with the very core of the modern problem of politics. To state its limits and shortcomings does not amount to a refutation of Hobbes, but to a discovery of what it was that could interfere with his vision, which was otherwise nearly always clear-sighted, and indeed almost devastatingly so.

Sovereignty for Hobbes was not simply an attribute of the State, a function exercised within it and in its name. It was the very 'soul' of the political body, of that mighty being which he symbolizes in Leviathan, the invulnerable and undefeatable monster of which it is said in the Bible (Job xli. 24–25): *Non est potestas super terram quae comparetur ei.* But this soul is 'an artificial soul', as the State is an artificial person. While perfecting on the one side, as Gierke pointed out, the idea of the personality of the State, Hobbes on the other dealt a death-blow to the traditional comparison of the State with an organism, as well as to all explanations of politics in terms of pure factual growth.[1]

They who compare a City and its Citizens, with a man and his members, almost all say, that he who hath the *supreme power* in the City, is in relation to the whole City, such as the head is to the whole man; but it appears by what hath been already said, that he who is endued with such a power, (whether it be *a man*, or a *Court*) hath a relation to

[1] See Part I, ch. 1, p, 17–20.

the City, not as that of the head, but of the soule to the body. For it is the soule by which a man hath a will, that is, can either will or nill; so by him who hath the *supreme power*, and no otherwise, the City hath a will, and can either will or nill.

A creation of man, not a natural product, the State exists in so far as there is an accepted rule for making and enforcing decisions, in so far as there exists a 'common power', 'representing' and 'impersonating' the wills of the single individuals and reducing them to harmony and unity. 'The *pacts* and *covenants*, by which the parts of this body were at first made, set together, and united, resemble that *fiat*, or the *let us make man*, pronounced by God in the creation.' Sovereignty, which is the soul of that body, is an artifact like the State, because it is the result of an artificial bond, of that 'authorization' and 'renunciation' that take place with the social contract. Sovereignty no doubt is closely linked with force, but is not to be confused with it. When it 'departs' from the State, then, and only then, 'is the commonwealth dissolved', for this means that the bond of obligation that held the State together does not hold any longer. This, and this alone, indicates the real 'death' of the State, of which defeat on the battle-field is only a token. 'For the sovereign is the public soul, giving life and motion to the commonwealth; which expiring, the members are governed by it no more, than the carcase of a man, by his departed, though immortal soul.'

Clearly, the State is for Hobbes not a mere phenomenon of force. Power—of which sovereignty is the highest and completest expression—is force, but force in some way qualified and harnessed. Indeed, the rise of the State coincides with the rise of law: for the transition from the 'state of nature' to the 'civil state' is in fact nothing else than the transition from the rule of force, where there is no 'security', to that of law, where at last human relations are secured and predictable. Of course, the rule of law without force would be void. 'Covenants, without the sword, are but words.' The State, therefore, is a system of force besides being a legal system. Leviathan, 'that mortal god, to which we owe, under the immortal God, our peace and defence', must have 'so much power and strength conferred on him, that by terror thereof he is enabled to form the wills of them all, to peace at home, and mutual aid against their enemies abroad'. Paradise lies in the shadow of the sword: but 'power' and 'strength' are not synonymous, and the sword alone is an inadequate weapon. There is, indeed, the greatest contrast between the well-ordered association secured to men by the 'terror' of the law, and the true reign of terror from which men have emerged and into which they would plunge again if the 'power' of law was not enforced by the 'strength' of the sovereign. For the state of nature is not an imaginary state. It is an ever-present menace. It lurks beneath the glossy surface of civilized life. It is actually there, for us to take notice of, in the 'condition of war' in which States are with one another: a condition that, even when it does not break into actual fighting, is still at any rate one of 'cold war', since they keep 'their weapons pointing, and their eyes fixed on one another', 'in the state and posture of Gladiators'.

Thus Hobbes's sovereign State may well be described, in Dante's words, as 'the horseman of human wills'.[1] Law itself, as the command of the sovereign, is nothing but an expression of will. Hobbes's 'voluntarism' seems to know no boundaries. His, we hear it often said, is the full heritage of Nominalism, of a tradition of thought which denied that the notions of right and wrong, of just and unjust, have any meaning except as mere terms of reference. 'Where there is no common power, there is no law, no injustice.' And if, on the other hand, law does not derive its legal quality from its intrinsic content, but merely from the will of the sovereign, there is obviously no way of conditioning its value by any objective standards, be they of 'justice' or natural law, or even of positive morality. This does not, of course, exclude the possibility of assessing laws as 'good' or 'bad' according to standards of appropriateness or of utility. It means only that our approval or disapproval has nothing to do with the 'validity' of law, which is a purely formal criterion. The last nominalist, Hobbes can equally well be described as the first legal positivist.

Yet when all this is said, it is of the utmost importance to notice some further points which are often neglected. Just as the State is not pure force to Hobbes, so sovereignty is not arbitrary will; quite the contrary. To begin with, not any will can create the law, but only that will which has been 'authorized' to that end, the will of the 'sovereign representative' acting as *persona civitatis*. And even though this will, inasmuch as it is sovereign, is *legibus solutus*,

---

[1] 'Cavalcatore de la umana voluntade' (*Convivio*, IV, ix, 10): the description refers to the Emperor as the source of the law, according to the Roman doctrine.

it cannot violate the very reason for which it 'was trusted with the sovereign power, namely the procuration of the safety of the people'. This may well seem to interpolate a judgement of value into what had sounded so far to be a purely formal and descriptive approach. Yet it may also and very well be explained merely in terms of non-contradiction: for if the mark of the civil state, as contrasted with the state of nature, is the 'security' of law and the 'foresight' which it entails, surely there is no civil state, no sovereign, no 'State', when that security and foresight are lacking.

Perhaps we might try to put these remarks in a more modern idiom. Hobbes's notion of sovereignty is infinitely more complex and subtle than is usually believed, certainly much more complex than Austin's. It is based not on fact but on principle. 'Authorization', not 'habitual obedience', is what 'makes' the sovereign. To conceive, as Hobbes does, of State and law as coeval, means that there are legal limitations on the sovereign power, even though these limitations consist of disabilities rather than of duties. It implies that the sovereign is qualified to legislate under certain existing rules, even though these rules are built-in in the system and confer upon him an unrestricted power. It sanctions the position of the modern State as sovereign *qua* independent: that independence is not, however, a question of force alone, but presupposes the absence of a higher and different system of rules conferring power on the national sovereign. In short, Hobbes's theory of sovereignty is a description of the State in terms of power, not of might; it is an attempt to show that the State can be understood only as a legal system.

Seen in this light, and in the historical perspective in which we have so far been conducting our inquiry, the conclusion can only be that there is nothing particularly extravagant or unheard-of in Hobbes's theory of sovereignty. True, the last fetters within which Bodin sought to contain Leviathan have fallen apart. The laws of nature and of God are not properly laws until they are interpreted and sanctioned by the sovereign. There is no 'fundamental law' in the State except the one which imposes on the subjects the duty of obedience. But the tokens of sovereignty—unity, indivisibility, absoluteness—are the same for both Bodin and Hobbes. Both authors voice the demand, in a period of bitter civil strife, for a stable and lasting solution of the problem of divided allegiance: a solution which cannot be found unless the *locus* of power is first assessed, unless it is clearly stated whose commands are 'laws', to whom they may be lawfully addressed, and for what end, and within what limits. In stressing the need for a strong, definite, and centralized government, Hobbes may seem merely to follow in Machiavelli's footsteps. But his approach is entirely different from that of the political realist. For him the modern State does not rest on the monopoly of force only, but of law. In making sovereignty the basic attribute of the State he was paving the way for the notion of the State which is still, whether we like it or not, the one with which we labour today: of the State that combines unity of power at home with independence abroad—of the 'national State' under whose banner the world has moved during the last three centuries.

What then can possibly be the explanation of the 'scandal' caused by Hobbes's teaching, of the almost unanimous execration with which it was received by his contemporaries and by his own fellow countrymen on both sides of the fence, conservatives as well as revolutionaries? I have already made it clear that I have no intention of discussing the greatest cause of that scandal, the philosophical premises on which Hobbes's political theory rests— his 'nominalism', his agnosticism, his deliberate challenge to all the accepted taboos of his time. No doubt these premises have to be taken into account for a correct understanding of Hobbes's notion of the State, and I have already pointed out how thoroughly subversive that notion was of the traditional view of the relation between State and justice. But since our discussion here is restricted to Hobbes's analysis of power, the question is not so much whether those premises were right or wrong, as whether that analysis was accurate and fair, and how much of it has survived and has become part and parcel of our political heritage. Now to a question of this kind the only possible answer is that what has survived is precisely what corresponded to a correct analysis of a factual reality. For it seems difficult to deny that the modern State has effectively secured for itself the monopoly of both law and force which Hobbes described under the name of 'sovereignty'. In this sense, Hobbes's 'invidious truths' have turned into today's generally accepted truisms: and they will remain such, at any rate until a new political situation, which may already be in process of development, has taken the place of the one we still live in. Here and now, as things stand, it would not enter anyone's head to doubt that the laws of the State, whether good or bad, are 'valid' laws; nor would anybody venture to maintain that the use of force is not the exclusive prerogative of State power. Sovereignty, as defined by Hobbes, still remains the essential characteristic of political experience.

But just at the very moment when Hobbes seems to hold up the mirror to the future, and to be about to reveal all the secrets of the modern notion of the State, his excessively logical mind, his passion (one would almost be tempted to say) for carrying on his argument to the bitter end, blur and obscure the picture. It is, therefore, not surprising that the 'lesson of facts' does not wholly correspond to the excessively abstract model he erects to interpret that lesson. Three points in particular deserve to be kept in mind if we want to ascertain how greatly the modern notion of the State departed and still departs from Hobbes's notion.

First and foremost, with regard to the structure of power. Hobbes and Bodin, as we saw, both emphasized unity as the main attribute of sovereignty: unity, which implies the indivisibility of power. Except in times of upheaval and civil war, the sovereign (be it 'a man' or 'an assembly of men') is always one and one only. The 'rights of sovereignty' cannot be divided except at the risk of shattering the very existence of the State, as happened in England during the 'horrible calamities' which brought a great nation to the edge of ruin. But Hobbes completely overlooked Bodin's careful distinction between the seat and the exercise of power, between the form of the State and the form of government. He thus not only closed the door, which Bodin had left open, to the possibility of combining the unity of sovereignty with a variety of different ways in which sovereignty may be brought to bear upon its subjects. He also, had his notion of sovereignty carried the day, would have made it impossible ever to conceive of the 'division of power' in its modern, constitutional sense, according to that doctrine which, as we shall see, was to come to maturity in a period when the notion of sovereignty was generally held and practically unchallenged.

The second point of departure lies in the manner of conceiving the legal system. Hobbes's doctrine that law is coeval with the State and that there is no law where there is no common power— the doctrine, that is, that there is only one unique type of law, the command of the sovereign—was in marked contrast even in his lifetime with the theory of international law which was being given final shape by such great lawyers as Grotius. For Grotius, law did not stop at the level of the State. It extended also to international relations. No doubt States are sovereign in the sense that they are creators of the law within their own boundaries. But if law is in essence a pattern of regularity, a way of harnessing and controlling force, there is no contradiction in saying that States can be subject, even if only voluntarily, to a law that they normally respect in their relations with other States and which, after all, confirms, and even further legalizes, as it were, their sovereignty. By defining law exclusively as a command, Hobbes not only shut himself off from all possibility of understanding the nature of international law; he also impoverished the very concept of law as well as that of a legal system. An echo of his views is still present with us in the difficulty we find in dissociating the concept of law from that of the State, in constructing a model which may fit not only international law but other kinds of legal experience. But some recent theories, of which we shall have more to say, are a clear indication that we are moving further and further away from the teaching of *Leviathan*. The modern doctrine of the plurality of legal systems, if accepted, provides a much richer, more complex, and more fully developed view of the phenomena peculiar to law than the rigid monism of the Hobbesian and Austinian model.

Finally—to complete the list of the several points where Hobbes's forecast of the future was belied by historical events—his demand for a thoroughly unified society found an insurmountable obstacle in the survival of one of the views which he had more directly challenged and fought against. This was the Christian conception of a type of association which cannot be accounted for in purely political terms, the idea of the Church as a visible organization, distinct from and independent of the State. It was precisely here that Hobbes's teaching had sounded more revolutionary, rejecting as it did, with ruthless determination, any possible dualism within the unity of the sovereign State. '*Temporal* and *spiritual* government, are but two words brought into the world, to make men see double, and mistake their *lawful sovereign*.' To set up a spiritual against the civil authority amounts to creating 'another kingdom, as it were a kingdom of fairies, in the dark'. 'A Church . . . is the same thing with a civil commonwealth, consisting of Christian men.' Rousseau, the first complete theorist of the 'ethical

State' in the modern sense of the word, lavished his praise on
Hobbes for this radical denial of the traditional dualism. 'Of all
Christian writers,' he wrote, 'the philosopher Hobbes alone has
seen the evil and how to remedy it, and has dared to propose the
reunion of the two heads of the eagle, and the restoration throughout of political unity, without which no State or government will
ever be rightly constituted.'[1]

Nevertheless, the greatest caution is advisable when speaking of
the novelty of Hobbes's views in this respect. The idea of State
and Church forming one single body had been clearly put forward
in England at the time of the breach with Rome. Indeed, some of
its exponents, and perhaps the whole 'Tudor theory' of Church and
State, seem to foretell Hobbes's point, and propound it with the
same vigour and clearness. On the other hand, the idea of a single
society in which Church and State coincide, may also, in some of
its aspects at any rate, be viewed as an inheritance from the
medieval conception of the *respublica christiana*. The real novelty,
even in Hobbes's days, may rather be seen in the view, which
was gradually taking shape, of State and Church as independent
societies, each in its own way 'perfect' and complete: a view that
has paved the way for our modern, pluralistic society, a society
radically different from the one Hobbes had in mind.

Unity, uniqueness, and oneness: no power, no law, no society
except with the State and within the State. No better description
could be given of the gist of Hobbes's political theory, no better
explanation of why that theory went straight to the core of the
modern problem of politics, contributing more than any other to
shaping the modern notion of the State. Indeed, Hobbes's State
is the modern State; but it is also, and at the same time, its *reductio
ad absurdum*, almost its caricature. The myth of Leviathan was an
inspiration; but it was a warning too. On closer inspection, the
'mortal God' could be seen to be nothing more than a splendid
machine built and set in motion by men for the use of men. In
good time, the menace of Leviathan unfettered could be thwarted.
The delicate mechanism could be improved, perfected, and controlled. We may well be glad that neither power, nor law, nor
society, was ever thoroughly moulded according to the pattern
which Hobbes had outlined. But we should never forget the debt

---

[1] Rousseau, *Social Contract*, IV, ch. 8 (trans. by G. D. H. Cole).

we owe him for our notion of the State as the creature of law, as the embodiment of power, and not of might only.

REFERENCES

Hobbes, *Elementa Philosophica De Cive* (1642), Preface and chs. vi and x (quotations given from the English version made by Hobbes, with the title *Philosophical Rudiments concerning Government and Society*, London, 1651); *Leviathan, or Matter, Forme and Power of a Commonwealth* (1651), Dedication, Introduction, and chs. xiii, xvi, xvii, xviii, xxi, xxvi, xxix, xxx, xxxix. Austin, *The Province of Jurisprudence Determined*, Lecture vi.

I shall not even try to list the many works, old and new, from which I have drawn inspiration for this chapter: it would take too much space and would be a waste of time, since many good bibliographies are available. But scholars usually tend to focus attention more on the philosophical than on the legal side of Hobbes's political theory—witness the heated debate which has recently taken place on Hobbes's concept of obligation.

I would therefore like to record the particular stimulus I have derived for the interpretation of Hobbes here offered from the work of two outstanding contemporary legal philosophers, Professor H. L. A. Hart and Professor N. Bobbio. The latter's Introduction to his Italian translation of Hobbes's *De Cive* (2nd edn., Turin, 1959) has provided many of the views, developed in this chapter, concerning Hobbes's 'modernity'; while the former's discussion of the problem of sovereignty in *The Concept of Law* (Oxford, 1961, ch. iv, § 3, ch. vii, § 4, and ch. x, § 3) has been of much help in confirming and further clarifying the interpretation of Hobbes's concept of sovereignty which I had already outlined in the Italian edition of this work.

7

THE 'MIXED STATE' AND THE 'DIVISION OF POWER'

How can power be controlled without contradicting the logic of sovereignty, with its emphasis on unity, indivisibility, and absoluteness? Clearly, a question of this kind presupposes an acquaintance with that logic. The question could not have been asked had the doctrine of sovereignty not provided the challenge. The discomfort aroused by Hobbes's teaching was highly significant. That teaching had seemingly struck at the very root of the old conviction that all power corrupts and that absolute power corrupts absolutely. Political writers set themselves the task of 'hooking' Leviathan. They tried all possible means of restoring the supremacy of justice and natural law which Hobbes had imperilled. They set about defining the scope and ends of the State anew, exploring the deepest foundations of political obligation. They even overlooked, in so doing, the soundness of some of the grounds which Hobbes had himself provided. Legal theorists went the other way round. They elected to meet Hobbes on his own chosen territory. They focused attention on the problem of power. The question for them was not so much to confute Hobbes as to take the sting out of his teaching. It was a question of finding out whether power might not be ordered in such a way as better to ensure that 'security' posited by Hobbes himself as the necessary and minimal condition for the State's existence. Here, then, was the constitutional problem of the modern State in a nutshell: to control power without destroying sovereignty. The modern theory of the division of power provided an answer to that problem. It was a typical post-Hobbesian product. This, however, is no excuse for ignoring some of its most interesting and illustrious precedents.

The idea of resorting to some constitutional device in order both to reinforce the stability of the State and to prevent its power from becoming arbitrary is no novelty in the history of political thought. Once again we are brought back to the Greeks, on whom first dawned the thought of combining the advantages of the different simple types of constitution in such a way as to prevent the State from 'degenerating', that is, from turning from a 'good' into a 'corrupt' form of government. The idea of a 'mixed constitution' was a commonplace of Greek political thought. It was developed at length by Plato in Book III of the *Laws* and by Aristotle in Book IV of the *Politics*. The mixed constitution did not represent an ideal for Plato or Aristotle. Even Aristotle had no doubt that 'the best [constitution] must be the one which is administered by the best'. But, as a system adaptable and practical 'for the majority of States and men', Aristotle recommended 'a middle or mixed type of constitution' or *polity*, a moderate form of democracy, which for many reasons he held to be the most likely to be beneficial and stable. Even here, however, Aristotle seems to be inspired more by moral and political than by strictly legal considerations. The mixed constitution he envisaged was not so much a combination of those particular elements of each simple form that relate to the exercise of power, as a blending of the principles which inspire and are proper to each of them. His aim does not seem to be to effect the control of power so much as to strike the right balance between virtue, wealth, and numbers.

From a 'juridical' point of view the theory of the mixed constitution developed by Polybius in Book VI of his *History of Rome* is much more interesting. After giving a penetrating criticism of the various simple forms and describing the perpetually revolving cycle in which they follow one another, Polybius praised the wisdom of those constitutions where the elements of the various simple forms were united. He instanced on the one hand the classic example of the Spartan constitution, the work of the genius of a single lawgiver, and on the other hand the practical illustration provided by the existing Roman constitution, which, unlike the Spartan, was the product of age-long trial and experience. In republican Rome, according to Polybius, the royal element was represented by the Consuls, the aristocratic by the Senate, the democratic by the assemblies of the people. Polybius attributed the strength and stability of the Roman State to this combination of the three types of government. Many writers have seen in his theory the oldest expression of the idea of the balance and mutual control of powers in the State.

About one century later Cicero, in Books I and II of the *De Re*

Publica, developed the idea of the mixed constitution as the *optimus status rei publicae* on lines very similar to those of Polybius. For him too the highest praise of the constitution of republican Rome was reserved for the happy combination of the three basic forms of government it afforded. There is a very interesting comment of Cicero's on this point, although the fragmentary condition in which his treatise has come down to us does not allow us to be quite certain of the correct interpretation of the passage where it occurs. Cicero seems to indicate that the mixed constitution ought to consist not in the mere overlapping of the outward countersigns of the different forms of government, but in a precise assignment of functions to the different parts of the community. 'This you should bear in mind, as I said from the beginning: that the stability of the State cannot be preserved unless there is a fair balance between right, duty and office (*aequabilis . . . compensatio et iuris et officii et muneris*), so that there may be enough power in the magistrates, and authority in the decision of the elders (*principum*) and liberty in the people.' The view here expressed takes on a more precise meaning when it is put alongside another famous passage in the *De Legibus*, where Cicero says that, 'by a fair distribution of rights—power resting in the people and authority in the Senate—it is possible to maintain the State in concord and moderation'.[1] The ultimate source of power for the Romans was, as we know, the people. But this would not seem to exclude, indeed would seem to be perfectly compatible with, the performing of the governing functions by several appropriate media.

The theory of the 'mixed State' or of the 'mixed constitution' (the distinction between the two concepts does not appear to have any special relevance before Bodin's time) was taken up again and developed with strong approval by medieval political writers. St. Thomas Aquinas may serve as an example for all the others. He returned repeatedly to this idea. He started with the typically medieval preference for kingly government as the best form of government. But he soon added that monarchy should be 'tempered' (*temperata*), and that a 'mixed régime' was the best. He even went into detail describing the various ways in which this mixture could be effected. Two points are of special interest in Aquinas's

---

[1] 'ut . . . possit ex temperatione iuris, quum potestas in populo, auctoritas in senatu sit, teneri ille moderatus et concors civitatis status' (*De Legibus*, III, § 28). I have already referred to this passage in the Introduction, p. 7.

theory of the mixed constitution: the request that the people should have a say in the appointment of the ruler, and that laws should be enacted by the whole community. These points take on a particular relevance when set against the background of medieval views concerning the nature of law and the source of power.

The theory of the mixed State was particularly well adapted to explain and interpret the complex constitutional structures that had taken shape in the various European countries by the end of the Middle Ages. These structures were the result of a slow transformation of older ideas about the relation between power and law; they were closely linked to the presence and the collaboration of several 'estates' in the 'body politic'. No wonder the idea of the mixed constitution achieved its greatest popularity and success at the beginning of the modern era. To confine ourselves to one country alone, we find it hailed by one of the earliest theorists on the English constitution, Sir John Fortescue, writing in the latter half of the fifteenth century. Indeed, Fortescue borrowed almost piecemeal the notion of the *regimen mixtum* from St. Thomas Aquinas. He used it as a tool to prove the excellence of the English constitutional monarchy. In the following century Richard Hooker described the English State as 'a threefold cable' composed of the king, the nobility, and the people; and he further stated—in true medieval fashion—that the power of the king was limited by the law, which was laid down by 'the whole body politic'. Another writer of the period, Sir Thomas Smith, went so far as to declare 'that common wealthes or governements are not most commonly simple but mixt', a view which did not prevent him from saying, with a clear grasp of the notion of sovereignty, that 'the most high and absolute power' in England was held by Parliament, 'for everie Englishman is entended to bee there present'. However, the theory of the mixed constitution or State was by no means exclusively characteristic of England. It was a common topic of Renaissance thought and was to survive throughout the seventeenth and the eighteenth centuries.

This was the theory, rooted in tradition, and in appearance, at least, confirmed by experience, which Bodin and Hobbes set out to criticize and reject. Their platform was the concept of sovereignty. Practical considerations, of course also played a part in their criticism. Mixed States, States 'in between' (*di mezzo*), as Machiavelli had called them, are unstable and brittle: so much had already been shown convincingly by the Florentine Secretary. But the main point for both Bodin and Hobbes was that a mixed State is logically unthinkable because of the unity and indivisibility of power. According to Bodin, a composite type of State is bound to produce a conflict which force alone can settle. Its existence is an illusion, because sovereignty always rests in one place only. Hobbes was no less categorical. While in the *De Cive* he still seems to admit the possible existence of mixed types of State, in *Leviathan* he flatly asserts that 'there can be but three kinds of commonwealth'—monarchy, aristocracy, and democracy. 'Other kind of commonwealth there can be none: for either one, or more, or all, must have the sovereign power, which I have shown to be indivisible, entire.' It would be doing an injustice to Bodin and Hobbes to neglect the fact that their attitude was certainly influenced by the tragic experience of their times as much as by the abstract demands of a particular theory. Both were writing with their eyes fixed on the sight of their countries torn by civil war. But these wars, which the opposed parties tried to justify as a struggle for the old, mixed constitution, or in the name of the traditional principle of the Rule of Law, were to them nothing else than a struggle for sovereignty. 'Division into opposite armies' would never have happened had 'sovereign rights' not first been divided. 'And this division is it, whereof it is said, *a kingdom divided against itself cannot stand.*'

But if Bodin and Hobbes were agreed in condemning the idea of the mixed State, Bodin, as we saw, differed from Hobbes in distinguishing between form of State and form of government. Bodin held that the form of State is in every case simple; but the form of government can be complex. A monarchy, for example, can be governed 'democratically' (*populairement*) if the monarch gives a share in office to 'everyone equally', or 'aristocratically' if he gives a share only to a few. Similarly, an aristocracy can be governed in a 'monarchic' or in a 'democratic' fashion, and so forth. With this distinction between the *locus* of sovereignty and the exercise of power Bodin paved the way to the recognition of the fact that, notwithstanding the unity and indivisibility of sovereignty, power can be distributed in various ways in accordance with particular conditions of time and place, and even in accordance with the ends pursued by the State itself. It was precisely a concern with the 'ends' of the State that fostered the rise of the modern doctrine of the distribution or 'division' of power. But, to secure these ends, political theory had to come to grips with the niceties of legal theory.

In Locke and Montesquieu, the founders of the doctrine, the aim of the division of power was the attainment of a particular value; we shall consider this value below under the name of 'negative liberty'. But, characteristically enough, the doctrine itself, with its detailed description of the 'three powers', legislative, executive, and judicial, was nowhere put forward as an abstract deduction from a preconceived pattern—as what would be called nowadays an 'ideology'. On the contrary, the division of power was presented—implicitly by Locke, expressly by Montesquieu—as inherent in a particular, historical type of constitutional system, the system which, rightly or wrongly, Montesquieu believed to exist in England. Similarly, the doctrine was not advanced, as is commonly believed, as a downright attack on the concept of sovereignty. Indeed, the existence of sovereignty was taken for granted. What the doctrine implied was a new and original view of the manner in which power could be distributed and organized within the State, a view which has become the keystone of the modern conception of the State as a legal system. The problem with which Locke and Montesquieu were concerned was that of the constitution, not that of sovereignty. With them it was not a question, or not only a question, of determining where sovereignty resides or to whom it ultimately belongs, but of determining how sovereignty can be made to work in the best possible way through different agents. As Madison seems to intimate, in his celebrated remarks on Montesquieu, it would be more appropriate to speak of a 'division of power' rather than of a 'division of powers'.

Let us look at the matter more closely. According to Locke, three things distinguish a 'civil state' from the state of nature: an 'established, settled, known law', a 'known and indifferent judge', and an executive power 'to back and support' both laws and judicial decisions. These, then, are the different channels through which the 'power of the society' is brought to bear upon its members; but they are also the necessary means to society's achieving its end, which is the preservation of the 'lives, liberties and estates' of those members. For Montesquieu, on the other hand, in order that the liberty of the citizen may be assured, that is 'that tranquility of mind, arising from the opinion each person

has of his safety', the State must be 'moderate', and there must be
no possibility that power might be 'abused'. To attain this end,
''tis necessary that by the very disposition of things power should
be a check to power'. Now in his chapter on the English Constitution Montesquieu says quite clearly that three powers are found
in all States: the legislative, the executive, and the judiciary. But
'political liberty', he immediately adds, exists only in those States
in which these powers are not all 'united in the same person' or in
the same 'body of magistracy'. All States, according to Montesquieu, fall into two categories. Following in the footsteps of
Machiavelli, he abandons or modifies Aristotle's threefold division
of monarchy, aristocracy, and democracy. Basically, States are
either republics or principalities, though the latter can be either
'monarchies' or 'despotisms', depending on whether power is
exercised in accordance with stable laws or in a capricious and
arbitrary manner. In determining the form of State, the essential
factor is in any case sovereignty—*la souveraine puissance*.

If then all three powers exist in all States, this can only mean
that it must be possible, according to Montesquieu's scheme, to
apply the mechanism for separating them and confronting them
with each other in republics as well as in monarchies. What is
needed, in order to achieve that stability of law in which freedom
consists, is not to wreck sovereignty but to control it by adequately
disposing the exercise of power. Despotism is, of course, out of the
question, since it is by definition an arbitrary government in-
tolerant of law. But it will be perfectly reasonable to expect liberty
to prevail equally well in republics as in monarchies, liberty in the
sense of the rule of law guaranteed by the division of power. There
is no clear indication in Montesquieu of a preference for one form
of State rather than another. His statement that 'in a free State . . .
the legislative power should reside in the whole body of the people'
must not be misread as a vindication of popular sovereignty. There
is a simple reason for this. Montesquieu was deeply steeped in the
law. He was a lawyer much more than a political theorist. Unlike
Bodin, he did not hold that the whole of sovereignty was contained
in the legislative power.[1] Unlike Rousseau, he had no axe to grind

---

[1] Locke's position is more uncertain. He sees the legislative as the 'supreme
power', but admits that in some cases the executive power vested in the person
of a king 'may also be called supreme'. Behind both legislative and executive
there is, of course, for Locke the 'supreme power of the whole community'.

in favour of democracy. Sovereignty, with Montesquieu, seems to be equally present in the legislative, the executive, and the judiciary. All three in their discordant concord constitute the life of the State: 'these three powers are forced to move, but still to move in concert.' As a legal structure the State is one, however divided its power.

My main contention in this chapter is that the division of power is not incompatible with, indeed that it actually presupposes, a clear notion of sovereignty. A view such as this is in many ways quite unorthodox. And yet I believe that it offers the only possible solution to a number of riddles relating to modern State-theory.

To begin with, there is no other way of explaining how the doctrine of the division of power could be outlined and achieve its greatest success at a time when the idea of the sovereignty of the State had carried the day and was generally accepted. Once it is granted that sovereignty is the mark which distinguishes the State from other institutions, and positive law from other laws, it is hard to believe that the division of power should have aimed at questioning the very existence of the State by exploding the notion of sovereignty.

A second point to bear in mind is that, as I have tried to show, the division of power, in its technical details at any rate, is a legal, not a political, theory. It does not provide an answer to the question who should be the holder of sovereignty, but only to the question of how power should be organized in order to achieve certain aims, whoever is the ultimate holder of sovereignty. The theory is consistent with any political form, except, of course, with arbitrary government. The Constitution of the United States provides the best case in point. Here the constitutional system which Locke and Montesquieu advocated was laid down, prefaced by the phrase 'We, the people'. The strongest vindication of popular sovereignty goes hand in hand with the most forcible assertion of the division of power. But constitutions enacting that division are not the exclusive privilege of modern democracies. Enlightened monarchs, some of them at any rate, accepted them long ago and even tried their best to secure them.

Finally, and this point is perhaps the most important of all, though often overlooked, the very aim of securing those ends for which the division of power was devised would never have been achieved had not the sovereignty of the State been secured also.

Only by knowing for certain who has the power to command can that 'tranquility of mind' be attained which Montesquieu praised so highly as the condition of political liberty. But of tranquillity of mind, that is 'certainty of law', there can be none unless we know that the different channels through which power is brought to bear on us are the legitimate interpreters of the power of the State; and unless in turn the State is strong enough not to allow any other power to lay claim to our allegiance. That the division of power is the backbone of the modern, liberal notion of the State, all are agreed. But few bear in mind that the very rise of the modern, sovereign State was an essential condition of the liberty we enjoy and cherish.

To grant and accept these points is not easy. It would seem to be particularly difficult to the Anglo-Saxon mind. Englishmen are as fond of quoting Sir Edward Coke's famous dictum, 'Magna Carta is such a fellow that he will have no sovereign', as Americans are of repeating Justice Wilson's no less famous statement in *Chesholm* v. *Georgia* (1793) that 'to the Constitution of the United States the term sovereign is totally unknown'. And yet Britain and the U.S.A. are sovereign States, exactly in the sense in which Hobbes described sovereignty. Both Britons and Americans know very well where their allegiance lies, in whose name laws are enacted, decisions reached, orders given. They proudly assert that theirs is a democracy. The division of power which modern democracies practice and respect has secured that rule of law which is, after all, the very condition of power. By controlling and regulating power it has further established and guaranteed that safety and security of the citizen which is the condition of liberty. But sovereignty—as Hobbes well saw—is the necessary prop of that safety. The legislative, the executive, and the judiciary are all in their own way its expression. Their harmony, and at times even their rivalry, are still the best insurance against the 'abuse of power'.

REFERENCES

Plato, *Laws*, III, 691d–692c, 693d and e. Aristotle, *Politics*, III, 1265ᵇ, 1288ᵃ; IV, chs. viii–xi; v, 1302ᵃ. Polybius, *History of Rome*, VI. Cicero, *De Re Publica*, I, §§ 35 and 45; II, §§ 23 and 33; *De Legibus*, III, § 28. Thomas Aquinas, *De Regimine Principum*, I, ch. vi; *Summa Theologica*, 1ᵃ2ᵃᵉ, qu. xcv, art. 4; 2ᵃ2ᵃᵉ, qu. cv, art. 1. Sir John Fortescue, *De Natura Legis Naturae*, ch. xvi; *De Laudibus Legum Angliae*, passim; *The Governance of England*, chs. 2 and 3. Machiavelli, *Discorso sopra il riformare lo Stato di Firenze*. Richard Hooker, *Ecclesiastical Polity*, VII, xviii, 10; VIII, viii, 9. Sir Thomas Smith, *De Republica Anglorum*, Book I, ch. 6; Book II, ch. 1. Bodin, *De la République*, II, ch. 1. Hobbes, *De Cive*, ch. vii, § 4; *Leviathan*, chs. xviii, xix, xxix. Locke, *Second Treatise of Government*, ch. ix, §§ 123–6; ch. x, § 132; ch. xii; ch. xiii, § 151. Montesquieu, *Esprit des Lois* (English trans. by T. Nugent, 1750), Book II, ch. 1; XI, chs. 4 and 6. James Madison, *The Federalist*, nos. xlvi and xlvii.

The 'unorthodoxy' of the views proposed in this chapter is best realized in comparing them with the quite opposite views on the relationship between the concept of sovereignty and the doctrine of the division of powers which Gierke set forth in ch. III, § iii, 1 of his classic work, *Johannes Althusius und die Entwicklung der naturrechtlichen Staatstheorien*, Breslau, 1880–1913 (Eng. trans. by B. Freyd, *The Development of Political Theory*, London, 1939). Gierke's views carry the greatest weight and have been largely followed.

8

THE PLURALITY OF LEGAL SYSTEMS

Is the whole of legal experience contained in State law, and is it only the 'terror' inspired by Leviathan which establishes and secures the observance of that regularity of behaviour that we have hitherto associated with the idea of law? At a first glance, the Hobbesian view seems to be fully confirmed by the facts, if the process of formation of the modern State is considered in an historical perspective. A progressive monopoly of power by the State, with complete control over the output, protection, and execution of the law, corresponded to, and was supported by, the monopoly of force on the part of what Machiavelli had called the 'new principality'. There is perhaps no more eloquent witness to this state of affairs than Montesquieu, the greatest theorist of controlled and divided power: 'Formerly every village of France was a capital; there is at present only one large one: every part of the State was a center of power, at present all has a relation to one center; and that center is, in some measure, the State itself.' In Montesquieu's eyes, the modern State had arisen on the ruins of feudal particularism, when Europe was 'divided into an infinite number of petty sovereignties'. For the author of the *Esprit des Lois* the real danger of modern despotism lay in this 'uniqueness' of law which had taken the place of the plurality of the old legal units, of the *prérogatives des corps*, of the *privilèges des villes*.[1]

It was precisely these 'prerogatives', these 'privileges'—these 'liberties' in the medieval meaning of the word—that Hobbes had denounced as portents of the dissolution of the State. The sovereignty of the State tolerates no *imperium in imperio*. Leviathan,

[1] For this very reason Montesquieu recommended the preservation or the renewal of 'intermediate powers' (*pouvoirs intermédiaires*) which 'canalize' power and slow up its impact, just as the 'weeds and little pebbles that lie scattered along the shore' hold up the onrush of the sea: an idea which was cherished by a small number of nineteenth-century liberals, and which anticipates the desire, now so strongly felt in many parts of Europe, for decentralization and for the revival of local and regional autonomy.

and Leviathan alone, is the supreme source and arbiter of law. There is only one legal system, or else there is none. Law as a discipline of human intercourse comes into being and ceases with the State, since only the State can impose on its subjects the *law*, which is 'obligation', while upholding in the face of other States its *right*, which is 'liberty'.

There is written on the turrets of the city of Lucca in great characters at this day, the word LIBERTAS; yet no man can thence infer, that a particular man has more liberty, or immunity from the service of the commonwealth there, than in Constantinople.

The liberty of the commonwealth . . . is the same with that, which every man then should have, if there were no civil laws, nor commonwealth at all. And the effects of it also be the same. . . . Every commonwealth . . . has an absolute liberty, to do what it shall judge, that is to say, what that man, or assembly that representeth it, shall judge most conducing to their benefit. But withal, they [the commonwealths] live in the condition of a perpetual war, and upon the confines of battle, with their frontiers armed, and cannons planted against their neighbours round about.

The uniqueness of State law does not, however, imply for Hobbes that no other legal systems exist. There are, indeed, as many systems as there are sovereign States. But these systems are structurally identical. They have no relevance to one another. Rather, they are rivals and potential enemies. The multiplicity of legal systems means only that Leviathan's sway is limited in time and space: that the power of the State extends only to a particular people and within a particular territory. But this does not contradict the essential uniqueness of legal experience. It is simply the result of the existing fragmentation of politics and of the present anarchy in international relations. For Hobbes there is no law where there is no 'common power', a will superior to all other wills, capable of imposing obedience to its commands by force.

The reduction of all law to State law was the direct consequence of the imperative conception of law. It is closely linked with the authoritarian structure of political relations as relations of command and obedience. It is quite impossible even to conceive of a real plurality of legal systems unless other interpretations of legal experience are granted, unless the existence of other and different kinds of social relations is recognized as possible besides that between imperative command and enforceable obedience. Such a recognition does not necessarily upset the legal construction of the State so far analysed. It merely sets a limit to its validity. If anything, it contributes to a better understanding of the proper sphere of reference of that notion of sovereignty which, as we have seen, sums up the idea of 'legalized force', of the 'power' the State claims as its exclusive prerogative.

The existence of law outside and above the State, so emphatically denied by Hobbes, was upheld with unparalleled vigour and conviction in Hobbes's own lifetime by the founder of modern international law, Grotius. In Grotius's view, international relations are not relations of pure force. States do not act solely from interest and lust for power. They are not in a Hobbesian state of nature.

There is no City so strong and of itself sufficient, but may sometimes stand in need of Foreign Aid, either by way of Commerce or to defend it self against the united forces of many Foreign Nations confederate against it: Therefore we see, that the most potent Princes and States have always been desirous of Leagues, which would be of little use or force were all Laws and Justice confined within the bounds of any one City only. Most true it is, That as soon as we recede from the Law, there is nothing that we can certainly call ours.

This sounds like an answer to Hobbes; in fact, these words were written more than twenty years before *Leviathan* was published. Clearly, according to Grotius, a legal system is conceivable in conditions of equality as well as in conditions of authority. Relations between States do not fit within an authoritarian pattern. The laws they observe are not the commands of any sovereign. The 'Law of Nations' or *ius gentium* is 'more extensive than that which is Civil'. It 'derives its authority from the joynt consent of all, or, at least, of many Nations'. It should be noticed that this law, too, like the positive law of the State, is created by men: it is a *ius voluntarium*. It is not, or not only, a rational demand, an abstract 'natural law' construction. Of course, since it cannot secure confirmation from a higher or 'sovereign' power, it has to be ultimately warranted, according to Grotius, by justice or natural law, by the rule *pacta sunt servanda*. But, in so far as it is positive law, it is valid, and can be laid down with certainty, to the extent to which States in fact regard themselves as bound by it and respect it, uniformly regulating their behaviour and their mutual relations according to its rules: in short, in as far as *pacta sunt servata*.

International law, as I have tried to show by going straight back to the source of all modern theories about it, still remains the classic example of a legal system structurally different from the one we associate with the State, which centres on the principle of sovereignty. But international law is by no means the only example that can be brought to disprove the theory of the uniqueness of State law, and to support the notion of the plurality of legal systems. In times nearer our own this notion has been put forward and popularized, at any rate on the Continent of Europe, by the so-called 'theory of the Institution'. According to this theory it is possible to speak of 'law' and to recognize the existence of a legal system, not only in regard to the international community or to the Church, but wherever 'social relations' take definite shape in a 'factual organization'. This can happen with any kind of human association, whatever its purpose (even if the purpose is criminal): what matters is that its members should form what is called a 'concrete unity', thanks to a body of rules which holds them together and determines their mutual relations. It is not, however, these rules, but the organization itself which constitutes the legal system. The 'institution' exists before the rules and moves them 'like pawns on a chessboard'.

The institutional theory, in the version which has most widely influenced contemporary legal and political thought, thus appears to challenge not one but two of Hobbes's basic tenets. On the one hand, it affirms with uncompromising vigour the possibility of a plurality of legal systems, as against Hobbes's idea of the uniqueness of State law: there can be laws outside the pale of the State, without the existence of a 'common power'. On the other hand, the institutional theory leads to a pluralistic view of society radically opposed to Hobbes's notion of the essentially unitary structure of the State. It would almost seem as if we were presented with an interpretation of history entirely the opposite of the one even Montesquieu had accepted. The modern State would never quite have succeeded in unifying society. Multiplicity, not oneness, is the mark of historical progress. The claim of the State to be the sole centre of power must be rejected as unwarranted by facts and dangerous in principle. Such views might well be said to imply a definite ideological commitment. They have been aptly

described as 'one of the many ways in which legal and political
theorists have sought to resist the growing invasion of the State',[1]
its pretence of being the sole arbiter of all human relations. In this
chapter I shall deal only with the impact of pluralism on the theory
of law, not on the theory of society. The last, and third, point on
which Hobbes's model of the modern State has been either belied
or improved deserves careful and separate treatment.

As far as law is concerned, the supporters of the institutional
theory could hardly be more emphatic in stating that, in order to
understand the real nature of a legal system, it is necessary to
abandon the notion of law formed 'solely on the model of State
law'. If anything, they may be criticized for not having drawn
out all the logical conclusions from this premiss. Whilst recognizing, on one side, that the State is 'the most important of institutions', that it is the 'legal macrocosm', the 'most highly developed'
form of human society, they also maintain, on the other, that there
is no difference in quality or 'structure' between the legal system
of the State and the other legal systems: for every legal system is
by definition an 'organization', and the very concept of organization implies—so they say—a relation 'of superiority and of corresponding subordination'. Now surely this last proposition plays into
the hands of Austin and Hobbes instead of contradicting them. Let
us admit that Hobbes was wrong in not recognizing the possibility
of the existence of legal systems different from that of the State.
Nevertheless, his analysis of the characteristics properly belonging
to the State system is not thereby invalidated, so long as we accept the authoritarian model on which he based it. To assert the
plurality of legal systems and yet to conceive of these systems as
fashioned according to the authoritarian model may thus either
mean to assert the existence of other, and rival, 'sovereign powers',
or else it entails some further inquiry as to the way in which these
systems are related (as they are in a federal State) to the ultimate
holder of sovereignty. But in neither case does it imply a denial
of the very peculiar position the State holds with regard to the
laying down of the law and to its enforcement, which was the main
characteristic of the doctrine of sovereignty.

The modern upholders of the institutional theory may very
probably be right when they say that 'all force which is effectively
social and thus comes to be organized is thereby changed into law'.

[1] N. Bobbio, *Teoria della norma giuridica*, Turin, 1958, p. 16.

But they will be compelled by the very evidence of facts to admit that it is only in the 'power' of the State that the complete equation of force with law is achieved, and 'sovereignty' was the name invented to indicate that equation. They may be right too when they stress that a relation of superiority and subordination is implicit in every organization. But if this is so, they must obviously recognize that the relation of command and obedience in the organization of a State has characteristics of its own, which distinguish this relation from any other. Finally, they may even be right in describing legal systems as 'moving' legal rules 'like pawns on a chessboard'. But the fact remains that only the State is in a position to create or 'produce' legal rules simply by an imperative *fiat*. The State does not only 'move' the rules: it 'imposes' them with all the force at its disposal. Were it only for these two last attributes—the creation and the imposition of law—the legal system of the State stands out as something quite peculiar in the plurality of legal systems. Should there be any doubt that the monopoly of force is the pre-requisite of the monopoly of power, the political realist is always at hand to provide support for the doctrine of sovereignty. So long as we take our stand on the imperative ground, the Hobbesian and Austinian model remains unassailable.

There is, nevertheless, much to be learnt from the institutional theory. It has undoubtedly helped to broaden our understanding of both State and law by stressing—as used to be stressed by the old adage *ubi societas ibi ius*—that legal phenomena are not exclusive to the sphere of the State, that rule-controlled behaviour is characteristic of all social experience.[1] Further, if properly construed, it must inevitably lead to the abandonment of the imperative conception of law, or at any rate to the recognition that the simple relation of command and obedience does not adequately account for the complexity of law, even of State law, since there are indeed laws which are 'directives' rather than 'imperatives', which are 'accepted' rather than 'imposed', and whose 'sanctions' do not necessarily consist in the possible use of force on the part of a 'sovereign'. If I conform to the rules of a game, or to those of my club, or to those of the Church (and I may perhaps conform to these rules much more carefully than I do to the laws of the

[1] This last point is brought out very well by Peter Winch, *The Idea of a Social Science and its Relation to Philosophy*, 3rd imp. London, 1963, ch. ii.

State), I do not do it simply because these rules are laid down in international conventions about the game, or because they were agreed to in a meeting of members, or because they have been laid down by the highest Church authorities. If I do conform, it is because for me, unlike others of my fellow citizens, these rules are 'valid' rules, even though they may not be so within the legal system of the State or in the current sense of a law's being valid. Certainly, as things stand today, I could not be 'compelled' to keep these rules, or at any rate not as I should be if they had the might of the State behind them. Perhaps only the Mafia or the Ku-Klux-Klan are prepared to use sanctions as effective as those the State has at its disposal, if not more so. But should we then not say that, in their case, what we are confronted with is a true *imperium in imperio*?

As a matter of fact, there may be nothing to prevent the 'organized social force' of a particular 'institution' from acquiring a strength and an efficiency as great as, and perhaps even greater than, the strength and efficiency of the State. There may be nothing to prevent a particular organization from successfully opposing the State, from disputing its monopoly of force, and substituting its own for the State's power over all or part of its 'territory' and of its 'people'. In a case of this kind could there be any doubt that the 'institution' itself would be on the way to becoming a 'State'? Surely, international law would have little hesitation in answering in the affirmative. Surely also that State, or more precisely its advocates and lawyers, would soon end by claiming that very attribute which legal theory has for many centuries indicated by a name, viz. sovereignty. Once again, Hobbes's logic would come into its own. Leviathan would score its final vengeance. Needless to say, events of this kind are not of everyday occurrence.

But a similar, though different, case might equally well arise on a different level. Suppose a new and different organization of international relations were to replace the existing one. Suppose a 'common power' were set up, able to impose by force the rules which today are left to the discretion of the sovereign States and to the dubious sanctions of the international community. Would not the whole structure of that community thereby be changed, and would not this 'super-State' end by itself becoming *the* State, and fall a prey to the same logic of sovereignty which has hitherto been considered as pertinent only at the national level? All we could do in such a case would be to hope and pray that, in organizing the new Leviathan, account would be taken of the experience of the old one. Surely all the delicate mechanisms by which the power of the Nation-State has been brought under control may equally be needed if the World-State ever comes into being.

REFERENCES

Montesquieu, *Esprit des Lois* (Eng. trans., as quoted), Book II, ch. 4; VIII, ch. 6; XXIII, ch. 24. Grotius, *De Iure Belli ac Pacis*, 1625 (Eng. trans. by W. Evats, 1682), Proleg., § 22; Book I, ch. xiv. 1.

As a theory of law the 'Institutional Theory' discussed in this chapter has had a much wider influence in Continental Europe than in English-speaking countries, although in some respects it has close analogies with the pluralist theories which were popularized in England by Harold J. Laski. My references are to the Italian version of the theory, chiefly represented by Santi Romano, rather than to the French, headed by Maurice Hauriou, the real founder of the theory (cf. the article by W. I. Jennings, 'The Institutional Theory', in *Modern Theories of Law*, London, 1933). Unlike Hauriou and his disciple Georges Renard, Romano presented his theory as a strictly 'positive' theory of law, without any reference to religious beliefs or to 'natural law' premisses. The passages cited in the text are taken from S. Romano's influential book, *L'ordinamento giuridico* (1st edn., Pisa, 1917; 2nd, with additions and notes, Florence, 1945), part i, §§ 5, 10, 12–14, 19; part ii, §§ 25–32.

9

CHURCH AND STATE

THERE is one last problem left for discussion, a problem different from that of the unity of power and the uniqueness of State law. This is the problem Hobbes raised when he declared that sovereignty entails a structure of society so closely unified that there is no room left for any kind of independent association within the political body, and that any split in such oneness is a deadly threat to the State. Hobbes's illustration of this point is as usual strikingly imaginative: 'another infirmity of a commonwealth is . . . the great numbers of corporations, which are as it were many lesser commonwealths in the bowels of a greater, like worms in the entrails of a natural man.' Rousseau is no less emphatic: 'it is . . . essential, if the general will is to be able to express itself, that there should be no partial society within the State, and that each citizen should think only his own thoughts.' The pattern is clear: corresponding to the single, indivisible power of the sovereign State there must be a unified society, which in its turn includes the whole body of citizens, all equal and equalized in a common subjection. There must be one society only, as there is only one law and only one holder of power. And yet, as we have seen, the modern State has tolerated a quite different situation. Power has been divided. Other laws beside those of the State have been recognized as possible. The question then is: do we live in a unitary or in a pluralist society? Surely, even the staunchest supporter of 'monism' is forced to admit now, three centuries after Hobbes, that his plans on this head also failed to materialize in their entirety.

The first and most decisive proof that the modern State has not carried through Hobbes's demand for the 'one society' is provided by the survival of a type of organization distinct from that of the State, its rival and sometimes its enemy: the organization of the Church or the Churches. The Christian view of the world is essentially dualistic. As a Christian, man is a citizen not of one, but of two cities. The fact of his subjection to the State, of his earthly citizenship, does not weaken the existence of another, more important bond of allegiance, of another, more exacting fellowship —the fellowship of the Church.

This divided allegiance was deplored and denounced as a threat to the State from Machiavelli to Hobbes, from Rousseau down to certain modern 'secularists'. 'Jesus', Rousseau remarked, 'came to set up on earth a spiritual Kingdom, which by separating the theological from the political system, made the State no longer one, and brought about internal divisions which have never ceased to trouble Christian peoples.' Would it have been of any use to reply to Rousseau that the special destiny of the West has lain precisely in this 'internal division', and that the tensions resulting from it may have been one of the chief reasons for many Western achievements? Much more decisive is the fact that even the modern State has ended by adapting itself to this division. As long as our society remains a Christian society it is bound to remain at heart, if not actually by definition, a divided, pluralistic society.

However, as I have pointed out, a distinction must be made between the different meanings of pluralism. Pluralism of law does not necessarily imply a pluralism of societies. It is one thing to recognize the existence of rules which may be binding on us though independent of the State; it is another to think of society as split into two or more organized wholes. To admit the possibility of laws with a different structure and grounds of validity different from those of State law is something other than to assert the factual existence of different types of human associations, not only formally, but substantially distinct from one another. Some caution of this kind is necessary, I believe, in dealing with the dualism of State and Church which has played such an important role in the course of the centuries. That dualism has been taken to mean two quite different things: a dualism of powers and a dualism of societies.

The traditional theory of State and Church, the one against which the main thrust of Hobbes's attack is directed, was essentially a theory of the dualism of powers. The medieval vision of society, at least as regards the relation between the religious and the political sphere, was not a pluralistic vision but one of unity. Church and State were conceived to be one in the *respublica christiana*: more exactly, the 'spiritual' and the 'temporal' powers were viewed as the two necessary props, as two departments, as it were, of a single and universal society composed of the same members united by the same faith. No doubt there was a difference in ends between the sets of rules controlled by and emanating from each of the two powers: one set of rules being concerned with peaceful and orderly life in this world (*temporalis tranquillitas*), the other with the service of God and the attainment of salvation (*aeterna felicitas*). But it was precisely because of their different ends that the temporal and the spiritual power could be conceived as complementary. Their harmony and co-operation were seen as the indisputable conditions for the well-being of the world. One day, under the impact of a new analysis of power, even the traditional dualism would begin to be questioned. The age-old symbolism in which it had been expressed (the sun and the moon, the two swords, etc.) would sound increasingly stale, as can be seen in Dante's curiously entangled use of it in the *Monarchia*. The final crisis came when the 'theocrats' dared to assert that dualism must be reduced to unity in the fullness of power of the Pope. However, the basic premiss of medieval political thought remains throughout that of the single Christian society. From that society those who do not share the common faith (*qui foris sunt*) are automatically excluded. Jews may be tolerated, but as a foreign body. Religious orthodoxy is the condition of political allegiance. Any menace to that orthodoxy, to the Church, is a menace to the State. To persecute heretics is not only a religious duty for the Christian prince. It is equally necessary by 'reason of State', for heresy is the most serious challenge to unity and uniformity.

Now there can scarcely be any doubt that, in its beginnings at any rate, the Protestant Reformation started from premisses which were closely similar to those just described. It was in the name of religious uniformity that the Reformers appealed to the temporal rulers, and that the princes in turn set out to 'reform' the Church. Where the spiritual guide had failed, the temporal should take over. What mattered above all was to safeguard the oneness of society, even at the cost of breaking up the unity of Christendom and of destroying once and for all the dualism of powers which in medieval eyes had formed its necessary counterpart. These were indeed the views that were forcibly set forth in the two great documents which mark the beginning of the Reformation in England, the *Statute of Appeals* (1533) and the *Act of Supremacy* (1534).

The opening words of the *Statute* deserve careful scrutiny, even though they are certainly not without medieval precedents.[1] The first and basic statement is a vindication of sovereignty: 'this realm of England is an Empire.' The King of England enjoys 'the dignity and royal estate of the Imperial Crown of the same'. But sovereignty does not only mean full independence on the international level. It assumes a very special character when referred to internal matters, when applied to a society whose structure still remains, notwithstanding its dual aspect, fundamentally one. England in fact is said to be governed 'by one supreme Head and King ... unto whom a body politic, compact of all sorts and degrees of people divided in terms and by names of Spiritualty and Temporalty, be bounden and ought to bear, next to God, a natural and humble obedience'.

Here then are all the consequences of the oneness of society clearly outlined. The distinction between 'spiritualty' and 'temporalty' is not a distinction between two organizations. It is merely a distinction of 'names'. It is precisely because society is and must remain one, that Henry's claim to the fullness of sovereignty sounds like both a reminiscence of Boniface VIII and an anticipation of Hobbes. The demand was for a further step in unity, on lines similar to those which the 'theocrats' had followed in the Middle Ages; but it was also a demand for the full control of the single, national society, on lines which foreshadowed the Hobbesian model. In fact, once the unity of Christendom was broken, the oneness of society could only mean that the national Church completely coincided with the national State. This was the doctrine laid down in the Peace of Augsburg (1555): *cuius regio eius religio*. It was also the doctrine which inspired the Elizabethan Settlement and which Archbishop Whitgift expressed in a sentence corresponding almost word for word with that of Hobbes: 'I make no difference betwixt a Christian commonwealth and the Church of Christ.' There is no room for dissent in a State based on religious orthodoxy. Still less is there room, when a State of this kind claims the fullness of sovereignty, for allegiance to a 'foreign potentate' such as the

---

[1] Two of the main concepts laid down in the *Statute* can already be found clearly outlined in France two centuries earlier than in England: the idea of the full sovereignty of the national ruler (*rex in regno suo est imperator*) and that of the kingdom as one single body (*omnes et singuli, clerici et laici, regni nostri tamquam membra sicut in uno corpore vere viventia*). On this last point see Wilks, *The Problem of Sovereignty*, Cambridge, 1963, p. 431 and note 2.

Pope of Rome. The official religion must be the religion of every citizen. Conformity is the token of political loyalty. Uniformity must be enforced with all the means at the disposal of the State.

No wonder that a doctrine such as this—which its bitterest enemies denounced as *machiavellistica et turcica*—should have caused deep misgivings in many religious minds. It was from the protest of the Christian conscience against the control of the State over Church matters that the modern notion of religious liberty was ultimately born. But that liberty would never have been a practical proposition had not a different and entirely new conception of society finally carried the day. In England, as well as in many other European countries, Catholics and Protestants alike helped to foster that new conception when they upheld, against the doctrine of the 'one society', the existence of 'two Kingdoms', and strenuously defended the autonomy and independence of the Church versus the State. Few of them, however, interpreted that existence as a recognition of a possible separation between Church and State, still less did they envisage the possibility of a society based on heterodoxy rather than on religious uniformity. On the contrary, they all agreed in maintaining that the two societies were closely interrelated, and that the State had no higher duty than that of protecting and defending the Church and of respecting the law of God as interpreted by ecclesiastical authority.[1]

Religious liberty in its modern, constitutional, meaning was not the child of Christian 'dualism' alone. It was the product of a complex historical growth in which theory and fact played an equally decisive part. As a theory, it could trace its real ancestry to the small band of chosen spirits who dared to oppose the dominant theory of uniformity and of religious as well as political intolerance, stressing the impossibility of coercing beliefs and the inviolable rights of man's conscience. As a fact, it was the result of a new structure of society, the structure which emerged from the fierce

---

[1] More clearly perhaps than by any other contemporary writers, the notion of State and Church as two complete and self-sufficient societies was set forth by the Jesuits, and in particular by Cardinal Bellarmine. But the principle of the indirect power (*potestas indirecta*) of the Church in temporal matters re-established the bond of interdependence between the two societies, and the subordination of the State to the Church. As an opponent of the new Roman doctrine was quick to remark: 'quod una manu abstulit Papae Bellarminus, id altera dat.'

battle waged against the traditional doctrine by those 'seditious' groups, by those 'fanatical' sects, which Hobbes considered no less dangerous to the sovereign State than the Church of Rome, with its claim to universal lordship. Now for the first time the task of reforming the Church was indicated as possible 'without tarying for anie', without waiting 'till the Magistrate command or compell'. Now, indeed, the purely spiritual nature of the Church was proclaimed, and the absolute impossibility of the State's intervening in matters of religion. Now, at long last, the spell of religious and political uniformity was broken. Such, more or less clearly grasped in its full implications, was the doctrine which inspired those Independents from whose ranks came a statesman of Cromwell's stature. Such was the doctrine fully incorporated two centuries later in an ambitious plan for the complete renovation of his country by another great statesman, Cavour, and summed up by him in one single sentence: 'a free Church in a free State', *libera Chiesa in libero Stato.*

Of course, the recognition of the self-sufficiency of State and Church was not the only source of our modern, pluralistic view of society. But it certainly contributed more than anything else to bring about the final collapse of the notion of the 'one society'. For a society where State and Church are seen as independent wholes, a society in which minorities are respected and free to organize themselves according to their wishes and needs, a society where complete uniformity of behaviour and thought is no longer required for the welfare of the State—a society such as this is no longer a monistic society. Surely Hobbes's model of the modern State has been thoroughly discredited on that score. Rousseau, as we have seen, was of a quite different opinion. Like many Continentals down to the present day, he still believed that the only healthy society was that in which no allegiance existed other than allegiance to the State, and that democracy should spell unanimity. But, as Tocqueville noticed in his memorable journey overseas, democracy had taken a different turn in countries where there had been a strong tradition of dissent and autonomous group life, where minorities had been allowed to play their part in all spheres of life, from religion to economic organization, from self-government to education and culture. Unlike the countries which clung to the pattern of conformity and unity, these countries showed an unparalleled vitality and vigour, and the greatest resilience in the hour of trial. For a couple of centuries, at any rate, the path of social progress seems to have lain on the side of pluralism rather than on that of oneness.

And yet we can never be sure that Hobbes's ghost has been finally laid to rest. Two questions still come to mind whenever we compare our notion of the State with the model which he framed. The first question is: what changes has Leviathan undergone by adapting itself to a pluralist society? The second: are we not witnessing in our own days disquieting signs of a revival of that model, which we thought had been discarded once and for all? Surely the sun is setting in many places on independent group life, and the shadow of an all-absorbing but necessary State control is gradually spreading to what used to be left to the initiative of single individuals. Governments are taking upon themselves more and more the role which Tocqueville feared most of all: that of an 'immense and tutelary power' catering for all our needs;[1] and even though the vigour of individual and group activities has not yet abated in Western societies, the problem still remains of how the unity of the State can be reconciled with the pluralism which they profess to uphold and to cherish.

The only way of answering such questions properly is to return once again to the analysis of power, of that legal nature of the State which has been the subject of our inquiry so far. Surely the sovereignty of the State is no less efficient in countries with a marked pluralistic structure than it is in those where society is more homogeneous and uniform: just as it is no less present in those countries where power is constitutionally divided, or in those where the multiplicity of legal systems is admitted as a matter of course. The Italian Constitution of 1947, for example, has adopted the division of power; it expressly recognizes the validity of international law; it guarantees the independence (and even the 'sovereignty') of the Catholic Church, as well as freedom of worship, of association, and of individual enterprise. Nevertheless, it would not occur to anyone to deny that Italy is an independent and sovereign State. This can, therefore, only mean that none of the essential attributes which Hobbes had grouped together as belonging

---

[1] It is interesting to find the phrase *autorité tutélaire* used by the Abbé Siéyès, on the eve of the French Revolution, to describe his ideal of a society in which all citizens are equal before the law and there is no 'hierarchy of power' other than that of the State.

exclusively to the State has yet been explicitly renounced. To say that the State is sovereign means that the 'fullness of power' is still at its disposal, and that at any moment it can, if necessary, bring into its service that monopoly of force which it alone, among all groups and associations, possesses. Indeed it might well be pointed out that it is precisely because the modern State is strong (stronger perhaps than Hobbes's Leviathan ever was), and because its law is the only law that can be enforced by measures which are really compulsory, that it has been able to agree to the division of power, to the recognition of other laws of a different character from its own, and to the pluralistic structure of modern society, with its infinite variety of interests and aims. In fact, it might even be argued that, just because of its strength, the modern State can secure certain benefits which would be denied to the individual in the Hobbesian scheme: such are those 'liberties of the citizen' (including religious liberty) that modern political theory has laid down as the reason for the existence of the State, the foundation of its power, and the final aim of its activities.

We are thus brought in the end to the problem of values, which so far we have tried carefully to avoid. The very fact of admitting a pluralist society raises the question: how do we distinguish between group and group, between organization and organization? what, to put it quite bluntly, is the proper sphere of the State? Take the distinction of State and Church as separate societies: how can we discriminate between them, unless we know which ends each may rightly pursue? It is all very well to speak of a 'wall of separation', as the Americans do: but how can that wall be built, unless one knows exactly where the boundaries run? Questions such as these can never be solved on a purely descriptive level, by defining the State as the ultimate holder of power or by merely taking stock of the fact that it possesses the monopoly of coercive law. It is questions such as these which provide evidence of the limits of the purely legal approach to the State, however important that approach may have proved to be from the point of view both of history and of theory. They evince the necessity of transferring the problem of the State to a plane altogether different from that on which we have hitherto taken our stand. It will no longer be a question of assessing whether might is effective or whether it is legal, but whether power is legitimate, whether, in other words, it is exercised with a proper title and within its proper sphere.

REFERENCES

St. Thomas Aquinas, *Summa Theologica*, 1ᵃ 2ᵃᵉ, xcviii. 1; 2ᵃ 2ᵃᵉ, x, 8 and 11; xi, 3; xii, 2. John Whitgift, *Of the Authority of the Civil Magistrate in Ecclesiastical Matters* (in *Works*, 1851, III, 313). Robert Browne, *A Treatise of Reformation without Tarying for Anie* (1582). St. Robert Bellarmine, *Tractatus de Potestate Summi Pontificis* (1610), ch. v. Hobbes, *Leviathan*, ch. xxix. Rousseau, *Contrat Social* (Eng. trans. by G. D. H. Cole, London, 1913), II, ch. 3; IV, ch. 8. Emmanuel Siéyès, *Essai sur les privilèges* (1788). Alexis de Tocqueville, *De la démocratie en Amérique* (Eng. trans. by H. Reeve, London, 1838–40), part II (1840), iv, ch. 6.

On the theory of Church and State and the growth of religious liberty there is an immense literature which cannot possibly be listed here. I should like, however, to profess my indebtedness to such old and yet still valid essays as Lord Acton's *The History of Freedom in Christianity* and *The Protestant Theory of Persecution*, as well as to J. N. Figgis's 'Respublica Christiana' in *Churches in the Modern State*.

More particularly, I should like to mention in this connexion the work of a great and inspiring teacher whose pupil I had the good fortune to be nearly fifty years ago. His name was Francesco Ruffini, and his book, *Religious Liberty*, was published in English (with a Preface by J. B. Bury) in London in 1912.

10

LEGALITY AND LEGITIMACY

THE words 'legality' and 'legitimacy' do not seem to have a well-differentiated meaning in current legal language and thought. Legal and legitimate are used indifferently to describe the way in which State activity conforms to the particular rules of the legal system or to the general directives which the Constitution lays down. For my part, I hold that 'legitimacy' is a convenient expression for describing in general terms the criteria for the 'validity' of power, its 'title' for issuing orders and demanding obedience from those who in turn hold themselves under obligation to obey.[1] In this sense legitimacy presupposes legality, the existence of a legal system and of a power issuing orders according to its rules. But it also provides the justification of legality, by conferring on power the chrism of authority: it is a further 'plus' sign added to the force which the State exercises in the name of the law. Indeed, if I am not mistaken, the very root of the word 'authority', derived from the Latin *augēre* (to augment), clearly suggests the idea of the conferment and possession of a special qualification, which 'authorizes' whoever is invested with it to exercise a particular power or right. In order to eliminate all considerations of legitimacy from our study of political phenomena, we should have to avoid the use of the word 'authority' altogether, and to speak only of 'might' and of 'power' in reference to the State.

There is no need to go very far back in history to discover that in traditional political theory the problem of the relationship between legality and legitimacy was long held to be one of the basic problems concerning the State. During the sixteenth and seventeenth centuries the subtle distinctions drawn by medieval writers with regard to unjust or 'tyrannical' power, and especially the distinction between the two kinds of tyranny, *ex parte exercitii* and *ex defectu*

---

[1] With a slight shift of emphasis, this is also the way in which Max Weber defines 'validity' and 'legitimacy'. For a further discussion see the list of references, below.

tituli, were still very much alive. Power, according to this theory, which had been fully developed by Bartolus and by Coluccio Salutati, could be unjust, that is tyrannical, on account of the use that was made of it, i.e. of the way in which it was exercised. But it could also be unjust, and was held to be so even more definitely, because of a flaw in its origin, when the ruler or the government had no proper title to govern or to rule. The practical consequences of this distinction were manifold: for example, the rules drawn up about the possibility of civil disobedience or open resistance differed according to the type of tyranny involved. So did the views held on the way in which 'legitimation' of power could take place. Some writers held that it could consist only in a formal 'investiture'; others that the original flaw could be healed by the regular exercise of power according to accepted rules of law. The quest for the legitimation of power has never ceased to be one of the main concerns of political theory, even though the word 'legitimacy' may sound rather obsolete nowadays. There are men still alive, however, who can remember a time when the principle of 'dynastic legitimacy' was still widely accepted in Europe, and the appeal to 'national legitimacy' is one of the favourite arguments of President de Gaulle. As for resistance to a rule which is unjust and tyrannical, examples are certainly not lacking in our time, and they alone would suffice to prove that the problem of the foundation of power is one that cannot be avoided in any discussion of politics, not to mention the notion of the State.

It is precisely at this point, however, that the line of argument we have followed so far seems to come to an end. Legal theory has helped us to understand and construe the State as a legal system; but the problem of the ultimate foundation of that system is not one which that theory purports to solve. The relation between legality and legitimacy finds no place among the topics normally discussed by jurists. The grounds of obedience, its limits, and, generally, the whole problem of political obligation, are usually considered, together with the problem of justice, 'meta-legal' questions: matters to be left to philosophers, if not to personal opinion or to political preference; problems long discarded from legal theory proper, together with the whole paraphernalia of natural law and natural rights. There would be no objection to this negative attitude if the question were only one of definition: the definition of the subject and scope of legal science. For it is obvious that lawyers, trained as they are to confine themselves strictly to the study and assessment of positive law, should not be blamed for refusing to handle such issues as cannot be solved in terms of positive law alone. The case of unjust or tyrannical power, let alone the case of resistance, is one no longer envisaged in constitutional documents. The legal system does not contain any provisions concerning it. If it did, the issue would no longer be left to personal opinion. Those provisions would be provisions of positive, not of natural, law.

Such, more or less, is the answer we should probably receive from most lawyers if we asked them point-blank: it is all very well to conceive of the State as a legal system, but why does the legal system derive its validity from the State? As I pointed out from the start, their strict adherence to the law, without further questioning, has in itself a certain dignity: it ensures that the job of expounding and applying the law is done with the utmost devotion, and certainly nobody would deny that, in our civilized world, this job is done exceedingly well. But it is not too difficult to detect behind this complete dedication a deep commitment to legality as something worth preserving at all costs. In other words, the defence of legality (*dura lex sed lex*) is itself an indication of a choice, of the acceptance of a value considered by the lawyer to be inherent in the very existence of a legal system, one which, as such, also provides the ultimate justification of the State.

Max Weber's comment on this point is illuminating and decisive: 'today', he remarked, 'the most usual basis of legitimacy is the belief in legality, the readiness to conform with rules which are formally correct and have been imposed by accepted procedures.' Weber had noticed that most modern societies, and more particularly the State, are 'legal' societies, societies where 'commands are given in the name of an impersonal norm rather than in the name of a personal authority; and in turn the giving of a command constitutes obedience to a norm rather than an arbitrary decision, a favour, or a privilege'. Hence Weber concluded that 'rational legitimacy', which he identified with legality, was the only type of legitimacy to survive in the modern world. In it 'every single bearer of power of command is legitimated by the system of rational norms, and his power is legitimate so far as it corresponds with the norms. Obedience is thus given to the norms rather than to the person.'

These remarks of Weber's throw a great deal of light on the problem with which we are here concerned. They certainly explain why the respect, indeed the cult, of legality plays such an important part today, not only in legal theory but in current views of the State. Let it also be added that there are good and sound reasons for this fact. The principle of legality is closely bound up with the modern conception of the State. The very notion of the constitutional system was born, as we saw, from the struggle against arbitrary rule and from the need to restrict the action of the State within precise legal limits. The old idea of the Rule of Law was transformed into an institutional practice. Special devices were set up or gradually developed (such as 'administrative justice' on the Continent and 'judicial review' in the United States) for the purpose of safeguarding legality against abuse, not only by the executive power but by the legislative as well. The idea that legality is the foundation of the State was the inspiration of formulae such as Government under Law, *Stato di diritto*, *Rechtsstaat*, which are generally accepted today as the best descriptions of what the modern State is or purports to be, and of the reason why its commands are accepted as legitimate. As Dean Pound once put it in humorous vein, the modern man's notion of the State (and not only the lawyer's) may be expressed with a paraphrase of the Psalm: *Propter legem tuam sustinui te, Domine*—'Because of thy law am I content with thee, O State.' Legality seems indeed to have become, as Weber pointed out, the modern version of legitimacy.

But if this be the case, the question arises: what kind of legitimation does legality offer? If all our analysis thus far is correct, legality is inherent in the notion of power as force exercised according to, and in the name of, the law. There is no denying that this 'normalization' of force can in itself represent a benefit or a value. In unravelling Hobbes's views we found that it was precisely that normalization or regularity in human relations which constituted for him the highest benefit of political association. We also found, no doubt, that the price Hobbes asked us to pay for the preservation of peace and security was a high one: but all values are bought at a price, and in Hobbes's day many of us would probably have been willing to pay that price to see law and order restored, and an end put to chaos and anarchy. The point which must now be cleared is precisely this assumption of value. For, indeed, no sooner is mention made of a value assured by the State than the strictly formal approach is abandoned. The question is no longer one about the presence of power, but one about its purpose and scope: no longer one that can be answered in purely descriptive terms, but one that presupposes a choice and necessarily entails prescription. We do not limit ourselves any more, as lawyers appear to do, to taking stock of the fact that laws exist which ensure the regular exercise of force; but we commit ourselves to a particular view about the object, the content of law itself, about the end that norms pursue and that justifies their existence. This is the stumbling-block of all strictly legal theory of the State, the reason why the principle of legality cannot by itself alone fulfil the task which used in the past to be fulfilled by that of legitimacy. For legality to provide legitimacy as well, it must necessarily refer not only to the formal structure of power but to its intrinsic nature. In other words, what is required is clearly to indicate what kind of legality we have in mind when we praise the State for ensuring it.

Now there seems to be hardly any doubt that an indication of this sort can be traced in the principle of the Rule of Law, at any rate as it is usually understood in the Anglo-American tradition, and as it is gradually influencing legal thought in other countries also. In the discussions held in Chicago in 1957 'it seemed to be generally agreed that "the Rule of Law as understood in the West" involved more than the mere compliance of the sovereign power in a State with the rules of the positive law of that State. There was, in fact, a large measure of agreement that the rule of law has some positive content capable of being expressed in terms of fundamental values'.[1] Less than two years later the International Commission of Jurists, in the Congress it held in New Delhi, agreed to define the rule of law as 'the realization of the appropriate conditions for the development of human dignity'. Clearly, the emphasis here is on the content of the law, on the purpose of legality. There is not merely a request for the formal correctness of the particular rules or the single decisions which compose a legal system. There is a request for the conformity of these rules and decisions to the values that are posited as necessary for the existence

---

[1] J. A. Jolowicz, Digest of the Discussion, Chicago Colloquium on 'The Rule of Law as understood in the West' (Sept. 1957), in *Annales de la Faculté de Droi d'Istamboul*, t. ix, 1959.

of a free society.[1] We are provided with a touchstone which enables us to evaluate the 'legal quality' of law, the substantive aspect of legality. Legitimacy and legality are identified, but only in as far as legality is itself an assertion of values.

But views such as these would still find much difficulty in being accepted on the Continent of Europe. Here the notion of the *Rechtsstaat*, or government under law, when not wilfully deformed so as to justify the most perverse kinds of tyranny, ended by losing in the hands of our jurists that content of value which alone justifies the identification of legality with legitimacy. The theory of the *Rechtsstaat* was developed in the nineteenth century by German jurists in particular. It then spread in various ways in Europe, and was regarded with great favour in Italy. In its beginnings, at any rate, it sounded almost synonymous with the theory of constitutional government. It was intended to account for States founded on the principles of liberalism, if not of democracy. But later, particularly under the influence of the so-called 'positive theory of law', the notion of the *Rechtsstaat* completely altered its meaning and character. Once 'ethical neutrality' was accepted as the condition of scientific work, once all and every reference to value and content was declared to be irrelevant and even obnoxious to the understanding of the law, the one and only justification of any legal system was found to be 'efficacy', that is, its factual existence: and every State, in as far as it is a legal system, can by definition be considered to be a *Rechtsstaat*. The problem of legitimacy thus underwent a radical change. The 'principle of effectiveness' became 'the new rule of legitimacy'.[2] The most that could be done was to distinguish between a 'legal' and a 'moral' legitimation of power.[3] But moral legitimation is obviously not a matter for the lawyer to discuss: in fact, it is usually considered by orthodox positivists a matter of ideology, if not merely of personal opinion. Legal legitimation is the exclusive concern of the theorist: and from his point of view it does not make much difference whether the cohesive principle of the legal order is found in a 'basic norm' or in an 'institution'. 'Normativism' and 'institutionalism', the two schools of thought which divide Italian legal

[1] N. S. Marsh, 'The Rule of Law as a Supra-National Concept', in *Oxford Essays in Jurisprudence*, ed. by A. G. Guest, London, 1961, pp. 240–5.

[2] P. Piovani, *Il significato del principio di effettività*, Milan, 1953.

[3] N. Bobbio, *Teoria dell'ordinamento giuridico*, Turin, 1960, p. 64.

positivism today (and not Italian positivism only) agree on this point. The 'principle of legitimacy' means to Kelsen that the 'validity [of a given system of norms] is determined only by the order to which they belong'. When, as in the case of a successful revolution, 'the total legal order . . . has lost its efficacy', this merely indicates that a new legitimacy has set in: 'the principle of legitimacy is restricted by the principle of effectiveness'.[1] Romano, the staunchest Italian supporter of the institutional theory, reaches the same conclusion: 'An illegitimate legal system is a contradiction in terms. Its existence and its legitimacy are one and the same thing.'[2]

Now it would be only too easy—and it has been done many times—to level at such views the accusation of justifying the *fait accompli*. They seem to end by making force, not justice, the last resort of legal as well as of political life. But perhaps this kind of criticism of the positivists' standpoint is not really quite fair. Their doctrine is merely a refined and elaborate statement of what is implicit in all purely factual approaches to the problems of politics and law. In frankly declaring that the problem of the 'good law' or the 'good society' is a 'meta-legal' question, they provide the best justification for the very sort of inquiry we ourselves have pursued so far. We have tried to understand the positive contribution which both political realists and lawyers had to make to the understanding of the complex phenomenon of the State. We should never have been able to do so unless we had started by putting our preferences as it were within brackets, and had deliberately adopted a descriptive rather than a prescriptive type of discourse. Let us not forget, either, that many present-day positivists are men of high moral convictions. There can be no doubt of their being—as the phrase now runs—morally as well as politically 'committed'. If they cling to the views I have described, it is because they deem it a token of intellectual honesty to profess them. They will repeat with Austin that 'the existence of law is one thing; its merit or demerit another'. The question of the validity of law is to them a different question from that of moral obligatoriness. Professor Hart puts their case very well when he asks: in

[1] H. Kelsen, *General Theory of Law and State*, Cambridge, Mass., 1946, pp. 115–22.

[2] S. Romano, *Principî di diritto costituzionale generale*, 2nd edn., Milan, 1946, pp. 192–3.

what way is it better, when faced with an iniquitous State, to say 'This is not law, this is not a State', rather than 'This is law, this is a State, but too iniquitous to be obeyed or respected'? 'The certification of something as legally valid', Hart remarks, 'is not conclusive of the question of obedience.' Many contemporary positivists would probably agree with him when he adds that the 'official system', the State, must in the end be submitted to some further 'scrutiny' before its power is recognized as morally binding and as worthy of the respect and the loyal allegiance of its citizens.[1]

But what can this scrutiny mean, except that the possession of power is not the final word about the State? Surely the whole structure of normative propositions which constitute a legal system can very well be represented as a set of hypothetical imperatives, of rules concerning the use of force if and when the system so disposes. Power, as we have tried to define it, would in this case be merely force once removed. And laws could hardly be called obligatory: indeed, what Justice Holmes called the 'bad man's' notion of law would no doubt provide a more adequate description of the reason why men obey. It seems to me that for laws to be obligatory, that is, true ought-propositions and not mere statements concerning the use of force by the State, a value-clause must be inserted somewhere in the system. The whole structure must be invested with some kind of authorization or legitimation. It will be necessary to assume that the State is the holder not only of power but of legitimate power, or better still, of authority; that the 'aura of majesty' that surrounds the 'official system' can be somehow explained and justified.

The search for a legitimate basis of power is not an empty and senseless search. It is the fundamental quest of political philosophy. A theory of the State which takes no account of it is necessarily incomplete. It is no use protesting that such notions as legitimacy or authority are emotionally loaded, that they are at bottom irrational and certainly incapable of definition with the precision and severity of scientific language. This emotional and irrational character has never been denied by those few thinkers who have been inclined to investigate the idea of legitimacy, and to take it more seriously than a mere ideology, a political formula, or a noble lie. 'There is something miraculous in the awareness of legitimacy', wrote Benjamin Constant after the gravest crisis which has shaken

[1] H. L. A. Hart, *The Concept of Law*, Oxford, 1961, pp. 203-7.

France in the course of her history. At the height of another and more recent crisis, the Italian writer Guglielmo Ferrero thought that the time had come to invoke those 'invisible genii' which hold States together, and to restore the 'legitimate power' without which 'there can be no escape for the world'. This is the language of imagination, perhaps even of rhetoric. But the fact that rhetorical language is not an exact language does not necessarily deprive it of meaning. There may be ways of, and reasons for, recommending our preferences, since we cannot prove them as scientific truths. Is there such a thing as a 'democratic legitimacy'? Can the modern State appeal to authority beyond the force and power it undoubtedly owns? Can we account for the soundness of our institutions, or at any rate for the ideals that inspired them and for the aims they pursue? On the answer to this question depends in the last resort the possibility of constructing in our age a theory of the State worthy of the name.

REFERENCES

The Weber quotations on legality and legitimacy are taken from his two works, *Wirtschaft und Gesellschaft* (Eng. trans., as given in the Introduction) and *Die Wirtschaftsethik der Weltreligionen*, in *Gesammelte Aufsätze zur Religionssoziologie*, vol. I (Eng. trans. in *Essays in Sociology*, ed. by H. H. Gerth and C. Wright Mills, 1947).

As I have pointed out in the text, I consider Weber's remarks of paramount importance for the treatment of the problem discussed in this chapter, and far more enlightening than much that has been written on the subject in more recent days. In fact, the political scientist's notion of 'legitimate power' is in most cases merely a description of the correspondence, in a given society, of the structure of power to the prevailing 'political formula' or 'ideology'. It would seem as if the strict behaviourist approach made it impossible, or at any rate difficult, for empirical political science to appreciate the importance of the normative framework, i.e. of legality, as a necessary step for the proper understanding of the problem of legitimacy.

See, however, for a further discussion of legitimacy, the standard works of Lasswell and Kaplan, *Power and Society*, London, 1952, ch. vi, §§ 6.3–6.5 and of S. M. Lipset, *Political Man*, London, 1960, ch. iii, as well as the articles on the subject in the volume *Authority*, ed. by C. J. Friedrich (*Nomos* I, Cambridge, Mass., 1958); and, on the relationship between legality and legitimacy, C. Schmitt, *Legalität und Legitimität*, Munich and Leipzig, 1932; G. Burdeau, *Traité de Science Politique*, III, Paris, 1950, §§ 57–63; M. Duverger, *Droit Constitutionnel et Institutions Politiques*,

Paris, 1955, ch. 1; and the article by O. H. von der Gablentz, 'Autorität und Legitimität im heutigen Staat', in *Zeitschrift für Politik*, N.F., V (1958). Professor C. J. Friedrich has recently returned to and amply discussed the subject in a chapter of *Man and His Government*, New York, 1963, part ii, ch. 13.

For the Marxist's use of the notion of legitimacy a short article of Lukàcs is revealing. According to Lukàcs, the only legitimate power is that of the proletariat, whose task it is to 'get rid both of the cretinism of legality and of the romanticism of illegality' (G. Lukàcs, 'Légalité et Illégalité', 1920, in *Histoire et Conscience de Classe*, Paris, 1960).

Reference has also been made in this chapter to the following much older works: Bartolus of Sassoferrato, *De Tyrannia* (*c.* 1350) and Coluccio Salutati, *De Tyranno* (*c.* 1400). (Both writings can be read in English translation in E. Emerton, *Humanism and Tyranny: Studies in the Italian Trecento*, Cambridge, Mass., 1925); Benjamin Constant, *De l'esprit de conquête et de l'usurpation dans leurs rapports avec la civilisation européenne* (1814).

Guglielmo Ferrero's *Pouvoir* was first published in French in the U.S.A. in 1942 (Eng. trans. by T. R. Jaeckel, New York, 1942).

PART THREE

AUTHORITY

1

LAW AND ORDER

THE first, the easiest, and the most widespread legitimation of power is that which involves the need for order, and describes order as the greatest benefit which can be secured by the State. We need only turn to current language to find the word 'order' used in this sense. 'The preservation of order', 'the forces of order', the 'new order' as opposed to the 'old': how often we come across these and other similar expressions in newspapers and speeches, not only in those of a markedly conservative bent! Order is a magic and exquisitely political word, loaded with an evocative power which the word 'legality' does not possess. No doubt, in English at any rate, law and order are usually linked together. But it is the notion of order, not that of law, which arouses emotion, and never fails to awake a response in people's imagination and desires. For indeed, in the popular mind, order is opposed to disorder, or, as is also said, to anarchy. Order is normality, safety, peace—even peace at any cost. Thus understood, order does not too obviously coincide with legality. The general who reported to the Czar 'Order rules in Warsaw' is not likely to have been a lawyer. To him, law simply meant martial law. Yet it was in the name of law that he justified his recourse to force. A certain degree of ingenuity, perhaps even a kind of professional distortion, is needed to enable us to declare that order is in its own way a rough, primitive form of legality, and to see in it at least the beginning of that control and normalization of force which we singled out as the distinctive mark of the State. The appeal to order, and to the benefits it entails, implies the transference to the plane of values of the notion of power, a notion which, as we have seen, is in itself indifferent and neutral.

The classic example of such a transfer is still that of Hobbes. As we saw, Hobbes identified the State with legality, that is with an order which guarantees safety and peace. But this order is at the same time a value: indeed, it is the highest value attainable in this world by men. It therefore constitutes not only the essence

of the State, but its justification. We need not, however, be
Hobbesians—that is we do not need to accept Hobbes's premisses,
his predominantly pessimistic view of human nature—in order to
take the step from maintaining that the State exists to guarantee
law and order to demanding that this order should be established
because it is a good thing. There is a sense in which every political
philosopher, one could almost say every good citizen, indeed every
man who willingly obeys the laws, implicitly makes Hobbes's
reasoning his own. He does so in so far as he 'accepts' order not
only as a fact but as a value, that is, as something which not
only exists, but should rightly exist, and from which he derives a
positive advantage.

Thus, if we turn to political theories of the past, we find hardly
any which cast doubt on the merits of law and order. The myth
of the 'state of nature' was neither a subversive nor an anarchical
myth, a means of disproving the value of order. It certainly was
not such for Hobbes, who used it to stress the need for the State.
But neither was it such for 'those who of old sang of the age of gold
and of its happy state',[1] taking a more optimistic view of human
nature. Men in that condition of happy innocence obeyed the law
without constraint and lived together in peace and harmony. But,
like the hierarchy of Heaven, they bore witness to an order, to that
order which, according to St. Augustine, is the condition of peace:
pax omnium rerum tranquillitas ordinis.[2] Nor are utopian dreams
necessarily anarchical. Utopias, the models of a perfect society,
in which at certain moments in history men sought an escape and
refuge from reality, do not imply a denial of order; far from it.
They are expressions of an aspiration after a better or different
order, after an order which may well be more rigorous and exacting than that which actually exists and is laid down in positive
legal systems.

But, it may be objected, it is one thing to dream of the lost happiness of a fabulous age, or to imagine perfect constitutions in
far-off, unknown lands, and quite another to justify the State as a
coercive machine. In the one case we assume the existence of an
order which rests on the evidence of reason, in the other we
refer to an order which is distinguished by the use of force. But
this objection clearly misses the point. For the value of order is

---

[1] Dante, *Purg.* XXVIII. 139–40.
[2] 'Peace for all things is the tranquillity of order.'

something quite different from, and independent of, the way in which order takes shape and is established. There will always be a question of deciding whether order is or is not something desirable before we decide whether it can and ought to be imposed by force or achieved by some other means. And here everyone seems to agree, Hobbesians and anti-Hobbesians, political realists and seekers after Utopia: that order is desirable and necessary; that it has a positive value; that it is what distinguishes men from beasts and makes their life worth living.

We have to travel to the very threshold of our modern world to find this view deliberately challenged. What we then come up against is a depreciation of order, or to be more exact an emphasis on its purely negative side. Order sets limits to the power of the individual to act: hence it entails the sacrifice of something that is unique and precious. It is contrary to the 'true nature' of man, and as such it is an evil: what is worse, an unnecessary and perhaps an avoidable evil. Such are the views which crop up for the first time in the eighteenth century, almost in contrast, as it were, to the final establishment of the modern State, to its complete monopoly of power. They are set forth in fables and myths according to the taste of the century. Yet these fables have not lost a certain poetical truth, an endearing freshness and candour. They deserve to be remembered not only because they foreshadow later theories, whether anarchical or liberal, deliberately hostile to the State, but because they register certain demands with regard to order and law which have become part and parcel of our attitude towards power. Three authors in particular come to mind in this connexion, each telling a different tale, but each pointing to similar conclusions: that order is not necessarily a good thing, that men might be better off without it, and that there are certainly a number of values which legislation cannot secure and can even hinder.

Of these three authors, Montesquieu, with his Story of the Troglodytes, is the least remote from tradition. The Troglodytes, a small people of Arabia, having killed their king decide to devote their lives solely to the pursuit of their particular interests. The consequence is complete confusion and insecurity—Hobbes's state of nature. Even the doctor, who has been refused fair payment, refuses in his turn to cure them when an epidemic overtakes and decimates them. The few survivors are thus converted to 'humanity', to 'justice', and to 'virtue'. Happiness and prosperity, peace at home and bravery in face of the enemy, flourish again. But the Troglodytes decide to give themselves a leader once more. They turn to a venerable old man, who weeps on learning that the choice has fallen on him. ' "I shall die with grief for having seen the Troglodytes born free, and now to see them in subjection. . . . I see, O you Troglodytes, what it is. Your virtue begins to be too heavy for you. In the condition you at this time are, you must be virtuous in spite of yourselves. You cannot subsist without it, but would fall into the miseries of your forefathers. This yoke seems hard to you. You had rather submit to a prince, and obey his laws, less rigorous than your morals. You know you may then satisfy your ambition, acquire riches, and languish in vile luxury; and provided you avoid committing great crimes, you will have no need of virtue." He stopped a moment, and his tears flowed faster than ever. "Ah! what would you have me do? How can I lay my commands on a Troglodyte? Would you that he should do a virtuous action because I command it? Would he not do it himself, and from an instinct of nature only?" '

The moral of Montesquieu's story seems fairly simple. Government is redundant for men who are truly virtuous. In fact, government may be an excuse for dispensing with virtue altogether. If men followed reason there would be no need for the State. This moral is not substantially different from that of the old fable of the golden age. For what is redundant is the coercive machinery of the State, but not order as such; quite the contrary. It is the rule of reason that makes the peaceful, happy coexistence of human beings possible. They are better off without the State, but only in so far as they are reasonable.

To find the very benefits of law and order denied we must turn to another myth, that of the happy savage. We must turn to Rousseau's startling interpretation of the state of nature, which is radically different from that of all his predecessors. For Rousseau the nature of man does not lead, as it does for Hobbes and Spinoza, to the war of all against all. But neither does it entail a rudimentary, peaceful society, as it does for most theorists of the state of nature. Man left to himself does not stand 'in need of his fellow-creatures' nor has he 'any desire to hurt them'. A simple hut and the few tools needed to sustain daily life are all that is necessary for leading a 'free, healthy, honest and happy' existence. Self-interest, the multiplication of needs, contact with other men, have laid the roots of slavery. In a word, it is society which has depraved and perverted man. History is but the tale of the progress of inequality.

But this, as is well known, is not for Rousseau the end of the story. The *Discourse on the Origin of Inequality* finds its counterpart in the *Social Contract*. Rousseau's final message is not the destruction of order, but the building of a new and better one. The basic problem of politics is that of finding the means of enabling man to be 'as free' in society as he was in the state of nature, of helping him to recover the equivalent of his natural independence under the form of civil liberty. This is the problem which Rousseau faces in the *Social Contract*, where the citizen is guaranteed against any form of 'personal' dependence by his 'total alienation ... to the whole community', i.e. to the State. Thus, we shall see, Rousseau ended by definitely turning his back on the happy savage, and perhaps even opening the road to the ethical State or to modern totalitarianism.

But Rousseau's peculiar interpretation of the state of nature does not for that reason lose its importance nor its fascination. The myth of the happy savage struck deep into the imagination of his sophisticated contemporaries. The gospel of the return to nature could easily be turned into an open invitation to anarchy. An appeal of this kind can be found, for example, in Diderot's *Supplément au Voyage de Bougainville*, which gives perfect literary expresssion to the longing for escape, to the quest for the exotic, of an age which, under a veneer of civilized refinement, was pervaded by thrills of rebellion and by an unquenchable thirst for renewal. We almost seem to hear already the chidings of a Marx or the oracular utterances of a Pareto. 'Look carefully at all political, civil and religious institutions. If I am not deceived, you will find the human race crushed from age to age beneath the yoke which a handful of rogues has sought to lay upon it. Beware of the man who would impose order. To create order always means to make oneself master of others at their expense.'

According to Diderot, among the nations of Europe only the Calabrians, the inhabitants of the southern tip of Italy, had managed not to let themselves be imposed on by 'the flattery of legislators'. He praised their 'anarchy', the genuine and happy condition of primitive, as yet uncivilized, peoples. He pointed out that 'their barbarism' might well be 'less vicious than our urbanity', and that, at any rate, 'the heinousness of a few big crimes about which so much fuss is made' was amply compensated by our 'petty wickedness'. Significantly enough, a similar argument was used, only a few years after Diderot, by one of the earliest prophets of Italian nationalism, Vittorio Alfieri. Steeped in the reading of Machiavelli, Alfieri openly undertook to defend the 'enormous and sublime misdeeds' which were Italy's special privilege. They were to him a sign that Italy 'possessed even now, more than any other European country, an abundant supply of fierce and fiery spirits. Such characters needed only the room and the means to achieve great things.' Here, indeed, an 'ethics of heroism' is proclaimed, which was soon to become a cherished motif of the Romantics, and could lead one day to the cult of the superman and to the open defence of violence.

All that remained to be done, in addition to eulogizing anarchy, was to pronounce the vindication of the anti-social nature of man, of egoism, of the pursuit of personal profit, with no further regard for the traditional view, which Montesquieu's Troglodytes had to their cost learned to know and respect, that virtue and justice are the foundation of society. This is the theme of the most caustic of all eighteenth-century apologues, Mandeville's *Fable of the Bees*. Mandeville's purpose is to show that 'private vices . . . may be turned into public benefits'. 'Fraud, luxury and pride', combined with 'hunger', are the springs of political life. The prosperity of the State, like that of the hive, is founded on the greed of its members, on the exploitation of one set of human beings by another. 'Such were the blessings of that State; Their Crimes conspir'd to make them Great.'

It is, however, noticeable that Mandeville, in spite of all his cynicism, still uses the traditional vocabulary of morals. Vice remains vice, evil is still evil. It took some time for these vices to be called economic virtues. Mandeville's point is merely that 'what we call evil in this world . . . is the grand principle that makes us sociable creatures'. What he does in effect is to propose a new set of values. He turns the tables on Hobbes's state of nature. Man's basic instincts no longer need to be thwarted by the iron claw of Leviathan. They are a constructive force, full of the promise of progress. All that is needed is to let them loose, the less hampered the better. Competition, the struggle to win power and wealth, should take the place of the old aspiration after law and order. In a world such as this the State is reduced to a purely negative role. It may well turn out in the end to be nothing but an instrument of power for those who take control of it, and an insurance of survival for those who are unable to do so.

Three myths, three different worlds. In each of them the modern reader can recognize as in a distorting mirror some familiar trait. In each there are to be found particular features which have in some way contributed to the shaping of modern man's attitude to the State. In an age such as ours, which has known and knows the most extreme forms of idolization of State power, it may seem paradoxical to suggest that the State is devalued. And yet it might well be asked whether the two views which hold the field in State-theory today—political realism, which reduces the State to force, and legal positivism, which acknowledges its presence in every effective system of law—do not in fact imply such a devaluation. The truth is that there is no point in talking of devaluation or valuation in considering theories which deliberately take their stand on the plane of neutrality, in discussing a type of argument whose purpose, as I have repeatedly pointed out, is to remain accurately descriptive. But this does not alter the fact that, as we saw, value judgements are often made even by realists and positivists: Machiavelli and Hobbes are outstanding examples. Nor does it alter the fact that a judgement of this sort is certainly present in that substitution of the idea of order for that of legality, which we observed taking place in everyday language and from which we started out in this chapter.

A value judgement was certainly made by all those—and they are the majority of political philosophers—who in the course of centuries stressed the concept of order as the first and foremost legitimation of power: though not any kind of order, but only one that is 'just' and 'right'. Here the Augustinian definition of order is more significant than any other: 'order is a disposition of equal and unequal things giving to each its place.'[1] This definition in turn clearly echoes that given by the Roman lawyers, of justice as a 'firm and enduring will to give each one his right'.[2] In both cases the accent is no longer on what is, but on what ought to be. Order is not merely a situation of fact, it is an ideal state of affairs, something to be striven after, which provides a standard for

---

[1] 'Ordo est parium dispariumque rerum sua cuique loca tribuens dispositio.'
[2] 'Iustitia est constans et perpetua voluntas ius suum cuique tribuendi.' (*Dig.* I, I).

judging a given situation. Order, indeed, is equivalent to justice; and since the State is the guarantor of order, justice alone can be the foundation of the State, the reason for its existence: *iustitia fundamentum regnorum*.

This approach is entirely different from any we have hitherto encountered. From this new standpoint the State is no longer merely a force that imposes itself, nor a power exercised according to any law whatsoever. It is a power 'authorized' to exact obedience in view of the attainment of certain definite ends. Thus the analysis of the concept of order has changed the mood of our whole inquiry. Henceforth we must be prepared to meet definitions and theories which are anything but neutral. A momentous step has been taken in political discourse, the step from description to prescription.

REFERENCES

St. Augustine, *De Civitate Dei*, Book XIX, ch. 13. Montesquieu, *Lettres Persanes* (1721), Letters xi–xiv, quot. from the English trans. by Ozell (1722)—spelling modernized. Mandeville, *The Fable of the Bees, or Private Vices, Publick Benefits*, 2nd edn., 1723: 'The Grumbling Hive' or 'Knaves turn'd Honest' (pp. 9 and 23); 'A Search into the Nature of Society' (p. 428). Rousseau, *Discours sur l'origine et les fondements de l'inégalité parmi les hommes* (1755), trans. by G. D. H. Cole, London, Everyman's Library, 1913, *passim*; *Contrat Social* (1762), same edn., Book I, ch. vi. Diderot, *Supplément au Voyage de Bougainville* (1772), in *Œuvres*, ed. Pléiade, pp. 1029–30. Alfieri, *Del Principe e delle lettere* (1778–86), ch. xi.

For the interpretation of Rousseau, and especially of the apparent contrast between the *Discourse on the Origin of Inequality* and the *Social Contract*, I am greatly indebted to R. Derathé, *J. J. Rousseau et la science politique de son temps*, p. 151, as well as to E. Cassirer, *The Question of J. J. Rousseau*, trans. by P. Gay, New York, 1954.

For Mandeville's paradox and the 'reformation of the language of morals' that it implied, and which was achieved by the Utilitarians, see E. Halévy, *The Growth of Philosophic Radicalism*, trans. by M. Morris, London, 1928, pp. 15–16 and 33.

For the meaning attributed respectively to Utopianism and Anarchism I refer to R. Ruyer, *L'Utopie et les Utopies*, Paris, 1950, and to G. Woodcock, 'Anarchism: The Rejection of Politics', in the volume *Power and Civilization*, ed. by D. Cooperman and E. V. Walter, New York, 1962.

2

NATURE AND CONVENTION

In what sense and under what conditions is it possible to define as 'right' and 'just' the order which is achieved in the State by means of the legal system? The question, put in such terms, may sound preposterous to modern ears. Yet it is one that has been asked ever since the dawn of civilization and that still, however differently worded, troubles the mind of man. To provide an answer to that question has long been considered the special task of political philosophers; it is an answer that must be given, were it only to prove that political philosophy still exists. In fact, the issue is twofold. To ask in what sense law and order are said to be 'right' is clearly a question about definition. It implies the admission that, at a certain point in our attempt at defining the State as the guarantor of law and order, we have abandoned the purely factual approach and have introduced some reference to values. But to ask, on the other hand, under what conditions the order set up by the State is 'just' involves us in an assessment of those values. Clearly, we must first ascertain if, and when, and how, value judgements are resorted to in defining the State, before we proceed further to examine the nature and character of such judgements.

To define the State as a 'right order' may mean one of two things. It may mean either that the State is the bearer of a value called 'justice', or that it is simply an instrument, a means of achieving that value. At any rate, in both cases State and justice are inseparably linked. Aristotle's statement on this point can be taken as paradigmatic. 'Justice', he says, 'belongs to the *polis*; for justice, which is the determination of what is just, is an ordering of the political association.'

Let us briefly follow Aristotle's argument. At the beginning of the *Politics* we are told that only in the State can man achieve the perfection inherent in his nature. Outside the State man is a being either above or below humanity, 'either a beast or a god'. Man is by

nature a political animal (*politikon zōŏn*): this means that political
life is the natural condition of mankind, whereas its absence is an
impossible, almost a monstrous, condition, just as a man who is
unable, or has no need, to share in the benefits of political association can hardly be called a man. For 'man, when perfected, is the
best of animals, but if he be isolated from law and justice he is the
worst of all'.

Everything obviously hinges on the concept of nature. For Aristotle it is the end which determines the nature of beings. The
nature of a thing is its condition in the final, perfect, stage of its
development. To say that the State is natural does not, therefore,
merely mean that in fact men do live in political societies. Aristotle
certainly does not refuse to resort to factual confirmation in order
to prove the 'naturalness' of the State. Experience teaches us, he
says, that man is the most sociable of all animals, the only one
gifted with speech; that men are differently endowed, and that the
household, with all its inequalities, is the kernel from which historically the State draws its origin. But the chronological order is
reversed when we come to consider the end, that is the justification,
of the State. Even though the naturalness of political life is empirically warranted, and even though it is possible to retrace the
growth of the State in the development of human associations, the
historical perspective is completely altered by means of the concept
of nature described above, which puts the centre of gravity at the
point of arrival, not at the point of departure. Therefore, whatever
may have been the sequence in time, the State is logically and
morally prior to, indeed more 'natural' than, the family or the village
out of which it has grown; for it is the condition of the family's
and the village's existence and well-being, just as the whole is
the condition of the existence and well-being of the parts. The
State is the bearer of a good which has the value of an end, for
the individual as well as for all subordinate groups. This good
is justice. 'Justice', Aristotle repeats in the *Nicomachean Ethics*,
'exists only as between men whose relations to one another are
governed by a system of law.'

Yet, in presenting the State as the achievement of justice, Aristotle had no intention of justifying any and every kind of State.
He had too deep a sense of the variety and relativeness of concrete
political forms, and of their remoteness from the ideal type or
model which alone would ensure the complete coincidence of

justice and the State. Such a coincidence does not and cannot occur except in the 'good' State, just as the virtue of the ordinary citizen is not, and can in no way be, the same as that of the good man, that is as virtue in general, except in a good constitution. The fact remains, however, that justice is the essential value-connotation of the State, and that the State is not only an instrument of this value, but its embodiment. It is a value that is, so to speak, immanent in the State, and can be attained by the individual only through a full and active participation in political life. The 'ethical' nature of the State is the corollary of this immanence: the idea that the State not only guarantees an external, formal order, such as the one which is set up by law, but provides the conditions for a life lived in accordance with virtue, i.e. for the realization of moral life. Thus Aristotle assigns the highest possible task to the State, at the cost of belittling morality: for the fulfilment of the moral ideal, tied as it is to the City, is bound to be peculiar and partial, that is, lacking that universal character which we usually associate with moral values as such.

The political philosophy that has for centuries dominated Western thought, far more effectively than Aristotle's, gives an entirely different account of the relationship between State and justice; and it is one that has to a much greater extent affected our history and our ways of life. How did this change come about in the centuries immediately following Aristotle, how were new values revealed, and by whom? This is not the place to retell the highly dramatic story, in what would necessarily be a totally inadequate way. What matters is to emphasize that the discovery of these new values led to a new and quite different way of justifying the State. While in Aristotle the attribution of value to the State had found expression in the doctrine of its 'naturalness', now the State no longer appears as something natural, but as something conventional. The argument follows a line expounded by the Sophists and taken up again by the Stoics; it is based on the contrast between *physis* and *nomos*, between what is natural and permanent and what is conventional and subject to change. Nature no longer means a final point of development, but on the contrary an initial condition; and it is to that condition that we must turn if we want to understand why the State came into being, the reasons that justify its existence, and the role it plays in human affairs. Thus, in defining the State as a conventional institution, the value-connotation was no longer in-built, but brought in as it were from outside. It was a matter of knowing the particular grounds which made the State necessary, or useful, or desirable, and which alone could account for the change from the original to the present conditions of mankind. In the traditional version of the theory the State exists for the implementation of certain values which are universal and unchanging—'natural' in the sense that they correspond to the very nature of man. These values find expression in the 'law of nature', that law of which God himself, according to Cicero's famous definition, is the author, and reason the interpreter, which is not bounded by the walls of the City but is valid for all nations and all times.

At first sight this may well appear to be a wholly negative attitude, one of almost deliberate depreciation of the State. Deprived of the value of being itself an end, the State is reduced to being simply a means of attaining values which are given, not made. Justice is no longer immanent in law and order; it transcends the level of politics: it is realized only if and when the State is modelled on a higher order and on a higher law. But a closer examination reveals that depreciation is not a correct description of this kind of approach. Rather, it implies a positive appreciation of the possibilities offered to men of building up a 'just' order, and of the responsibilities laid upon them for doing so. The 'true city', to use a wonderful image of Dante's, may not be achieved here and now; yet it may be possible to perceive, at least in the distance, its towers and spires.[1] Since the State is a human contrivance, the central problem is a problem of origins. Only by assessing the origins of political bondage can man know why he must choose to live in the State and obey its laws.

So numerous over the centuries have been the interpretations of these origins—offered in the various accounts of the State's 'conventionality'—that it would take volumes to list them. In the Christian Middle Ages the idea of sin could offer a perfectly adequate explanation of the transition from the state of innocence to the actual conditions of mankind in political life. It could even colour man's need to submit to law and order with the light of resignation, transforming into a duty what in purely factual terms

[1] Onde convenne legge per fren porre;
convenne rege aver che discernesse
de la vera città almen la torre'   (*Purg.* XVI. 94–96).

was a painful necessity and an inescapable fate. With the coming of a new age, the claim for individual independence was on the contrary to lead political philosophers to assert the need for an act of will—a 'social contract'—to explain and to justify the rise of political institutions, as well as to determine their limits and ends. It is only in our own day that the theory of the conventionality of political life appears to have been finally contradicted by the evidence of the so-called social sciences, and particularly by anthropology. They all seem to agree in maintaining that the existence of some form, however rudimentary, of political organization is a phenomenon which can be empirically proved, for it is found among all peoples in all ages. Therefore, so the argument goes, there can be no doubt that we ought to speak of the State as something natural, not as something conventional or artificial.

But this kind of argument would have had little hold on traditional political philosophers. And indeed it misses the most important point in the contrast between convention and nature, as well as its real contribution to the modern theory of the State. No doubt the relation between the 'state of nature' and the State (or 'political' or 'civil state') could be and was conceived as a relation of sequence in time. This, at any rate, was the way in which the Stoics and the Fathers of the Church conceived of it; so also did the Roman and Byzantine jurists, as did the medieval political philosophers, who, before Aquinas rediscovered Aristotle, could make no use of the Aristotelian notion of the political nature of man. This way of thinking was further encouraged by the story of Eden in the Bible and by the never-forgotten myth of the Golden Age. Even at a later stage, at the time when the doctrine of the social contract carried the day, political theorists (many of them, though not all) continued to think of the state of nature as the initial condition, corresponding to the happy infancy of the world, a condition which they believed could be found once more in the newly discovered lands full of virgin promise: 'in the beginning all the world was America', according to Locke's stirring phrase.

But, as had been the case with Aristotle, so with the theorists of the state of nature or of the social contract, the empirical or historical confirmation of the condition referred to as 'natural' was only of comparative importance. What mattered was the value attributed to those conditions as setting up a standard or model, as helping to bridge the gap between what was and what ought to be.

As we know, the historical sequence is completely reversed when Aristotle speaks of the State as natural. Similarly, when the Stoics, the Fathers, the medieval philosophers, the theorists of the social contract, or even the modern Utilitarians, take the opposite view, and maintain that the State is not a natural but a conventional institution, what they have in mind is not so much the historical sequence as the importance of showing that the State is a means of achieving certain ends. Hence it matters little whether the state of nature ever existed or the social contract ever took place. A judgement of value could never have been derived merely from the reference to a factual state of affairs. State of nature and social contract were normative concepts: their whole importance lies precisely in this. For only by conceiving the State as a human contrivance could the thought of harnessing Leviathan make any sense. Political institutions could then be reduced to their true proportions, their limits secured, their duties defined. The path could be kept open for the pursuance of values higher than politics, the ultimate values, which in order to be truly universal must apply to all men *qua* men.

The proof that this is not possible when the State is regarded as an end in itself and as the bearer of the highest values emerges clearly from the modern theory of the 'ethical State'. I have mentioned this theory before. Now is the time to come more closely to grips with it, even though, for the reasons I have already mentioned, it may well be doubted whether this theory is at bottom anything but a version of political realism writ large. For, indeed, if according to this theory the justification of the State ultimately lies in the very fact of its existence, then all those points hold good in regard to it which we discussed in considering the glorification of force as the ultimate answer to the problem of politics.

This in fact is the final outcome of the teaching of the man who may be regarded as the greatest exponent of the modern theory of the ethical State, as the real master of all those who in our time have personified the State as the supreme embodiment of justice. At first sight Hegel's teaching seems to follow closely in Aristotle's footsteps. Even his language differs only slightly from that of Aristotle. Both consider the State not only as the instrument, but as the condition, of man's perfection. 'Only as part of the State does the individual possess objectivity, truth and morality.' But, unlike Aristotle, Hegel and his followers do not admit the possibility of a difference between the real and the ideal, between what is and what ought to be. 'On some principle or other, any State may be shown to be bad, this or that defect may be found in it; and yet, at any rate if one of the mature States of our epoch is in question, it has in it the moments essential to the existence of the State. . . . The affirmative, life, subsists despite the defects, and it is this affirmative factor which is our theme here.' For this reason the State—the modern national State—was for Hegel not only the crown of our whole history but the highest positive expression of the moral life. The 'right' of the State knows no limit but that set by the force in virtue of which it makes itself felt in the face of other States. As in Hobbes, paradise lies under the shadow of the sword. But Hegel differs from Hobbes in that for him the sword not only guarantees survival and peace, but is the symbol of a new morality, of values which can be realized only in the State and to which the individual is wholly subordinate.

At one time the opposition between morals and politics, and the demand that the latter should conform to the former, were much canvassed. On this point only a general remark is required here. The welfare of a State has claims to recognition totally different from those of the welfare of the individual. The ethical substance, the State, has its determinate being, i.e. its right, directly embodied in something existent, something not abstract but concrete, and the principle of its conduct and behaviour can only be this concrete existent and not one of the many universal thoughts supposed to be moral commands.

The traditional view of the relation between State and justice is here turned upside down. A new political philosophy, or perhaps rather a new religion, was here proclaimed, which maintained among its dogmas that men were simply tools for creating the power and greatness of the nation, that States were responsible only at the bar of history, and that war was the health of the world.

The tragic happenings which have convulsed Europe within our lifetime ought to have made an end once and for all of this deadly philosophy. There would be no reason to mention it, were it not that it contains an indication of an historical and psychological situation which is without doubt characteristic of modern politics, or at least was so until not long ago. It is no use trying to cope with this situation simply by going back to the older view that the State is a human contrivance, an instrument, not an end.

The days when the State could be conceived as a remedy for sin are long past. But so are those when it was conceived merely as a machine deliberately assembled for the pursuit of definite aims. Today, the State is generally regarded as the expression of a cohesive bond which existed even before the legal organization of power. Political obligation may no longer be surrounded with a religious halo, as it was in the past. But neither is it the result of a simple calculation of the adequacy of particular means to particular ends, as it appeared to the theorists of the social contract or to the Utilitarians. Rather, it is a complex phenomenon, loaded with emotive and irrational elements, not easily reducible to abstract and clearly arguable terms. As the repository of a common heritage, the State is still to many people the object of blind dedication, which may prompt them to great sacrifices but also to great injustice; witness the slogan 'My country right or wrong'. Indeed, the name of this dedication is love of country, and the bond of nationality is in fact, as Hegel saw, the strongest pillar of the modern State as a nation-state. The idea of country and nation thus accounts for the evocative and sentimental aura which surrounds the modern notion of the State. We must therefore examine on what grounds and in what way the legitimation of power has been sought in such concepts rather than in that of justice, or at any rate conjointly with it.

REFERENCES

Aristotle, *Politics*, Book I, chs. i and ii; Book III, ch. iv; *Nicom. Ethics*, Book v, 6 (quotations given in Sir E. Barker's trans.). Cicero, *De Re Publica*, III, §§ 22, 33. Locke, *Second Treatise of Government*, ch. v, § 49. Hegel, *Philosophy of Right* (trans. by T. M. Knox), § 258 ann. and Add. 152; § 324, Add. 188; § 337 ann.

The contrast between the two different ways of conceiving the State, as a natural or as a conventional institution, has been analysed many times by historians of political thought. In my view the best and most comprehensive treatment of the subject is still, after many years, the one given by R. W. and A. J. Carlyle in their monumental *History of Medieval Political Theory in the West*.

As regards the 'ethical State', it is gratifying to notice that this doctrine never gained a strong foothold in England and in English-speaking countries. The most elaborate version to be found here—B. Bosanquet's *Philosophical Theory of the State*, London, 1899–1910—does not draw its inspiration from Hegel so much as from Rousseau. And it is in English that the most devastating criticisms of the theory have been made, such as those in L. T. Hobhouse, *The Metaphysical Theory of the State*, London, 1st edn., 1918, and K. R. Popper, *The Open Society and its Enemies*, already mentioned, vol. II.

In the concluding section of his book, *Reason and Revolution. Hegel and the Rise of Social Theory*, 2nd edn., London, 1955, H. Marcuse denies any connexion between Hegel's political philosophy and the Fascist and Nazi notion of the State. He is certainly correct in stressing the 'rational standard' and the concern for 'individual freedom'—in one word the liberal elements—on which Hegel's theory of the State still rests. Nazi ideology was the outcome of many other factors, some of which will be mentioned later in this book. But the Hegelian idea of the ethical State certainly played a decisive role in Italy under Fascism, and even received official endorsement in solemn documents and pronouncements of that time.

3

COUNTRY AND NATION

DURING the last decades many remarkable studies have been published on the problem of nation and nationality. This is a significant indication that the problem is still one of those with which our times are deeply concerned. I shall avail myself freely of these studies in my short account of the particular question which emerged at the end of the last chapter, the question of the relation between country, nation, and State.

One important point should be emphasized from the start. The ideas of nation and nationality are entirely absent from the definitions of the State which can be found in the writings of the three great thinkers who first mapped out the new landscape of the modern political world.

To begin with Machiavelli, it is quite clear that the State was to him something different and distinct from the nation. The great rhetorical peroration of the last chapter of *The Prince* should not deceive us. Machiavelli was no 'nationalist' in the modern sense of the word. What he had in mind was the setting up of a strong political unit in Central Italy. This alone could secure the liberation of the Peninsula from its 'barbarian' invaders. Indeed, it may even be doubted whether Machiavelli conceived of the whole of Italy as a 'nation'. He rarely uses that word. The State was to him exclusively a matter of force. It may face greater odds when its subjects are not all of the same region and language (*della medesima provincia e della medesima lingua*). But such odds can be overcome by a skilful ruler. The Romans managed to do so, and, according to Machiavelli, the Romans were always right.

Hobbes seems to hold a very similar view. He frankly admits that when the 'right of governing' is in the hand of 'strangers', this may be the cause of 'great inconvenience'. But, he adds, such inconvenience 'proceedeth not necessarily from the subjection to a stranger's government, but from the unskilfulness of the governors, ignorant of the true rules of politics'. It would seem, therefore, that, by observing those rules, even men 'not used to live under the same government, nor speaking the same language' can be moulded together into a common bond of citizenship: 'and this was it our most wise King, King James, aimed at, in endeavouring the union of his two realms of England and Scotland'. Neither language nor ethnic homogeneity is mentioned in the list drawn up by Hobbes of the elements that constitute the State. This too is significant. Clearly, Hobbes's State is not a Nation-state.

Of our three authors, Bodin is the most emphatic in asserting the irrelevance of what we nowadays call the 'national' element to the existence of the State. Power, he believes, is the one and only requisite. 'Wherefore of many citizens . . . is made a Commonweale, when they are governed by the puissant sovereignty of one or many rulers: albeit that they differ among themselves in laws, language, customs, religions, and diversity of nations.'

The question, then, can only be put in the following terms: when, in what way, and for what reasons did State and nation come to be so closely linked together as to turn the principle of nationality into the ultimate principle of legitimacy in the modern State?[1] But this question presupposes another: what is meant by 'nation' and 'nationality'? And here further difficulties arise. For indeed, apart from the strictly technical meaning of 'nationality' in English and in some other languages (where it is also taken in a more restricted sense as merely equivalent to citizenship), we cannot but agree with those scholars who, in trying to unravel the concepts of nation and nationality, have warned us against all sorts of pitfalls which make those concepts most difficult to define. In the end, the only competent guides in the jungle of so many different meanings are the linguists and the historians. It is to them that we must turn for help.

Now most of these scholars would agree that, contrary to the opinion which was generally held in the nineteenth century, the concepts of nation and nationality are a comparatively recent product of history. There is no denying, of course, that national consciousness has much deeper roots, and that it was the result of a long and obscure process which takes us back to the very

[1] The clearest and the final enunciation of this view is usually attributed, in Italy at any rate, to the Italian jurist Pasquale Stanislao Mancini (*Della nazionalità come fondamento del diritto delle genti*, 1851), who in turn drew his inspiration from Mazzini; but it can be found implicitly or explicitly stated in innumerable treatises on the State.

beginnings of our European community. It is certainly possible to find in the Middle Ages a clear awareness of the ethnical, linguistic, and, if we wish to call them so, the 'national' differences existing in Europe—provided we do not overlook the fact that the word 'nation' is used in medieval sources in a sense markedly different from ours.[1] The suggestion has been made that a reference to such national distinctiveness can be found in very old expressions such as *romanae nationis ac linguae*; indeed, that one of the first assertions of the great divisions of Europe was the treaty of 887 which sanctioned the break-up of the Carolingian Empire *inter teutonicos et latinos Francos*.

But one point alone is sufficient to show how remote this awareness of a national difference was from national consciousness in its modern acceptation. The recognition of the diversities of language, of stock, of customs, did not lead, at any rate for a long time, to a denial of a higher unity, that of the *respublica christiana*. Rather, such diversities were thought of as the natural differences within a large family, or as a distribution of functions and roles—even if particular 'nations' could claim that the task laid upon them was higher and nobler than that laid upon others, or that they were entrusted with a special mission, as was claimed by the French in the proud phrase *gesta Dei per Francos*. Perhaps the best illustration of this peculiar way of conceiving nationality is to be found in Dante. No one could possibly deny that Dante had a very strong national feeling. Italy stands out in his vision as a well-defined unit, with features, a language, a heritage of her own. But all his love for Italy did not prevent Dante from championing a supra-national political programme: the unity of the Empire, in which he was content to reserve for his country merely a privileged place. Dante's case is important, were it only because it provides further proof of the separation between the two concepts, of State and of nation, which we have already noticed in Machiavelli. Both Dante and Machiavelli, however different their reasons, seem to conceive the bond of nationality as something quite distinct from, perhaps even irrelevant to, the bond of citizenship, the political bond.

Nevertheless, it is precisely in the period which separates Dante

[1] *Natio* may either refer to the place of birth (as in Dante's phrase *florentinus natione non moribus*), or to some dubious ethnic or geographic division (as in the distinctions between 'nations' in medieval universities and Church councils). It hardly ever corresponds to citizenship or to political allegiance.

from Machiavelli, if not indeed earlier, that the ideas of nation and State can be seen gradually converging towards closer ties. But perhaps, in order to understand this process correctly, it would be as well to avoid such terms altogether when referring to that stage. The Swiss historian Werner Kaegi has recently suggested that 'nations' in the modern sense would probably not have come into being in Europe but for the unifying, centralizing action of political power. The determining factor in our history was the existence of 'centres of power', not nationality. This is a bold theory, but it is borne out by the facts. France is the classic example of a nation slowly shaped by the patient work of a dynasty bent on securing, unifying, and rounding off as it were, 'with a grandiose peasant mentality', that 'square plot of land'—the *pré carré*—which was the Kingdom of France. The job took eight hundred years to complete, but the result, at any rate for the French, was rewarding, and it still draws admiring comment from Frenchmen who in other respects are anything but friendly to the *ancien régime*. The case of England is both similar and different. Here the cohesive element was provided by Parliament, where what we call 'England' was forged. 'Parliament, indeed,' wrote Pollard, 'has been the means of making the English nation and the English state. It is really co-eval with them both. There was, it is true, an England centuries before there was a parliament, but that England was little more than a geographical expression. It was hardly a nation, still less a state.'[1]

No wonder then if, being itself partly a creation of power, national feeling was a weapon in the hands of those who actually held power and, by skilfully using it, laid the foundations of the modern State. Here again the process may have begun very early ('early modern nationalism', says Professor Post, 'arose, in the twelfth and thirteenth centuries, at the King's command'): but it is at the close of the Middle Ages that its main lines are more clearly discernible, and the ideas of State and nation come into direct contact. At the beginning of the modern era the 'new principality' undoubtedly knew how to make advantageous use of national consciousness; yet it also contrived to mould and to direct that consciousness to the pursuit of certain peculiar ends. 'New princes' unscrupulously exploited its dynamic possibilities: by doing so they also helped to bring into being that modern

[1] A. F. Pollard, *The Evolution of Parliament*, London, 2nd edn., 1926, p. 4.

phenomenon, the Nation-state. To this process Machiavelli is a
decisive witness. His sober realism never even contemplated the
possibility of a complete unification of Italy. Yet he did not hesitate to advise his prince to appeal to Italian national sentiment:
this, indeed, is the clue to the passionate rhapsody which concludes
his otherwise cynical and bitter little book.

But that coincidence of State and nation which was unthinkable
in Italy was being carried out, in Machiavelli's own day, in other
parts of Europe. The sixteenth century, the time of the birth of
the great Nation-states in Europe, was also the spring-time of
European nationalism. England alone offers ample evidence on this
point. Here, indeed, towards the close of the century, we are confronted with a real explosion of feelings that are at one and the
same time political and national: for it is hard to say which plays
a greater role, the pride of independence or the consciousness
of unity. They are the feelings which find their highest expression
in Shakespeare's immortal line: 'This blessed plot, this earth, this
realm, this England.'[1] They were the outcome of many factors:
England's geographical position, her comparative ethnic homogeneity, the breach with Rome, the religious Reformation, indeed
even the menace from abroad. But above all they found both a
pattern and a stimulus in the exceptional personality of that typical 'new prince', the great Elizabeth I, past-master in the art of
channelling the growing nationalism of her subjects within the
range of her crude power-politics, as well as of practising the
most ruthless personal rule, whilst at the same time scrupulously
respecting the most deeply rooted English political tradition,
that which saw Parliament as the representative of the entire
nation united round the Crown.

It might, therefore, seem rather puzzling that writers, such as
Machiavelli, Bodin, and Hobbes, should have passed over in silence
so important an element as nationality in their definition of the
State. But the puzzle can be explained when we remember that
the convergence of State and nation, which had at least in part
taken place in their days, was closely tied to the pursuit of a particular programme, and ultimately depended on the 'will to power'
of the new princes and the new States. Any change in that programme, and the two concepts could again fall apart. This is what
actually happened when from national unification the rulers of

[1] *Richard II* (1597), II, i.

Europe embarked on territorial expansion and on power-politics pure and simple. New ideologies were called upon to provide justification of the State's new course. The balance of power, dynastic succession, natural frontiers, all called a halt to the convergence of nation and State: for the balance of power, with its related theory of 'compensations', meant that 'peoples' could be bartered like flocks of sheep; while dynastic succession provided means for creating big multi-national units simply by the arts of diplomacy and marriage (*tu felix Austria nube!*); and the so-called natural frontiers, hardly ever corresponding to ethnical or linguistic boundaries, could not but lead to the inclusion of heterogeneous minorities inside the national State. Paradoxically, the idea of nationality seems to suffer eclipse at the very moment when the modern State was coming of age and the map of Europe was taking its familiar shape. Eighteenth-century statesmen neatly severed the practice of politics from nationalistic emotions. It was the century of Cosmopolitanism, the age of 'reason' and of 'lights'. And yet it is precisely in this century that the process of unification and centralization of the Nation-state received new impetus, and that the principle of nationality burst forth with a force hitherto unknown.

According to a view which is still largely held on the Continent, the modern doctrine of Nationalism is closely linked to a vision of history which profoundly altered the traditional view of man's place in the world. As against the old conviction of the basic immutability of human nature, and more especially as against the old aspiration to stress uniformity and regularity in order to enunciate laws which should be universally valid for all places and all times, the focus of interest shifted to what is peculiar and different, to individuality as the pivot and culmination of all historical events. Cosmopolitanism would have been superseded by Nationalism for this very reason: because the nation is all that is unique in the life of a people, its language, its traditions, its past. Hence the doctrine of Nationalism is also usually seen as an offshoot of Romanticism, of that great spiritual revolution whose roots are to be found in the eighteenth century, but whose full impact was perceived only in the nineteenth.

To this interpretation many serious objections have been raised: I am here concerned with one only. The rediscovery of the past and the emotional appeal of uniqueness, which were certainly a

feature of Romanticism, would not alone account for the birth of a
new political consciousness, nor for the virulent explosion of a new
kind of fanaticism, equal to, and perhaps even greater in vigour
than, that shown by religious fanaticism in the past. Above all
they would not account for the definite absorption of the principle
of nationality into the notion of the State. In the most recently
published study of 'State and Nation' Professor Akzin has rightly
cautioned us against the 'shallow' equation of Romanticism with
Nationalism. Irrationalism, traditionalism, organicism, all the paraphernalia of the new philosophy which swept Europe at the turn
of the century, did not necessarily lead to Nationalism, or at any
rate they did not lead to Nationalism alone. In a certain sense the
Holy Alliance was just as 'romantic' as Mazzini's Young Europe:
what divided them and set them against each other was a different
conception of the nature and purposes of the State. Nationalism
transformed nationality from an historical fact into a political ideology, into the one exclusive principle of legitimation of the State.
In order to do so it was necessary to affirm not only that nations
existed as separate and well-determined units, but that national
unity was an ideal to be sought after and fostered, and that the
only 'good' State was the Nation-state. Thus was the nation raised
to a dignity it had never possessed in the past, or rather to a dignity
which had been given a name in past ages, whenever there was
a question of locating the ultimate focus of allegiance and loyalty,
the highest good for which men could be called upon to sacrifice
their life. The Romans had called it *patria*. The nearest equivalent
in English is, I believe, not so much 'fatherland' as 'country'.
Consider how revealing daily language can be on that score. Not
even the most ardent nationalist would ever speak of a duty to 'die
for the nation'. But there is no need to be a nationalist to admit
the existence of a duty towards one's own country, a duty which
clearly indicates the attribution of a value to the Nation-state. Thus,
as Chabod has admirably shown, it was the notion of *patria* or
country which mediated between the idea of the nation and that
of the State. Patriotism provided the emotional and sentimental
halo which to this day surrounds the national State.

Like the idea of the nation and like that of the State, the idea
of country has a long history and a respectable pedigree. *Patria*
is an inheritance from classical culture. It is held out as the highest
object of love in a number of famous writings which like Cicero's

De Officiis, provided the mainstay of education in the West. Patriotism existed long before there were nations, let alone Nation-states. It was not unknown even at the time of the worst dis-memberment of Europe. It gained new impetus from the reading of the classics as well as from the leadership of kings in the new States. But patriotism was not necessarily linked to national con-sciousness or to political allegiance, even though in at least some parts of Europe it came to be associated fairly soon with the latter. *Pugnare pro rege et patria* was a familiar phrase in the Middle Ages; it has survived in English usage down to the present day. Not even personal loyalty, however, is an essential ingredient of patriotism. As always, Machiavelli's attitude is revealing. His *patria* was Florence, the city-state. His new prince was a lonely figure, trusting only to the sword. Nevertheless, Machiavelli's pages are filled with expressions of passionate love of country. Indeed, realist as Machiavelli certainly pretends to be, the emotion of patriotism carries evident weight in his work. His words to Guicciardini are often quoted: 'I love my country more than my soul.' The sweeping statement in the *Discourses* should also be remembered: 'When the safety of the country is ultimately in question, there must be no thought of justice or injustice, of mercy or cruelty, of praise or ignominy.' It is such statements as these, as I have pointed out,[1] that turn Machiavelli's hypothetical imperatives into categorical ones. The safety of the country is the end and the justification of the State.

But once again the confluence may have been purely accidental. Here is a typical eighteenth-century writer, a citizen of what was at the time the biggest and most powerful State in Europe. What does France mean to him? '*Un grand Royaume, et point de Patrie!*'[2] Listen to another writer, closer to Italy in space if not in spirit: 'My name is Vittorio Alfieri; the place where I was born, Italy; I have no country anywhere.'[3] For these men the ideas of State, nation, and country in no sense coincide. No State, however great and powerful, could provide them with a fatherland. The nation to which they belonged because they happened to have been born in it was not properly their country. *Patria* was that place only,

---

[1] Above, part I, ch. 4, p. 42.

[2] 'A great Kingdom, and no fatherland. . .' (D'Aguesseau).

[3] 'Il mio nome è Vittorio Alfieri: il luogo dov'io son nato, l'Italia: nessuna terra mi è patria.'

that community, that 'State', where a man could find the things
he truly valued. Hence, as the *Grande Encyclopédie* forcibly put it,
patriotism has no place under the yoke of a tyrant. Hence also, as
Voltaire gleefully concluded, one's country is wherever one lives
happily and well. *Ubi bene, ibi patria*; just as the nation is the fruit
of circumstance, and the State a conventional institution, so one's
country is the result of a choice. Such was the message of the age
of enlightenment, the conclusion against which Edmund Burke
was soon to launch one of his most bitter attacks.

Yet it was precisely this emphasis on choice, on a judgement of
value, which left the door open to portentous change. Burke might
appeal to a very different notion of the State by defining it as a
'partnership . . . between those who are living, those who are dead
and those who are to be born'. There still remained the need to
explain how that partnership could be 'consecrated', and for what
reasons it should be the object of dedication and love. This is what
the doctrine of Nationalism set out to do. And we shall never
appreciate the tremendous importance of the French Revolution
unless we realize that it was that revolution which gave the concept of nation an entirely new meaning, transforming it, as it were,
from a mere product of history into a deliberate construction, a
partnership not only of *mores* but of wills. This is the time when
we witness the final coincidence of the three ideas we have followed
throughout their erratic, independent course. 'The nation becomes
the country', but it does so because the nation is the expression of
self-determination, because the State no longer consists in the
mere whim of the autocrat or in the consolidation of the interests
of a few privileged classes, but in the sovereignty of the 'general
will'. Chabod is perfectly right in stressing that, even more than the
French revolutionaries, the true proclaimer of the new doctrine
was Rousseau. Rousseau may not yet have had before his eyes the
clear and coherent picture of national character which the doctrine
of nationalism outlined in the romantic age; but he certainly was
the prophet of the new religion which was henceforth to dominate
the modern world. Still more than the *Social Contract*, his advice
to the Poles is significant on that score. Patriotism is the true way
to salvation, for the individual as well as for the group. But
patriotism is both pride of nation and love of liberty, self-assertion
and respect for the law. The old adage *ubi bene, ibi patria* is here
completely reversed. It now reads *ubi libertas, ibi patria* and *ubi*

patria, ibi bene. A new world is dawning, where Democracy joins hands with Nationalism, and the State, hitherto the sum of cold calculations of power, gathers to itself a power hitherto unknown. For that power is no less than the outcome of a whole people's participation in those decisions which were at one time the privilege of the few.

Such, as I see them, were the reasons why nationality turned into one of the foremost grounds of legitimation in the modern State. And yet, in spite of the common background and the similarity of themes, there was soon once again to be a parting of the ways in this new world too. It was to come particularly as a consequence of the wholly different development of States and nations in the several parts of Europe, a difference which Sir Lewis Namier has very aptly emphasized. In those parts where amalgamation of State and nation had long been achieved, patriotism could find expression in a proud assertion of liberty, of the liberty won and sanctioned by means of free institutions which were held out for the admiration of the world. This may be said to have been the case with Britain, the 'mother of Parliaments'; it certainly was the case with revolutionary France. *'Ici commence le pays de la liberté'* read a placard once posted on the left bank of the Rhine. But where nations were still broken up into a multiplicity of political units, patriotism could not but take the shape primarily of a demand for unity and independence. The cause of liberty could wait. 'Germany is no longer a State', wrote Hegel in 1802: the supreme necessity, on which Fichte was to harp only a few years later in his *Addresses to the German Nation*, was that Germany should become one. In Italy, the priority given to independence over liberty was one of the most fateful choices of the *Risorgimento*. It may well have been one of the causes why free institutions were so precariously grounded in that part of the world.

But for the parting of the roads yet another reason can be given. To quote once again one of Chabod's illuminating suggestions, there would seem to have been from the beginning two possible ways of conceiving the nation: one based on purely 'natural' factors, the other on 'spiritual' elements; the one on something given, the other on something desired. The first of these two conceptions may have begun by merely stressing linguistic and ethnical differentiation as the distinguishing factors of nationality. It ended by extolling the most dubious biological factors, blood and race. The second conception, on the contrary, was based on the recognition of the importance of the cultural bond. It stressed the necessity of active individual participation if the nation was to be a living, spiritual unit; indeed, in Renan's famous phrase, a nation is nothing but a choice, a plebiscite of every day. Such a conception of nationality is not necessarily conducive to antagonism and hatred. On the contrary, it may permit the possibility of reconciling national differences with the complexity of human civilization as a whole. This possibility should be taken into account before a final judgement is passed on what it is the fashion nowadays to call the 'ideology' of the national State.

Certainly this peculiar ideology, even when it is not openly disparaged or deliberately condemned, cannot but appear to modern eyes—at any rate in Europe—as a thing of the past. But one lesson can be learnt from the very sketchy analysis I have attempted to give of it. This is that the 'State' cannot be understood simply as a structure of power, nor justified only by the help of abstract philosophical theorems. Its legitimation is interwoven with historical elements and irrational, emotional factors. We often hear it said that the new, the supra-national State, which is invoked and longed for today by so many, will be the signal for the final disappearance of those nationalisms which have brought Europe to the brink of ruin. But one thing at least can be said with certainty. Whenever the new State arises and establishes itself as a working proposition, it too will need an 'ideology' on which to lean, a faith capable of kindling men's imagination and warming their hearts. It will be essential, in other words, for this State to inspire men with a spirit of dedication as great as that inspired by the 'old' State, and for it to acquire in the eyes of its new citizens the value of a new and better *communis patria*.

REFERENCES

Cicero, *De Off.* I, 17, 57. Dante Alighieri, *De Vulg. Eloq.* I, vi ff.; *Mon.* II, iii, 16 and *passim*; *Ep.* VI and VII; *Div. Com., passim.* Machiavelli, *Prince*, chs. iii and xxvi; *Disc.* III. 41; Letter to F. Guicciardini of 16 Apr. 1527. Bodin, *Rép.* I, 6. Hobbes, *Leviathan*, Introd. and ch. 19 *ad finem.* D'Aguesseau, *XIXe Mercuriale* (1715). *Gr. Encyclopédie*, art. 'Patrie' (1765). Voltaire, *Dictionnaire Philosophique* (1771 edn.), art. 'Patrie', sects. 1–2. Rousseau, *Considérations sur le Gouvernement de Pologne* (probably composed in 1770–71, first published in 1782), ch. iv. Burke, *Reflections on the Revolution in France* (1790). Alfieri, *Misogallo* (1792), doc. 1. Hegel, *Die Verfassung Deutschlands* (1802). Fichte, *Reden an die Deutsche Nation* (1807–8). Renan, *Qu'est-ce qu'une nation* (1882).

Among the many studies of nation, nationalism, and patriotism that have been published in recent years I list here only those referred to in the text, together with those the reading of which should be considered indispensable. They are given in chronological order.

F. Chabod, *L'idea di nazione* (lectures delivered and mimeographed in 1943–4, and edited posthumously, Bari, 1961). H. Kohn, *The Idea of Nationalism*, New York, 1944. F. Hertz, *Nationality in History and Politics*, London, 1944. W. Kaegi, *Historische Meditationen*, Zürich, 1942–6, the first three essays. Sir L. Namier, 'Nationality and Liberty', a paper delivered in 1948 and now in the vol. *Avenues of History*, London, 1952. G. Post, 'Public Law, the State and Nationalism', an article published in 1953 and now in the vol. *Studies in Medieval Legal Thought*, 1964. B. C. Shafer, *Nationalism. Myth and Reality*, London, 1955. E. Kedourie, *Nationalism*, London, 1960. B. Akzin, *State and Nation*, London, 1964.

For further bibliographical references E. Kedourie's book and the volume ed. by K. W. Deutsch and W. J. Foltz, *Nation-Building*, New York and London, 1963, may be usefully consulted.

I hardly need to underline the deep impression made on me by Professor Chabod's war-time lectures. I should like to take this opportunity to acknowledge my general indebtedness to a friend and fellow countryman whose untimely death was a terrible loss to Italian culture. My study of *Frédéric Chabod et l'idée de nationalité* will shortly appear in a volume on *L'idée de nation* to be published by the Institut International de Philosophie Politique.

4

DIVINE RIGHT

'ORDER', 'justice', 'country', do not by any means account for the whole list of values to which recourse was, and still is, made in order not only to explain but to justify the existence of State-power. They are, however, the words which come up most often when political matters are discussed. Their recurrence is a sign of how easily standards of value intermingle with standards of fact in this type of discourse.

We must now turn to another kind of legitimation, which has not so much to do with the definition of the State as with the exercise of power. It is no longer a question of assessing the require-ments for the existence of the State, but the conditions and methods of its action. This action can in fact only be exercised through those men or those groups of men who hold power in the State and issue commands which are met with obedience. If we now ask what makes these commands not only effective but obli-gatory we are, as it were, shifting the focus of attention from the general problem of the nature of the State to the actual quality and deeds of the holders of power. Both that quality and those deeds must now be taken into account, and the question, once asked, leads to two further requests which insistently return throughout the long development of political theory. The first is a request to determine the ultimate foundation of power, what justifies the right that certain men claim over their fellow men. The second is a request to define the purpose of political power, together with its limits. Modern man, while still sensitive, up to a point, to this second request, is inclined to regard the first with indifference if not with scepticism or open irony.

Political theorists have given many different answers to the ques-tion of the ultimate foundation of power. These answers were variously influenced by the circumstances of time and place in which the question was raised, or in which the questioners found themselves when they tried to answer it. In this chapter a theory will be considered which occupies an important place in Western thought because it is directly connected with the religion that has been, and still is, dominant in Europe. It is a theory founded on certain precise dogmatic tenets of the Christian faith itself. Let me at once add that I have no intention of discussing in the small space available the much larger and more serious question as to whether Christianity had a political theory of its own. What matters is the fact that Christian teaching provided a distinctive answer to the problem of the legitimation of power. This answer is that which is given in a famous passage of St. Paul's Epistle to the Romans, ch. xiii.[1] This Pauline text is the starting-point of every Christian interpretation of politics, so much so that all Christian political theory may be regarded as one long uninterrupted commentary on it. The teaching of Romans xiii sounds clear and categorical. 'There is no power but of God', *non est potestas nisi a Deo*. Divine sanction transforms subjection into duty, power into authority. He who holds power is 'the minister of God'. He who obeys must do so not only because he is compelled, but 'for conscience sake', *propter conscientiam*. Political order is an 'ordinance of God'. To share in it means sharing in a plan willed and pre-ordained by divine Providence.

Yet however clear and categorical St. Paul's words, it is not so easy to assess the exact meaning of his doctrine. To begin with, St. Paul does not say to whom power belongs, nor does he tell us much about the particular nature of the power which some men exercise over others. The passage in Romans xiii does not explain how power was formed, nor how it came into the hands of any particular ruler. It simply states that Christians must recognize in power something not purely human, something which transcends, as it were, those who exercise it and endows them with a special character. That character is authority. The best description

---

[1] 'Let every soul be subject unto the higher powers. For there is no power but of God: the powers that be are ordained of God. Whosoever therefore resisteth the power, resisteth the ordinance of God: and they that resist shall receive to themselves damnation. For rulers are not a terror to good works, but to the evil. Wilt thou then not be afraid of the power? do that which is good, and thou shalt have praise of the same. For he is the minister of God to thee for good. But if thou do that which is evil, be afraid; for he beareth not the sword in vain: for he is the minister of God, a revenger to execute wrath upon him that doeth evil. Wherefore ye must needs be subject, not only for wrath, but also for conscience sake' (Rom. xiii, 1–5; cf. the parallel passages in Titus iii, 1 and in 1 Pet. ii, 13–17).

of this doctrine lies close at hand. It is a doctrine of the sacred character of authority, certainly not one of the divinity of power. The distinction is of great importance. The ancient world had known and widely practised the divinization of power. The deification of the ruler, imported from the East, became a fundamental institution of the Hellenistic monarchies and later of the Roman Empire. Christianity set its face directly against this pagan doctrine, just as in more recent days it was to oppose the divinization of the State with equal firmness. In the Christian view, power is God-given and God-like only in a devious, indirect fashion. The gift of God is not power itself, but the authority with which power is invested. Justinian, the Christian emperor, stated this view accurately when he claimed, in the Preamble of one of his great law-books, that he governed the Empire by God's authority —*Deo auctore.*[1]

There is no denying, however, that the doctrine of the sacred character of authority, while basic to the Christian vision of politics, did lend itself to very different interpretations. In regard to these differences, the contrast between early and medieval Christianity is revealing. For various reasons early Christian doctrine tended to interpret the Romans xiii passage in what might be called an 'absolutist' sense. The accent was laid almost exclusively on the providential character of power. The plan laid down by God must be accepted in whatever way it manifests itself. Divine sanction does not depend on the use made of power: good or bad, all power is of God. It follows that even evil power must be patiently endured. Passive obedience is the only road open to the Christian. Certainly, there may be cases when a Christian cannot and must not obey. But he can still practice obedience by passively submitting to the consequences which follow such a refusal. An interpretation of this kind was probably influenced by the particular conditions which prevailed in the late Roman world. Indeed, the Christian doctrine of the sacredness of authority could even be combined with some survivals of the old imperial cult. There is evidence of this, for example, in the use made by Christian emperors of expressions such as *nostra divinitas, divinum verbum, sacratae leges.* But this interpretation was also, and above all, due to a deeply pessimistic attitude towards political life and political institutions—the pessimism which, as we saw, pervades

[1] Constitution 'Deo Auctore', *Digest.*

St. Augustine's vision of history, and which, in later days, reached its extreme expression in Luther's conception that rulers and princes are the scourge of God.

But St. Paul's words were open also to a very different interpretation. To find it, we have only to turn to other periods in history and to open the books of the most representative writers of the Middle Ages. The point of departure was found in that important proviso which qualified the whole passage in Romans xiii: 'He [i.e. the holder of power] is the minister of God to thee for good' —*Dei minister est tibi in bonum*. Far from implying the divine character of any kind of power, the passage could be taken to mean that only that power is from God, only that authority is sacred, which is directed towards what is good, or, as these writers put it, which is founded on justice. The path to this new interpretation had already been traced by one of the Fathers, one who, indeed, as a Roman well trained in the law, valued highly precise language and subtle distinctions. In a passage which was to prove of capital importance for later theory St. Ambrose distinguished between the *ordinatio Dei* and the *actio administrantis*, between what is ordained of God and what is merely man's doing. Where power is concerned, the use made of it determines its character. Only the *munus*, the office, comes from God, and only a ruler who makes good use of power (*qui bene utitur potestate*) is God's minister.

The new interpretation thus rested on a clear separation between the divine sanction of authority as such, and the manifold aspects in which power manifested itself in actual historical experience. In medieval eyes the sacred character of authority was strictly dependent on its exercise. It was a source of duties rather than a source of rights. In the very act of surrounding political power with a religious halo, medieval political thought was limiting its action within the bounds of a clearly defined mission. The perspectives thus opened up were far-reaching. Completely different conclusions could now be drawn from St. Paul's own words: no longer the need for passive obedience, but rather (as most, if not all, medieval writers agreed) the lawfulness, even the duty of resistance. For indeed, if the exercise of power is an office, a task laid on the ruler, the duty of obedience in the subject is conditioned by the fulfilment of this task, and comes to an end when the task is no longer fulfilled or respected. Medieval political writers would hardly have been able to conceive that power came from God and should be obeyed simply because it existed, nor that a ruler could be invested with the chrism of authority simply because he held power.

This last point is particularly important, in that it enables us to distinguish the theory of the sacred character of authority from another theory, with which it is sometimes confused, the theory of 'divine right', or, as it has also been called recently, 'theocratic kingship'. As a matter of fact, or rather of definition, if the phrase 'divine right' were simply intended to describe the 'providential' character which power takes on, as we saw, in the Christian vision of politics, there would be no objection to its use in describing that vision. But in the current usage of historians the expression 'divine right of kings' has a much more restricted meaning. It is used to describe a theory which, even though its beginnings may be traced back to the Middle Ages, was not to come to full bloom till a later period. Figgis's summary of that theory can hardly be improved upon, only, perhaps, simplified, for our particular purposes. Divine right in fact entailed essentially three different claims, three separate though closely linked propositions. It meant first of all the extolling of monarchy as the best, or even the only, form of government sanctioned by God. Next, it meant the claim to absolute power for the monarch. Kings have to render account of their actions to God alone. They can exact unconditional obedience from their subjects. Last, but not least, divine right meant 'dynastic legitimacy', the assertion of a right to power acquired by birth, a right which is therefore independent of the subjects' consent and cannot be forfeited. When each of these three propositions is taken into account, it is not difficult to see how the theory itself was nothing else than the ideological justification of that absolute monarchy for which the doctrine of sovereignty had provided the legal foundation. James I and Bossuet gave the theory its most elaborate form. Like all ideologies, it certainly corresponded to the needs of an age. It was widely accepted, and survived to the days of the Congress of Vienna, if it does not still survive among a few belated champions of 'legitimism'. The point I wish to make here is that this theory is not necessarily linked with that of the sacred character of authority, and that it leads to totally different conclusions.

Consider first the claim that monarchy is a divinely ordained institution. Surely there is nothing to that effect in Romans xiii, nor was it the idea that all power is from God that inevitably led to theocratic kingship. The prevalence of monarchy over other forms of government, and the preference felt for it at certain times and places, were the result of special historical and political circumstances. No doubt, in the Middle Ages this preference could draw support from an appeal to both religious and philosophical arguments. An example of this kind of argument is the parallel, often stressed by medieval writers, between the rule of one king in his realm and that of one God in the universe. This argument can be found used by Dante as well as by St. Thomas Aquinas. Moreover, the sacredness of authority might well seem to emerge more clearly and forcibly in the government of one man alone than in the rule of many. It could, in that case, even be given a sort of visible shape, with the help of special institutions, by means of appropriate 'investitures' of a symbolic, charismatic character. Great liturgical ceremonies, such as those which took place in the anointing and coronation of the king, were specially devised by the Church to bring out this character: with the purpose, at the same time, of emphasizing the close relationship between the spiritual and the temporal sphere, and the ultimate dependence of the latter upon the former. But the excellence of monarchy in no way follows from the sacredness of authority. The gist of the Christian view is simply that all legitimately constituted power has a sacred character; that, whatever its historical origin or form, it must be viewed as ultimately going back to God's will, and hence as possessing, under certain conditions, divine sanction. The fact that a theory of this kind has survived, and that its survival can be reasonably accounted for, even when theocratic kingship has long disappeared, would in itself be significant. The principle of the sacredness of authority and of the duty of obedience has outlived the theory of divine right, which for some centuries seemed to be its corollary. Should there still be any doubts as to the distinction between the two theories, the teaching of the Catholic Church down to our own day should suffice to dispel them. For that Church has never ceased to preach respect for authority as a religious duty, nor has it hesitated to acknowledge any form of government, provided the rights of God and the Church were guaranteed and respected.

Nor are absolute power or passive obedience a logical consequence of the principle that all power is from God and that authority is sacred. There is no denying, of course, that in the first centuries of Christianity, as well as in later days, these principles were interpreted in a sense which definitely squared with the most exacting demands of the supporters of Absolutism. Indeed, the 'minister of God' of the Pauline text could easily be turned, by eager hands, into the representative of God—*Dei vicarius*. But a glance at the very different interpretation which, as we have seen, could be given to that text, is enough to prove that the sacredness of authority is not necessarily bound up either with a demand for passive obedience on the part of the subject or with one for absolute and irresponsible power on the part of the ruler. Besides asserting the lawfulness, even the duty, of resistance, medieval theory definitely rejected the principle of the irresponsibility of the ruler. It subjected the exercise of power to a whole series of limitations, which were not only moral, but legal. Indeed, it was precisely from such limitations that, as we saw, there was to arise in process of time that notion of constitutionally limited power which is the keystone of the modern theory of the State and the exact opposite of Absolutism.

As for the third principle, which crowns and completes the theory of divine right—dynastic legitimacy—it is obvious enough that this principle has nothing whatever to do with the Pauline text nor with a Christian vision of politics. Indeed, dynastic legitimacy is a comparatively late development, even in the theory of monarchy. Its origins are usually traced back to the Germanic *Geblütsrecht*, to ideas about the particular nobility or superiority of one race, which bestowed upon men of a certain lineage an unchallengeable right to power. This is no place for assessing its varying success in medieval theory and practice. All that needs to be said is that dynastic legitimacy seems to assume a growing importance with the consolidation of territorial kingship, developing alongside it in those countries where monarchs were the symbol of national unity, while it was neglected and even despised where monarchies had no roots, and loyalties had a different focus. One has only to remember Dante's invective against the 'evil plant' of the French monarchy, his sarcasm about the 'sacred bones' of its kings, to realize how alien the doctrine still was in many parts of Europe towards the close of the Middle Ages. As well as the doctrine of dynastic legitimacy, medieval political thought knew two other quite different theories concerning the foundation of power. On one side was the idea, which could be deduced both from the reading of the classics and from the Pauline text itself, that there must be a fitting correspondence between person and office, between minister and *munus*. On the other side was the theory, implicit, as we have seen, in the medieval notion of law, and warranted by Justinian's law-books, that the ultimate foundation of power is the will of the whole community. These three different principles of legitimacy—blood, fitness, and election—competed and were combined in various ways. For a long time the Church never hid its preference for the elective as against the dynastic principle; indeed, in one famous case, it did not hesitate to oppose the consolidation of succession to the Empire in one single family.[1] An understanding between the teaching of the Church and the theory of the divine right of kings took place only at a much later stage, and may be considered a matter of expediency rather than of principle.

We may therefore conclude that the most important contribution of Christianity to the problem of the legitimation of power was, broadly speaking, not a theory about its origin and nature, but about its foundation and validity. Christian teaching provided the background against which 'the powers that be' could be justified and sanctioned with the chrism of authority; but it left unsolved the problem of how in fact power comes into being, and where it should be located. Making use of a scholastic distinction, we might say that the theory of the sacredness of authority concerned the 'form', not the 'content' of power. 'Formally' (*secundum suam formam*), power as such always comes from God; but 'substantially', except in the improbable case of direct divine designation, power is a human contrivance. That these statements are not contradictory can be shown by the simple consideration that certain formulae which forcibly expressed the sacredness of authority have survived to our day, when the divine right of kings has long been discarded and there are few doubts left about the human origin of power. Such is the concise phrase 'by the grace of God', which goes back to Charlemagne (if not to earlier times), and can still be found engraved around the portrait of the Queen on the British coinage. On the Continent of Europe, down to the last century, sovereigns, who could have had no possible doubt that the will of the people was the source of their power, still thought it possible to appeal to a divine investiture. Napoleon III in France, Victor Emanuel II

[1] Decretal *Per Venerabilem* of Innocent III, 1202.

in Italy, styled themselves emperors or kings 'by the grace of God and the will of the People'. In doing so they were not contradicting themselves. They were following the lines of a traditional doctrine. The recognition of the sacred character of authority does not exclude but demands a further search into the origin of power. Unless one admits that power may be conferred directly by God, only two possible solutions remain. I shall examine these in the next chapter.

REFERENCES

St. Ambrose, *Expositio Evangelii secundum Lucam*, v, 29, in Migne, *Patrol. Latina*, vol. xv, cols. 1620–1. St. Thomas Aquinas, *De Reg. Princ.*, Book I, ch. 2; *Summa Theol.* 1ª, cIII, 3; *Summa contra Gent.* IV, 76. Dante Alighieri, *Monarchia*, Book I, chs. 7 and 8; *Purg.* xx, 46–60. James I, *Political Works*, ed. by C. H. McIlwain, Cambridge, Mass., 1918. Bossuet, *Politique tirée des propres paroles de l'Écriture Sainte*, Books II–VI.

Sir E. Barker, *From Alexander to Constantine, 336 B.C.–A.D. 337*, 2nd edn., Oxford, 1959. This is an admirable anthology of pagan and Christian writings concerning, respectively, the divinity of power and the sacred character of authority.

On the theory of monarchy in the Middle Ages, and on the institutions connected with it: M. Bloch, *Les rois thaumaturges*, 2nd edn., Paris, 1961; P. E. Schramm, *A History of the English Coronation*, Oxford, 1937; E. H. Kantorowicz, *The King's Two Bodies*, already mentioned.

On the divine right of kings two well-known works are still basic: J. N. Figgis, *The Divine Right of Kings* (1st edn., 1896), 2nd edn., Cambridge, 1922; F. Kern, *Gottesgnadentum und Widerstandsrecht im früheren Mittelalter*, Leipzig, 1914 (Eng. trans., by S. B. Chrimes, incomplete, *Kingship and Law in the Middle Ages*, Oxford, 1939).

With regard to 'theocratic kingship', mention of which is made in the text of this chapter, I wish to point out that the reference is to W. Ullmann's recent book, *Principles of Government and Politics in the Middle Ages*, London, 1961, and that the interpretation which I have proposed of Romans xiii, and of its impact on Christian political thought, is in many ways flatly contradicted by Ullmann's learned reconstruction. I have expounded in detail a defence of my view, and my disagreement with Ullmann's, in a lengthy review of his book published in the *Rivista Storica Italiana*, vol. LXXV (1963). Here it is enough to say that the main point of disagreement is Ullmann's view of theocratic kingship as directly linked to the Pauline text, and as the embodiment of a 'descending conception of government and law', diametrically opposed to, and therefore incompatible with, the 'ascending conception' of the human or popular origin of power.

5

FORCE AND CONSENT

To say that power has a human origin and is a human contrivance can mean two very different things. It can mean that the right to command belongs to one particular man, or to one particular group of men, to the exclusion of all others. But it can also mean that such a right does not belong to anyone in particular, but potentially to each and all. This is the alternative which seems to divide political theorists into two camps, and to make, in Mosca's imaginative phrase, the 'aristocratic' and the 'democratic principle' irreconcilable enemies. The view which I intend to maintain—developing a suggestion already put forward in the first part of this book (ch. 6)—is that the 'aristocratic principle', i.e. the assertion that men are not equal but unequal, cannot provide an adequate ground for the legitimation of power. Contrary to common belief, equality, not inequality, is a basic assumption of political theory.

When inequality is under discussion the obvious reference is to Aristotle. Together with the 'naturalness' of political life and as a corollary to it, the doctrine of the 'natural' inequality of men forms the keystone of Aristotle's *Politics*. Notice once again the peculiar meaning of the word 'natural'. To say that men are by nature unequal does not mean only that their inequality is evinced by experience. It means that diversity and differentiation are required in every kind of social aggregate in as far as it is a 'whole' composed of 'parts'. 'In all cases where there is a compound, constituted of more than one part but forming one common entity . . . a ruling element and a ruled can always be traced.' Therefore, since 'nature makes each separate thing for a separate end . . . there must necessarily be a union of the naturally ruling element with the element which is naturally ruled, for the preservation of both. The element which is able, by virtue of its intelligence, to exercise forethought, is naturally a ruling and master element; the element which is able, by virtue of its bodily power, to do what the other element plans, is a ruled element.' Starting from these premisses, Aristotle, as is well known, justified the institution of slavery. But he did so with an important proviso. Slavery, as sanctioned by law, may not correspond to slavery as laid down by nature. Its actual existence may not reflect the 'natural' disposition owing to which 'there are some who are everywhere and inherently slaves, and others who are everywhere and inherently free'.

The question now is: what part exactly, according to Aristotle, does human inequality play in political relations, and how important is it in determining the nature of power? We saw above[1] that Aristotle expressly mentions the case of individuals 'who are utterly superior to others', and to whom obedience must be yielded willingly, because 'they are a law in themselves'. This case may arise with one person only or with several, or even with a whole family or race. But Aristotle leaves us in no doubt that this case is exceptional, and that situations of the sort are altogether out of the common run. The normal situation is different. It is one in which men live together in conditions of approximate equality, since the *polis* is made of freemen, not of slaves and masters, and 'aims at being, as far as it can be, a society composed of equals and peers'. Indeed, in Aristotle's view, the very concept of citizenship is linked to that of equality: 'citizens, in the common sense of that term, are all who share in the civic life of ruling and being ruled in turn.' Hence the main problem of politics is precisely how best to govern these free and equal men, these 'citizens' who are such because they are qualified both to rule and to obey: and it is with this end in view that Aristotle suggests the various practical devices which are examined carefully and at length in the fourth book of the *Politics*. What matters for our purpose here is to underline that the political bond is quite clearly to Aristotle a bond between equals, not between unequals.

It is true, of course, that what Aristotle has in mind is an equality which springs, so to speak, from inequality, and presupposes it. Not only are slaves excluded from the dignity of citizenship, but also all those who do menial duties, like mechanics and labourers, whose only task is to provide the material basis of the life of the *polis*. To share in that life is a privilege reserved for the happy few —but these happy few must at any rate be approximately equal in capacity and disposition. Equality thus provides in a way the dividing line between political power and every other kind of

[1] Part II, ch. 1, p. 71.

power. For power exercised over and among men who are free and equal is something different from power exercised by a master over slaves, from 'despotic' power, as it is more properly called. Political power is a mark of distinction, reserved for civilized peoples like the Greeks, while unknown to barbarians, who because of their servile disposition are fit only for despotism, or at any rate are not yet ripe for a fully developed political life. This is a proud and haughty claim, one which sounds well in keeping with Aristotle's vision of human inequality. Yet we find that claim voiced down the centuries, adapted to new situations and set in a different key. We can trace it, for example, in the contrast drawn by a Christian writer, St. Gregory the Great, between the power of the Roman emperor and that of the barbarian ruler: one, the lord of free men; the other, the master of slaves. Nearer our own time, we find it still echoed in both Montesquieu's and Burke's praise of that 'spirit of liberty' which has given Europe its character, in contrast to the despotism which has enslaved and degraded the nations of the East. Surely, there is more here than simply a smug assertion of racial superiority. There is a deep insight into the true nature of political power and into the role that equality and freedom play in shaping it.

It was not Aristotle's teaching, however, but one which in many ways was exactly its opposite, that played the decisive part in moulding Western views about the origin and foundation of power. In sharp contrast to the idea of a natural inequality, this doctrine affirms the natural equality of all men. Only a few centuries after Aristotle, philosophers, jurists, theologians, all are agreed in proclaiming that 'as far as the law of nature is concerned, all men are equal'.[1] 'There is no change in political theory so startling in its completeness as the change from the theory of Aristotle to the later philosophical view represented by Cicero and Seneca. Over against Aristotle's view of the natural inequality of human nature we find set out the theory of the natural equality of human nature. . . . We are indeed at the beginnings of a theory of human nature and society of which the "Liberty, Equality and Fraternity" of the French Revolution is only the present-day expression.' Dr. Carlyle's famous dictum has been often challenged. It still carries great weight. But my intention is not to discuss once again its validity. Rather, it is to comment briefly on the meaning of the

[1] 'Quod ad ius naturale attinet, omnes homines aequales sunt' (*Dig.* I, 17, 32).

principle of human equality in political theory, and to assess its true impact on the problem of the foundation of power. The question is all the more important since we live in a world which takes pride in being built on the democratic principle, that is, on the assumption that, as far as political relations are concerned, equality is the rule. It is essential that we clarify that assumption if we wish to ascertain whether there is such a thing as a 'democratic legitimacy', a system of values capable of providing a justification for democracy, if not of making the world safe for it once and for all.

As far as the meaning of the principle of equality is concerned, one cannot but wonder how it should have given rise to so many doubts and to so much discussion. Obviously, the principle itself is one that cannot be verified empirically, i.e. proved by an appeal to facts. If anything, experience shows men to be not equal but unequal, and they are certainly not equal in political intercourse, where some command and others obey, some have power, some have little or none. The point which should be made from the beginning is thus fairly simple: it is that the principle of human equality, when referred to in political discourse, is a prescriptive, not a descriptive proposition, a statement about a rule to adopt and a course to follow, not about an existing state of affairs. I believe that this is precisely what was underlined in the old definitions of equality by means of such words as 'by nature', 'natural', and so forth. The very use of such expressions seems clearly to indicate the normative character of those definitions, which in turn could lead either to the criticism of existing inequalities as being 'against nature', or to a disparagement of factual inequality itself as being irrelevant to the normative standpoint and to the new perspectives which it disclosed. The statement that according to the law of nature or reason all men are equal was not intended to mean the absurdity that men are, or can be, equal in every respect and in all things. Rather, and more simply, it meant that certain inequalities sanctioned by society were wrong, and that at any rate, in spite of those inequalities, all men could claim certain particular rights which the law of nature or reason conferred upon them *qua* men. In much the same way, some modern constitutions lay down the principle of equality by stating that 'whatever their differences in sex, race, language, religion, political opinions, or personal and social condition, all citizens are peers in human dignity and equal before the law'.[1] Equality here means essentially non-discrimination. It has a negative rather than a positive value. In that ambivalence lies perhaps its greatest strength.

For indeed, if this last remark is correct, it can help us to explain why the idea of equality did prove, on the one hand, much less subversive of existing social structures than might have been expected, while providing, on the other hand, a powerful leaven of change and of progress in the political field. Thus we see slavery and other social inequalities surviving long after the idea of human equality had gained universal acceptance. But also we notice throughout our history a tendency to belittle the importance of such inequalities, or at any rate not to consider them as indicative of a basic disability with regard to all that is proper to man. From this to demanding that such inequalities should be considered irrelevant for political purposes was only one step. The taking of this step was made easier, oddly enough, by the very growth of a new type of power—the centralizing and levelling power of the modern State. Sovereignty, we know, entailed a formal equality in those who were subject to it.[2] It was merely a question of turning subjection into participation, and the gate would be opened for growing numbers to share in political life. It may have required centuries for the step to be finally taken; but how tempting it is to think (though it might sound somewhat rhetorical to say so) that there never died out in Europe the ideal of making every man a citizen, the ideal which Rome had pursued and which had gained for her the tribute of the poet: *urbem fecisti quod prius orbis erat*.[3] It is certainly a fact that that 'mark of distinction'—political life as a partnership in equality and freedom—which the Greeks had denied to some men and refused to recognize in others, has now come to be extended to almost all men in almost all countries. This did not happen because men, all of a sudden, discovered that they were equal. On the contrary, it happened because they realized that, however unequal, their inequalities could be overcome, or at any rate could be made irrelevant, through the abolition of privilege and the adoption of free, democratic institutions.[4]

[1] *Constitution of the Italian Republic* (27 Dec. 1947), art. 3.

[2] See above, Part II, ch. 5, esp. p. 100.

[3] 'Thou hast made a city of what was previously a world' (C. Rutilius Namatianus, *De reditu suo*, I, 66).

[4] In support of the interpretation here given of the principle of equality, no better authority can be invoked than that of one of its greatest apostles. Here

Closely connected with the meaning of equality is its impact on the problem of the foundation of power. Here too the idea acted as a powerful leaven, prompting political theorists to devise a number of different solutions in order to account for the inequalities inherent in political relations without sacrificing the basic normative principle of the 'natural' equality of men. Notwithstanding their differences, these theories all have, as we know, one common trait. They all stress the 'conventional' character of political institutions; they all try to explain, in some way or other, the transition from the 'natural' condition of equality to the inequalities which actually occur in human affairs. But the really important point, with regard to the legitimation of power, was the emphasis laid by some, though not all, such theories on the need, if inequality were to be politically relevant, of its being 'recognized' or 'accepted', if not actually 'agreed to' by explicit, open consent. Without such recognition, consent, or acceptance—so the argument ran—there can be no power; outstanding superiority is not enough to establish it firmly; something else is required. As Hume remarked, 'the sultan of Egypt or the emperor of Rome might drive his harmless subjects like brute beasts against their sentiments and inclination. But he must, at least, have led his *mamelukes* or *praetorian bands*, like men, by their opinion.' At this point little doubt can remain that the question is no longer so much about the relationship between equality and inequality, as about the comparative role of force and consent in the establishment of power.

are the words with which Abraham Lincoln, in a famous speech, explained the meaning of the statement in the *Declaration of Independence* about the 'self-evidence' of human equality.

I think the authors of that notable instrument intended to include *all* men, but they did not mean to declare all men equal *in all respects*. They did not mean to say that all were equal in colour, size, intellect, moral developments, or social capacity. They defined with tolerable distinctness in what respects they did consider all men created equal—equal with 'certain inalienable rights, among which are life, liberty and the pursuit of happiness'. This they said, and this they meant. They did not mean to assert the obvious untruth that all were then actually enjoying that equality, nor yet that they were about to confer it immediately upon them. In fact they had no power to confer such a boon. They meant simply to declare the right so that the enforcement of it might follow as fast as circumstances should permit. They meant to set up a standard maxim for free society, which should be familiar to all and revered by all,—constantly looked to, constantly laboured for, and, even though never perfectly attained, constantly approximated, and thereby constantly spreading and deepening its influence, and augmenting the happiness and value of life to all people of all colours everywhere.

Now the assertion that power is based on consent may be taken in two quite different senses. It may be taken merely as a description of what actually is the case whenever power is effectively grounded. Even the most despotic government, as Hume pointed out, is ultimately founded on acceptance, be it only acceptance by a handful of men. But it may also be taken as a request that consent be regarded as the one and only means of justifying what would otherwise be the result of force alone, viz. the inequalities inherent in social and political relations. Both interpretations are traceable in the age-long development of Western political theory, together with an increasing shift from the former to the latter. I have already discussed, in another part of this book,[1] the importance of the idea of consent in the Middle Ages. Its implications, we know, were for a long time legal rather than political. There was nothing revolutionary in the view that laws derive their force from their acceptance by those to whom they apply. It was only when the idea of consent finally came to be associated with that of an equal right in each individual to share in the establishment and exercise of power, that the distinctive features of modern democratic theory began to emerge into full daylight. Nowhere, perhaps, is the shift of emphasis more apparent than in the skilful, and in many ways perverse, use which Locke, in the *Second Treatise of Government*, makes of a number of quotations from Hooker, a writer whom he rightly selects as a representative of traditional views. What had for centuries been an accepted and harmless truism, that men are potentially equal and that consent is the only safe validation of power, was now transformed into a new and exacting theory of law and State.[2] Government by consent is the only legitimate government, because it is the only government which does justice to the basic rights of men.

We are now in a position to measure adequately the decisive part which the idea of human equality has played in our history; indeed, in looking back on it we cannot help being struck by the fact that the opposite doctrine of inequality should have failed to

[1] Above, Part II, ch. 4.
[2] To mention only two points in which Locke completely alters the meaning of Hooker's teaching: equality is to Hooker a source of duties, not of rights; and consent is the expression of the 'corporate' life of the whole society, not of single individual wills. But, of course, the greatest trick played by Locke on Hooker was that of presenting him as a forerunner of his own theory of the social contract.

gain ground amongst us for so long. It failed to do so in the teaching of Aquinas, who opened the door as widely as possible to Aristotle's vision of politics, and yet could never accept the view that natural inequality is a sufficient justification of man's power over man.[1] It failed to do so—which is perhaps still more significant— at the time when Europe's expansion was beginning, and when Aristotle's doctrine of natural superiority would have provided a welcome argument in favour of the right of the Europeans to conquer and subdue the newly discovered world.[2] It is only comparatively recently that the idea of human equality has been openly challenged as the traditional assumption of political thought. I think that it should not be too difficult to defend it, in view of all the evidence we have assembled so far.

Let us begin by brushing aside the extreme form of antiegalitarianism, racialism, since it does not succeed in providing a justification of power at all. That doctrine claims for certain races or nations a right to rule, but at the same time it rejects as irrelevant any recognition of that right on the part of those on whom the rule is imposed. It thus, openly or covertly, acknowledges that force is the only relevant factor in politics. Fortunately, such views have failed to gather sufficient strength to secure their triumph in Europe, although enough to set our old Continent ablaze. They are entirely alien to the Western political tradition. As Tocqueville wrote to Gobineau after having read his essay on the inequality of the human races, 'between your theory and mine there lies a whole intellectual universe'.

But there is, as we know, another version of anti-egalitarianism whose appeal is more subtle and insidious, and which therefore calls for some further scrutiny here. The 'élitist' theory began as an account of the inequalities existing in society. It ended by providing justification of those inequalities, by stressing the 'superiority' and the 'merits' of those who belong to the ruling class or *élite*. But the upholders of the 'élitist' theory are divided

---

[1] Inequality is no justification of slavery, which is to Aquinas, as to all Christian writers, a consequence of sin. It may provide a strong qualification for office, subject to legitimation in one of the two possible ways which Aquinas admits: investiture from above (*auctoritas superioris*), or from below (*consensus subditorum*).

[2] The existence of any such right was solemnly denied by the 'Congregation' of Spanish lawyers and theologians summoned by Charles V at Valladolid in 1550.

when it comes to explaining how *élites* are formed, and in what way they reach, or have reached, the power they hold. In fact— to use a fruitful distinction suggested by an Italian writer—there are only two possible alternatives: either the *élite* is 'imposed', or else it is 'proposed'. In the first case, clearly it is not the merits or the intrinsic superiority of the *élite* that matter, but its capacity to seize power, if necessary by force. In the second, which is obviously the case in modern societies, since those merits and that superiority call for recognition and acceptance on the part of those on whom the *élite* is to exert its power, there must be one point at least where rulers and ruled are on a footing of equality. In neither case does the 'élitist' doctrine offer a third solution, in addition to the old alternative of force or consent. Human inequality is no justification of power: rather, human inequality itself stands in need of being justified.

Thus it would seem that the principle of equality, together with the related notion of consent as the foundation of power, is the essential component of the idea of legitimacy in the modern world. And yet responsible voices have been raised to warn us that, with all its merits, equality is not enough. 'The nations of our time', wrote Tocqueville as a conclusion to his great study of democracy, 'cannot prevent the conditions of men from becoming equal; but it depends upon themselves whether the principle of equality is to lead them to servitude or to freedom, to knowledge or to barbarism, to prosperity or to wretchedness.' What else can this mean except that equality has its perils, and that consent is no sufficient guarantee of the preservation of the basic values of democracy, since it is possible to consent to anything, even to being no longer equal or free? Clearly, at this point the whole problem of the legitimation of power appears from a new angle and in a different light. It is no longer the origin, but the exercise of power which calls for attention. What matters is to determine the particular procedure of power, and the manner in which, next in importance to equality, freedom may be secured.

REFERENCES

Aristotle, *Politics*, Book I, chs. i–vi, and esp. 1252^a and ^{b}, 1254^a, 1255^a; III, xiii, 1283^b, 1284^a; xvii, 1288^a; IV, xi, 1295^b; VII, vii (quotations given in Sir E. Barker's translation). St. Gregory the Great, *Epist.* XIII,

34. St. Thomas Aquinas, *Comm. in quatuor libros Sentent. P. Lombardi* II, xliv, q. 2, art. 2; *Summa Theol.* Iᵃ, xcvi, art. 4; *Summa contra Gent.* III, ch. 81. R. Hooker, *Ecclesiastical Polity*, I (1594) ch. x. Locke, *Second Treatise of Government* (1689–90) §§ 5, 15, 74, 90, 91, 94, 134, 135. Hume, *Political Essays* (1741–2), iii, 'Of the First Principles of Government'. Montesquieu, *Esprit des Lois* (1748), Book XVII, ch. 6. Burke, *Reflections on the Revolution in France* (1790). A. de Tocqueville, *De la démocratie en Amérique*, Vol. II (1840), Conclusion (quot. in the Eng. trans. by H. Reeve, London, 1889); *Correspondance entre A. de Toqueville et le Comte de Gobineau (1843–59)*, Paris, 1909. J. A. de Gobineau, *Essai sur l'inégalité des races humaines*, Paris, 1854. A. Lincoln, *Reply in the Alton Joint Debate*, 1858. G. Mosca, *Il principio aristocratico ed il democratico nel passato e nell'avvenire* (1902), now in the volume *Partiti e sindacati nella crisi del regime parlamentare*, Bari, 1949.

For the discussion of the concept of equality special acknowledgement is due to S. I. Benn's and R. S. Peters's chapter, 'Justice and Equality', in their joint volume *Social Principles and the Democratic State*, London, 1959.

For the distinction between *élites* that are 'imposed' and *élites* that are 'proposed' I am indebted to the late F. Burzio's *Essenza e attualità del liberalismo*, Turin, 1945.

For a survey of the history of the idea of equality see S. A. Lakoff, *Equality in Political Philosophy*, Cambridge, Mass., 1964.

6

NEGATIVE LIBERTY

WHAT exactly is meant by saying that the purpose of power is to secure human freedom? How and why has the attainment of this end become one of the most effective principles of legitimation of the modern State? These are big and difficult questions to which a complete answer cannot be given in a few lines. But it is at least possible to map some landmarks in the development of political theory to guide our judgement in a discussion the importance of which hardly needs to be emphasized.

Historical evidence does not indicate clearly whether the rise of the modern State was in any sense necessarily connected with one of the various concepts of liberty which prevail at the present time. For Hobbes the 'liberty of the Commonwealth' consists, as we know, in its independence.[1] Machiavelli too, when speaking of political liberty (*vivere libero, stato libero*), seems to have this meaning especially in mind. Liberty was to him primarily the absence of foreign rule, and only secondarily opposition to tyranny. The rule of his 'new prince' was justified in so far as it succeeded in establishing a strong government, not in restoring a kind of liberty which he considered no longer possible, at any rate in Italy, in view of the prevailing corruption of political life.

Thus the ideology which presided over the rise of the 'new principality' seems very far from being one of a 'liberal' type. Yet it is worth while pausing for a moment's reflection before accepting this judgement as final. It can in fact be asked whether the very demand for a strong State, for a firm foundation of law and order, which is so evident in both Machiavelli and Hobbes, and which alone would suffice to explain the rise and success of absolute monarchy in Europe, was not in itself, notwithstanding every appearance to the contrary, a demand for a liberty of sorts. Take the famous sentence at the beginning of chapter xvii of *The Prince*, one of the most outspoken, and perhaps one of the most

[1] See above, Part II, ch. 8, p. 125.

terrifying, passages in Machiavelli: 'Caesar Borgia was reputed cruel; nevertheless, that cruelty of his repaired the Romagna, united it, and restored it to allegiance and peace.' Consider what are the benefits, the goods, the attainment of which justifies the merciless action of the new prince in Machiavelli's eyes: union, allegiance, peace. These are values we have already encountered. They are closely similar to those which Hobbes invokes in order to prove the need to forsake the state of nature and to enter the 'civil state'.

Indeed, nothing is more revealing than the list Hobbes draws up of all the good things that are missed in the state of nature, with the clear implication that they can be purchased by putting an end to that state, i.e. by setting up a 'common power', a 'State'.

In such condition [he writes in one of the best-known and most impressive passages of *Leviathan*], there is no place for industry; because the fruit thereof is uncertain: and consequently no culture of the earth; no navigation, nor use of the commodities that may be imported by sea; no commodious building; no instruments of moving, and removing, such things as require much force; no knowledge of the face of the earth; no account of time; no arts; no letters; no society; and which is worst of all, continual fear, and danger of violent death; and the life of man, solitary, poor, nasty, brutish, and short.

Here, as in a photographic negative, we get a clear picture of what are the values, the benefits which, according to Hobbes, are attained in the State. These values are both material and spiritual: they concern the comforts of life as well as the improvement of the mind. They are what in modern terms we should call 'cultural' values; and cultural values are always, in some way or other, associated with liberty, with the free display of human initiative and energy.

True, neither Machiavelli's nor Hobbes's State has much in common with the modern, 'liberal' State. The 'prince' of the one, the 'sovereign' of the other, know no brakes to their power. If freedom simply means independence, they alone are 'free', because their power is limited only by force and their will is the supreme law. Nevertheless, if the purpose of power is to guarantee peace and security, the all-embracing action of law must come to a halt at a certain point, if only to allow the enjoyment of all those goods which are the fruit of peace and security. The justification of law and order lies precisely here. Thanks to them, those obstacles are removed which would otherwise prevent that enjoyment if peace and security vanished. This is a wholly negative approach to the concept of liberty. 'The liberty of a subject', says Hobbes, 'lieth . . . only in those things which in regulating their actions, the sovereign hath prætermitted.' In other words, citizens are free only in that sphere which is not regulated by law: *silentium legis, libertas civium*. Let us, then, give this liberty its proper name. Let us call it 'negative liberty': but on condition that in this respect we number even Hobbes among 'liberal' authors.[1] For indeed the greatest philosopher of Absolutism seems to take a fairly generous view of what is or should be the liberty of the subject, if it includes 'the liberty to buy, and sell, and otherwise contract with one another; to choose their own abode, their own diet, their own trade of life, and institute their children as they themselves think fit; and the like.'

Thus, when from the origin of power we turn to considering its exercise, negative liberty appears as the first and perhaps the most significant justification of the modern State. Under that heading we can begin by listing both the removal of obstacles and the assurance of a sphere of individual independence, described by Hobbes himself as the task of the State. But evidently that liberty could not be held to be secure or complete until a third condition was fulfilled, until the line was firmly drawn where power must be brought to a halt, until, in one word, the limits of State action were definitely established. It seems almost paradoxical that here once again it is Hobbes who points the way. He does so where he analyses the conditions of a law's being good—since, as we know, laws can be good or bad, though by definition 'no law can be unjust'.[2] Among those conditions is that of being 'needful', by which Hobbes seems to mean that only such laws are to be approved which do not impose useless restrictions or burdens. 'For the use of laws . . . is not to bind the people from all voluntary actions; but to direct and keep them in such a motion, as not to hurt themselves by their own impetuous desires, rashness or indiscretion; as hedges are set, not to stop travellers, but to keep them in their way.' The analogy between laws and hedges is revealing. 'Good laws' are only those which are indispensable for securing

---

[1] According to Leo Strauss, a well-known student of Hobbes, the Hobbesian State is nothing else than the liberal State *in statu nascendi*.

[2] See above, Part II, ch. 6, p. 107.

men's peaceful coexistence. They should act as boundaries to that sphere which is reserved for the decisions of individuals alone. Once again we are confronted with the concept of negative liberty; but this time that concept is used as a legal standard, as a measure of the limits which the State should not overstep—though, of course, from Hobbes's standpoint, there is nothing to prevent it from doing so. It is fascinating to find the same analogy taken up by Locke. For laws to act as hedges is to him their greatest merit and their proper task. Indeed, it is precisely by doing so that laws, contrary to Hobbes's opinion, are the condition of liberty, since 'that ill deserves the name of confinement which hedges us in from bogs and precipices. So that, however it may be mistaken, the end of law, is not to abolish or restrain, but to preserve and enlarge freedom. . . . For liberty is to be free from restraint and violence from others; which cannot be where there is no law.'

Locke, of course, was and still is the chief philosopher of negative liberty. As a complete formulation of the liberal conception of the State, the *Second Treatise of Government* has probably been equalled only by another classic, John Stuart Mill's *On Liberty*. Mill's essay discusses in more up-to-date language the problem of the defence of the individual against the pressure of social forces unknown in Locke's day. But both writers, like all others who share the same liberal inspiration, are concerned to secure that sphere of individual independence which Hobbes, and many 'absolutist' writers after him, regarded as a gracious gift from the sovereign. No doubt the principles to which they refer in defining the duties of power and the limits of State action are widely different. Locke turns to the law of nature and of reason, which precedes the State, and to the natural rights of man, which are inalienable and imprescriptible. Mill appeals to the principle of utility, 'utility in the largest sense, grounded on the permanent interests of a man as a progressive being'. Further, in defining the ends to be secured the emphasis is different. To Locke the reason for the State's existence, or to use his own words, the reason why men join together in the 'social compact', is the 'preservation of their lives, liberties and estates', the three basic goods which he sums up in one 'general name, property'. Mill, on the other hand, draws up a long list of liberties which society must respect, but then he too sums them all up in a single sentence: 'the only freedom which deserves the name, is that of pursuing our own good in our own way, so long as we do not attempt to deprive others of theirs, or impede their efforts to obtain it.' What matters is that in both cases the legitimation of power is linked to an essentially negative concept of liberty. The purpose and at the same time the limits of State action are determined by the one and only value which must be established and secured: the free and unhampered development of the individual.

It would therefore seem logical at this point to conclude that the concept of negative liberty and the liberal conception of the State founded upon it are nothing but the product of a particular historical period and must be judged and valued as such. This is precisely what we often hear said when Liberalism is depicted as the typical expression of an age which saw the establishment of a social structure where unfettered individualism appeared to be the highest possible good. There is certainly much truth in this contention. There is no denying that the success of Locke's teaching corresponded historically with the rise of the commercial middle classes and the 'possessive individualism' which they professed, just as Mill's popularity was closely associated with the final triumph of *laissez-faire* and of the bourgeois way of life. But since calling Liberalism a 'bourgeois ideology' often conceals a polemical or even a hostile attitude, it might be as well to face the question in its most general terms, and to ask whether the fact that a given political theory was linked to a particular set of historical circumstances is sufficient ground for doubting its merits and its validity in a changed and more complex world.

Before even trying to answer this question properly, there is one remark which can and must be made concerning the 'bourgeois' character of negative liberty and of the liberal conception of the State. If this is a 'bourgeois ideology', it is certainly very different, both in its assumptions and in its implications, from that other and in many ways opposite theory—also described as bourgeois—of the governing *élites*, which we have already examined more than once in this book. Unlike modern 'élitism', classical Liberalism was tied, both logically and historically, to the principle of human equality. It claimed for every individual an equal share in the rights of man. Far from expressing a reactionary, or even a conservative, attitude towards the existing social structure, it was an instrument of progress, indeed even of subversion of that

structure, of the privileges and discriminations which that structure entailed.

This, however, is not the only merit of the liberal theory of
the State. Its greatest achievement was that of having created its
own instruments and institutions, which still constitute the firm
foundation of the modern State. These institutions have weathered
many storms, showing that they can be adapted to the needs of a
changed society. They seem, indeed, to have drawn fresh vigour
and inspiration from the very criticisms to which they have been
subjected, from the very menace of destruction with which they
have been faced in recent years. When examining those institutions
from a legal angle I pointed out that they were the result both of
historical development and of a deliberate commitment and choice.[1]
Now the men who made this choice made it in the clearest possible
manner, by means of those solemn 'Declarations' with which it
became and remains customary to preface constitutional Charters.
They laid down the values they considered essential for the legitimation of power, in the form of a vindication of 'rights'. But
those rights were, for the most part, negative liberties. They were
nothing else than limits appended to the action of the State. Nor
did they spring from the brain of these men, like Minerva armed
from the brain of Jove. They had been conceived of long before the
rise of bourgeois society, long before even the rise of the modern
State.

This, then, is the important point to be kept in mind when discussing the political theory of Liberalism: that the notion of
negative liberty was the exclusive product neither of abstract
theory nor of social conditions of comparatively recent date. The
'rights of Englishmen', which were to be an inspiration and a
model for so many Declarations of Rights in different countries,
have a long history behind them: they were 'historic' before becoming 'natural' rights. They were won in age-long struggles and
set down in famous documents, of which *Magna Carta* is only the
first in time. The English Declarations of Rights in the seventeenth
century have no abstract or universal character. On the contrary,
the emphasis is on precedent, on the fact that such rights already
existed and were sanctioned in the past, and that it was only a
matter of reaffirming them solemnly and of providing adequate
instruments for their defence. It took the American Revolution to

[1] See above, Part II, chapters 7–9.

convert these historic rights into natural rights. Undoubtedly the new spiritual climate and the rationalistic construction of the State which had found expression in Locke's writings had a share in this transformation. But an equal share was taken by the requirements of the political struggle. This no longer allowed the Colonists, once they had detached themselves from the mother country, to invoke the 'rights of Englishmen', and thus led them almost necessarily to claim these rights on general grounds as 'rights of man'. The great *Declaration* of the French National Assembly of 1789 purported to define both the rights of man and those of the citizen; but no sooner had the storm of revolution settled, than the same rights reappeared as historic or positive rights, or rights of the citizen rather than of man. If this proves anything, it can prove only that the vindication of rights was a way of defining the boundaries between the State and the individual, and that negative liberty had become a constitutional principle, the basic constitutional principle of the modern State.

Nor is it less important, on the other hand, that there should always have been great differences of opinion in fixing these boundaries, and that these boundaries have never been so much called in question as at the present day. A case in point is the discussion still raging on the Continent about the existence and precise nature of a new category of rights and freedoms, the so-called 'social rights'.

It is not easy to define these new rights in a few words. In substance, they amount to the demand that all citizens should in fact be able to enjoy those freedoms which by right are equal for all men. But a demand of this kind must in the end lead to the abandonment of the traditional idea of negative liberty as non-interference on the part of the State. Obviously, the promotion of social rights requires in the economic sphere not the abstention but the intervention of the State. This emerges clearly, for example, in the ruling of Article 3, § 2, of the Italian Constitution, which declares: 'It is the duty of the Republic to remove all obstacles of an economic and social nature, which by limiting in fact the liberty and equality of the citizens hinder the full development of human personality and the effective share of all workers in the political, economic, and social organization of the country.'

The concept of social rights and freedom thus brings us back to the question, to what extent the liberal conception of the State is linked to a particular type of economic and social organization. For there can be no doubt that it is difficult to reconcile this new concept of freedom with the interpretation of the liberal ideal which was given by the theorists of the bourgeois age, from Locke to Mill, and which inspired the constitutional Charters of the eighteenth and nineteenth centuries. This interpretation, as we saw, centred on the belief in the sanctity of private property and in the unsurpassed merits of full economic liberty. It is precisely that sanctity and those merits which are now called in question. They would have to be sacrificed if 'social justice' were to be realized. The conflict, to give it its proper name, is the conflict between Individualism and Socialism: and the problem of the survival of the liberal ideal is bound to be felt as particularly critical in societies which, like present-day Italian society, lie midway between the two. It is highly significant that two among the most distinguished leaders of Italian Liberalism should have been at loggerheads precisely on this point: the economist Einaudi maintained that Liberalism was inseparably tied to a *laissez-faire* structure of society, while the philosopher Croce maintained no less stoutly that liberal ideals and institutions could and should survive the radical social changes taking place in the modern world.

Faced with such a serious dilemma it is not enough to appeal to the experience of particular countries, like Britain for example, where the abandonment of economic Liberalism and the carrying through of courageous social reforms have apparently not weakened the old ideal of negative liberty, so well expressed in the saying 'An Englishman's home is his castle'. It is useful to go back to the crucial moment in the story of that liberty, to the time when it contributed decisively to the forming of the modern State in the shape of three basic demands: the removal of obstacles, the assurance of a sphere of individual independence, and the confining of State action within well-known, precise limits. I believe that it would be possible to speak of a threat to that liberty which has inspired modern constitutions only if one of these three demands were rejected. As long as there is no return to the attribution of absolute and unlimited power to the State, as long as the life and independence of the citizen are not at the mercy of arbitrary decisions, in a word as long as no attack is made on those constitutional guarantees which form the bulwark of modern liberty, we cannot hold that certain actions of the State can be called illiberal. Least of all can such an accusation be brought against State action directed to removing obstacles to the full development of human personality, or to the effective participation of all citizens in political life, when such obstacles are due to their particular economic or social condition, or to the privileged position of certain groups within the State. On the contrary, such action would seem to me to be a continuance, a strengthening of that liberating process which, as I have tried to show, though often overlooked, is one of the highest merits of the modern State.

It was, after all, to this liberating task, to this removal of obstacles which constitutes negative liberty, that the Head of a great and powerful nation appealed during the last war. When F. D. Roosevelt[1] proclaimed what came to be known as the Four Freedoms he was probably thinking only of offering a promise and hope to the peoples then crushed under the most horrible tyranny that history had ever witnessed. He was not outlining a political system, let alone a programme of social reform. But consider those freedoms in their constituent elements and in the historical perspective I have here outlined. The first and second—freedom of speech and expression, freedom to worship God each in his own way—are in the purest tradition of Liberalism; they might have been worded by John Stuart Mill. The fourth freedom, on the other hand—freedom from fear—expresses a much more elementary need; it almost evokes the spirit of Hobbes. As for the third freedom—freedom from want—this too is a negative freedom, at least if my argument thus far has been correct. But surely nobody would venture to brand it as a bourgeois kind of freedom when it has inspired, and continues to inspire, those classes and peoples who have hitherto been disinherited, and who now claim their share of the common human heritage, just as, only a few centuries ago, did the ancestors of those classes and peoples who prefer today (fortunately they are only few in number) to shut themselves up in a sterile egoism, raving about 'natural inequalities' and non-existent privileges of 'race' or *élite*.

[1] Message to Congress of 6 Jan. 1941.

REFERENCES

Machiavelli, *The Prince*, ch. xvii. Hobbes, *Leviathan*, chs. 13, 21, 30. Locke, *Second Treatise of Government*, §§ 57, 123, and *passim*. J. S. Mill, *On Liberty* (1859), Introd. and chs. iv and v.

On the concept of 'negative liberty' the most stimulating remarks recently made are undoubtedly those of Sir Isaiah Berlin in his Inaugural Lecture, *Two Concepts of Liberty*, Oxford, 1958; but see also M. Cranston, *Freedom: A New Analysis*, London, 1953, and the excellent essay by N. Bobbio, 'Della libertà dei moderni comparata a quella dei posteri', in the volume *Politica e Cultura*, Turin, 1955.

The definition of negative liberty as a bourgeois ideology is, of course, the usual criticism made by Marxist writers of the liberal theory of the State. But the phrase 'possessive individualism' comes from a recent book by C. B. Macpherson, *The Political Theory of Possessive Individualism: Hobbes to Locke*, Oxford, 1962.

The several writings of Croce and Einaudi concerning the relation between political and economic Liberalism have been collected in one volume: B. Croce–L. Einaudi, *Liberismo e Liberalismo*, a cura di P. Solari, Naples, 1957.

7

POSITIVE LIBERTY

THE concept of negative liberty, and the liberal theory of the State founded upon it, can be criticized for reasons different from, and better than, those which have been discussed in the preceding chapter. The point is whether this concept, in laying stress too exclusively on the limits of power, does not end by relegating to a secondary place, or at least by minimizing, the problem of how power is to be exercised, and precisely by whom. The model of the liberal State was set up once and for all by Montesquieu, with his description of 'moderate governments' as the only ones where 'political liberty' can be found—the 'political liberty of the subject' being 'a tranquillity of mind, arising from the opinion each person has of his safety'. The choice of this model rules out any preference for a particular form of political organization. It does not matter whether government is 'republican' or 'monarchical'. What matters is that power should not be 'abused', and this, as we know, can happen, according to Montesquieu, only where power is constitutionally limited. But if the test of a liberal government is that the rule of law should be secured and the area of private independence respected, strictly even an enlightened despot can satisfy that test. Frederick of Prussia was highly praised by Kant precisely on that score: for having enabled his subjects to use their reason and to speak their mind, thus removing all hindrances to the spread of enlightenment.

The claims advanced by modern man in the name of liberty are much more sweeping and complex. This is where we come up against what is usually described today as 'positive liberty', in relation to, if not in direct contrast with, negative liberty. The conceptual difference between these liberties is set forth in the following quotation from Sir Isaiah Berlin's recent Inaugural Lecture with a clarity I could hardly hope to improve upon:

The answer to the question 'Who governs me?' is logically distinct from the question 'How far does government interfere with me?' It is in this difference that the great contrast between the two concepts of negative and positive liberty, in the end, consists. For the 'positive' sense of liberty comes to light if we try to answer the question, not 'What am I free to do or be?', but 'By whom am I ruled?' or 'Who is to say what I am, and what I am not, to be or do?' . . . The desire to be governed by myself, or at any rate to participate in the process by which my life is to be controlled, may be as deep a wish as that of a free area for action, and perhaps historically older. But it is not a desire for the same thing. . . . The 'positive' sense of the word 'liberty' derives from the wish on the part of the individual to be his own master.

The distinction so sharply drawn by Sir Isaiah is no new one. At the beginning of the nineteenth century Benjamin Constant laid it down equally forcibly in his celebrated essay *The Liberty of the Ancients compared with that of the Moderns*. It can even, without too much effort, be traced back to Aristotle. Its tremendous importance for political theory lies in the fact that it forces us to face the question which liberals often eschew, the question of the relation between liberty and form of government. Indeed, the very definition of positive liberty indicates how closely this notion is linked to that of democracy. If liberty consists in having a say in all decisions that affect us, then, as Aristotle pointed out, it can be realized only in a system of government based on equality, where all citizens share 'in the administration of justice and in the holding of office'. In a system such as this 'the masses must necessarily be sovereign'. Positive liberty and popular sovereignty go hand in hand. It might even be said—Cicero said it in different words long ago—that one is the ideological justification of the other. Democrats have always maintained that 'in no other city except in one where the people has the supreme power can liberty find its abode: liberty, than which without doubt nothing is sweeter'.[1]

We have already encountered the doctrine of popular sovereignty in another context. Much has been written on it and many theories have been put forward concerning its history, some of which have indeed gone too far in claiming the uninterrupted continuity of the doctrine ever since its first appearance in classical antiquity. Two points are of interest to our present inquiry: the assumption of popular sovereignty as the exclusive legitimation of power, and the assertion of a necessary and unbreakable bond

[1] See above, Part II, ch. 2, p. 78.

between the concept of liberty and that of democracy. The clarification of these two points should help us to date with a certain precision the birth of the modern democratic State, or more exactly of the arguments which still lend it support.

As regards the first point, there can be little doubt that the claim put forward on behalf of popular sovereignty was closely associated, both logically and in time, with the emergence of those natural, original, and indefeasible rights of the individual from which the liberal idea of the State also drew its origin. Locke's political theory provides the best proof of that close association. Once again, as had been the case with equality, a notion that was entirely new was linked with the past, and could be thought of as sprouting from the trunk of much older theories. Both the medieval idea of consent, and the Roman doctrine of the derivation of power from the people, certainly contributed to the shaping of the modern theory of popular sovereignty. But if the bottle was old, the wine was an entirely new one. What was new was the presentation of popular sovereignty as an 'original right' of the people, corresponding to the 'natural rights' of the individual. What was without precedent was the abstract construction of the State as the result of a social contract in which each individual contributes his share of rights and of power. Indeed, what took place was a revolution in political philosophy: it might be called a 'Copernican revolution', to paraphrase a famous image of Kant's. But it was a revolution in thought parallel to one in action, and it is futile to argue which of the two was prior in time and played the decisive role in shaping the first democratic régimes worthy to be so called in the Western hemisphere. What matters is that the leaders of those revolutions were men who not only believed in the democratic principle, in human equality, in the will of the people as the only legitimate source of power, but attempted to build a society based on those principles, and were ready to fight for them if need be. 'Really I think that the poorest hee that is in England hath a life to live as the greatest hee; and therefore truly, Sir, I thinke itt's cleare, that every man that is to live under a Governement ought first by his owne consent to putt himself under that Government.' Colonel Rainborough's words are still remembered, as are those uttered by Lincoln on the battlefield of Gettysburg two centuries later, which also blazon forth a claim, an encouragement, and a promise 'that government of the people, by the people, for the people, shall not perish from the earth'. Democracy so conceived is a commitment, a choice. To define it is to prescribe it. It is an ideal accepted or refused even before it can be justified on rational grounds.

Now among all the arguments which can be, and have been, advanced in defence of democracy the idea of positive liberty is by far the most attractive, the most convincing, and at the same time the most ambiguous and the most liable to be misinterpreted or misunderstood. And Rousseau is of all political thinkers the one who has advanced that argument most cogently and drawn it with impeccable logic to its most extreme conclusions. For Rousseau the central problem of politics consisted in finding 'a form of association which will defend and protect with the whole common force the person and goods of each associate, and in which each, while uniting himself with all, may still obey himself alone, and remain as free as before'. 'This', Rousseau adds, 'is the fundamental problem of which the social contract provides the solution.' Through the social contract, with his entry into a 'civil state', man renounces his 'natural liberty', but only to find his true liberty, which is both 'civil' and 'moral', and consists in obedience to the rule of law: because man is free only when he is 'truly master of himself', and 'obedience to a law which we prescribe to ourselves is liberty'.

The notion of the social contract was thus stripped by Rousseau of any historic reference. It is, as Kant was to say, not an 'act' but an 'idea', the normative principle which allows us to conceive of political organization as implying not the sacrifice of liberty but its attainment. Liberty in the positive sense is in fact nothing else than self-government, autonomy. It cannot be realized except when the power which commands is the self-same power of him who obeys. The achievement of liberty in the State is therefore conditional on the sovereignty of the 'general will'. 'Subjects' become 'citizens' only in as far as they share in that sovereignty and partake of the general will. Their complete surrender to the State, to the 'country' (la patrie), secures them 'against all personal dependence'. 'In this lies the key to the working of the political machine; this alone legitimizes civil undertakings, which, without it, would be absurd, tyrannical, and liable to the most frightful abuses.'

No one, probably, has ever gone as far as Rousseau in presenting democracy as the only legitimate government; certainly few before him had ever given the notion of positive liberty the prominence it is given in the *Social Contract*. This is the reason why it is always necessary to return to Rousseau when we want to understand the relevance of the idea of liberty to modern democratic thought. But it is also the reason why from the first, let alone in its later applications, Rousseau's argument has been under constant and bitter attack. Indeed, Rousseau, the greatest theorist of positive liberty, has seemed to many people to sacrifice Liberalism to Democracy. Early in the nineteenth century the liberal writer Constant denounced the *Social Contract* as 'the most terrible auxiliary of every form of despotism'. Not long ago Sir Isaiah Berlin, in a memorable broadcast, defined Rousseau as 'the most sinister and most formidable enemy of liberty in the whole history of modern thought'.

The liberty which was felt to be threatened by democracy of the Rousseauian type was first of all negative liberty, the liberty that was dearest to the heart of all liberals of the old school. The danger was conceived to spring from what was called 'egalitarian' democracy. This at any rate was the threat which the men of the nineteenth century had particularly in mind. They knew nothing as yet of the very different dangers which were to be revealed in times nearer our own. Above all, they saw the menace to liberty in what they called the 'tyranny of numbers', which they believed was the inevitable consequence of the principle of equality. Logically, this principle is certainly inseparable from the idea of democracy. Demanding, as it does, that everyone should share in the exercise of power, democracy was inevitably bound to lead to the progressive extension of the franchise, to the assumption that one vote counts as much as any other, and to the need to solve eventual differences by having recourse to a simple numerical calculation, normally that of majority not further qualified. The fear of 'the despotism of the majority, which is nothing else than the right of the strongest', is a motif we find recurring in the writings of most early liberals, from Mallet du Pan to Constant and Mill. It was not dictated by any spirit of undemocratic reaction, but by a true concern for the proper working of liberal institutions and for the prevention of a new despotism, more exacting than the old.

A second threat which critics discovered in egalitarian democracy (the reference here is to constructive criticism only, not to that which was purely negative, and indulged in by reactionary writers) was that of the 'levelling of values', to call it by a modern name. This levelling was thought to be the inevitable result of the refusal to recognize the factual inequality of men, their different abilities, the role of self-differentiation in the dynamic of social life. The rejection of the aristocratic principle, some writers prophesied, would inevitably lead to a mass society with no standards left. Tocqueville, whom I have already mentioned more than once, is the nineteenth-century writer most clearly aware of this particular danger. He was, as he himself confessed, torn between his 'aristocratic instincts' and his 'rational belief' in democracy. His concern with the problem led him first to make use of his knowledge of democracy in America to produce a penetrating diagnosis of democratic experience in general. At a later stage it led him to trace the process of levelling in France to a time well before the Revolution, and to find its roots in the very structure of the *ancien régime* and in the rise of the modern bureaucratic, centralizing State. Faced by the inevitable progress of egalitarianism, Tocqueville declared that he was smitten by a kind of 'religious terror'. Yet his mind remained cool, his conviction unshakable: 'The question is not how to reconstruct aristocratic society, but how to make liberty proceed out of that democratic state of society in which God has placed us.'

The last and worst danger which has been seen to arise from an unconditional application of the democratic principle is that it can provide the ground for nothing less than a final and total renunciation of liberty. Rousseau himself gave warning of this danger when he criticized certain theories of the social contract, and particularly that supported by Grotius. Grotius in fact, by presenting the contract as irrevocable, used that very notion to justify Absolutism, or, as Rousseau puts it, 'to rob the peoples of all their rights and invest kings with them by every conceivable artifice'. The history of the nineteenth century, to say nothing of our own, certainly does not lack cases where popular sovereignty was used as an instrument for the establishment of dictatorships. Plebiscites, referendums, direct appeals to the electorate, have served, as we know only too well, to provide both the legal and the ideological justification for régimes which proved to be far more absolute than all the absolute governments of past ages.

These are serious arguments which deserve to be pondered, all the more because they do, in most cases, accurately fit the facts. Experience still seems to confirm Tocqueville's remarks concerning the difference between the egalitarian, levelling, democracies of the Latin type, and those which have been called 'deferential democracies' of the English-speaking countries. In these countries, and especially in Britain—which unlike the Continent of Europe was spared the great social upheaval of the French Revolution—a foreign observer is struck by what can only be described as the survival of many aristocratic elements in the structure of society. Such elements, together with the frame of mind which they foster, act as a corrective to the rigid logic of democratic egalitarianism, though it may well be that the most valid corrective lies in the spirit of independence that has long prevailed on these shores. However that may be, the case of Britain does seem to prove the possibility of reconciling positive and negative liberty, Democracy and Liberalism. Not only does the safeguard of individual rights, and of an area of free individual development, set a limit to the 'tyranny of numbers'. That very safeguard is a condition of the proper working of democracy: without negative liberty, the attainment of positive liberty, of real and not illusory self-government, will be retarded, if not impeded, throughout.

For indeed, if democracy is to work properly, obstacles must be removed that would prevent men from thinking and judging freely. They must be given the chance of discussing and weighing-up their leaders before confirming by their consent the power of the so-called *élites*. But for this to happen, the free play of political forces must be assured in the State. The principle of equality must be truly respected by guaranteeing to minorities the possibility of becoming majorities. Above all, we must never give to the decisions of majorities more than a purely pragmatic value, remembering, as the saying goes, that the only reason for counting heads is that it is easier to count them than to cut them off. Those decisions are human and fallible. They cannot entail a duty to submit to them as to an indisputable and ultimate truth. Subject to all these cautions, as is the case in modern constitutions, egalitarian democracy must not be confused with another, very different kind of democracy, which has only lately risen on the political horizon: 'totalitarian' democracy—the most terrible threat, in the opinion of many, to the ideal of liberty on which rests the modern notion of the State.

The key to this kind of democracy can undoubtedly be found once again in Rousseau, and in the ambivalence of that concept of positive liberty which, as we saw, plays a leading role in his construction of the State. The reason for this ambivalence and for the diverging interpretations which have been given of Rousseau's political thought can in turn be traced back to the ambiguity of his language, to what I should be inclined to call his skilful manipulation of words. Whether that manipulation was intentional is open to question: the fact remains that there is something deliberately obscure in Rousseau's presentation of his two central concepts, the social contract and the general will. The social contract is spoken of almost in terms of a mystical experience. It demands the 'total alienation' of the individual, offering in exchange a kind of rebirth, which will turn him from 'a stupid and unimaginative animal' into 'an intelligent being and a man'. Even more baffling is Rousseau's conception of the general will, which has called forth an endless literature. Clearly, the general will is for Rousseau not merely the rightful holder of sovereignty. It embodies a supreme ethical value: for it alone 'is always right', and only in obedience to it does man find the fulfilment of his moral life. For this very reason the general will does not and cannot for Rousseau coincide with 'the will of all', at any rate not without further qualification. The will of all can in fact express particular and variable interests, whereas the general will is 'always constant, unalterable and pure'. It does not show itself 'in long debates, discussions and tumult'; rather, it is best revealed in unanimity, in the greatest possible concert of minds. It is therefore necessary to put an end to the 'harmful divisions' due to 'parties' and 'sects' (Rousseau expressly borrows these words from Machiavelli). 'There should be no partial society within the State', in order that 'the people shall in no way deceive itself' and nothing may disturb the mysterious revelation of truth in each citizen's mind, thinking 'only his own thoughts'.

Nor is this all. The 'blind multitude', says Rousseau, needs to be 'guided'.

Of itself the people wills always the good, but of itself it by no means always sees it. The general will is always in the right, but the judgment which guides it is not always enlightened. It must be got to see objects as they are, and sometimes as they ought to appear to it; it must be shown the good road it is in search of. . . . The individuals see the good they reject; the public wills the good it does not see. All stand equally in need of guidance.

Rousseau leaves us in no doubt as to what he means by such guidance. He states in *Émile* that the best institutions are those which best succeed in 'denaturing' man. He repeats in the *Social Contract* that the shaping of a nation may require that human nature itself be changed. Such a formidable undertaking can be achieved only by training and by compulsion: souls must be taught as well as forced to fly. 'Whoever refuses to obey the general will shall be compelled to do so by the whole body. This means nothing less than that he will be forced to be free.' Indeed, the general will may appear to run contrary to my convictions and to my vote. But 'this proves neither more nor less than that I was mistaken and that what I thought to be the general will was not so. If my particular opinion had carried the day, I should have achieved the opposite of what was my will; and it is in that case that I should not have been free.'

The need of guidance, the wrongness of dissent; indoctrination, self-criticism, re-education: all the paraphernalia of this century's totalitarianism seem, alas, to be already contained in these statements of Rousseau. One can well understand why, in search of culprits, many respectable modern scholars should have seized gladly upon Rousseau, using him as a scapegoat for all our troubles as he had already been used more than a century and a half before. I believe that such views contain a certain amount of exaggeration and distortion; but I cannot here enter into a discussion both of what might be called the case for Rousseau's prosecution and of that for his defence. One point, at any rate, must be made: viz. that with Rousseau begins that manipulation of words I have already mentioned, which has led to such widely contrasting concepts of liberty and democracy as dominate our present world. What happened would seem to be that words belonging to the traditional vocabulary of politics were emptied of their content, and new meanings were substituted, which proved eventually to be quite the opposite of the old. It would, of course, be easy to produce countless examples of this kind of manipulation in our own time, simply by turning to current political propaganda. But it is only fair to recognize that the earliest and largest part of the responsibility for what has happened lies with political philosophers, and precisely with those who, starting with Rousseau and proceeding with Hegel, shared in the greatest manipulation of all: that which changed the liberal formula of the State as an 'instrument' of liberty into the totalitarian slogan of the State as the 'embodiment' of freedom. It is impossible not to feel perplexed, for example, on reading in De Ruggiero's *History of European Liberalism*—a book which is still very popular, even outside Italy, and whose author was without doubt a sincere believer in Liberalism—a statement like the following: 'We are today so much accustomed to the idea of the liberal State that we do not notice its paradoxical character, which was plain enough to its first inexperienced observers. The State, the organ of coercion *par excellence*, has become the highest expression of liberty.'

For my part, besides noticing the confusion which Hegelianism can foster even in a clear-sighted Latin mind, I believe that the only possible answer to this sort of argument is that, contrary to De Ruggiero's opinion, the first observers were not so far from the truth, or at least that they were reasoning correctly in terms of ordinary language and according to common sense. As with the opposition between force and consent, no dialectical artifice has ever succeeded in overcoming the opposition between coercion and liberty. 'To force men to be free' may seem to some people to be the greatest oracular utterance ever made by political philosophy. To my generation this sentence can only be a painful reminder of other similar phrases which could be read at the entrance to concentration camps. Better to give things their true names, to recognize facts for what they are. 'The organ of coercion *par excellence*' was certainly never in the past 'the expression of liberty', and need not be so today. There can and do exist democracies which deny individual liberty, just as there can be 'liberal' States where only a small number of citizens have any effective share of power. The State is, and can become, the expression of liberty only on condition that certain 'rules of the game' are respected. Negative and positive liberty constitute these rules, and this and nothing else is meant by saying that the purpose of power is to secure human freedom.

But if this is how things stand, then it is clear that we have not yet come to the end of our labours. Besides demanding respect for the rules, there may well be a question of asking what is at stake in the game: metaphor apart, it is a question of seeing whether it is possible to determine not only the form but the content of

State action, to establish, as was long believed possible, a firm and objective standard—the standard of the 'common good'—for the final legitimation of power. Writers with every kind of background have shared this belief. No better conclusion to our long journey could be found than a pause to reflect upon this venerable notion.

REFERENCES

Aristotle, *Politics*, III, i, 1275^a, ^{b}; xiii, 1283^b, 1284^a; VI, ii, 1317^a, ^{b}. Cicero, *De Re Publica*, I, §§ 31, 47. *The Clarke Papers*, Camden Society, New Series, XLIX, 1891, vol. I, p. 301. Locke, *Second Treatise of Government*, ch. xi, § 134. Montesquieu, *Esprit des Lois*, XI, chs. 4 and 6. Rousseau, *Contrat Social*, I, 6–8; II, 1–3, 6–7; IV, 1–2 (quot. in Cole's translation). Kant, *Beantwortung der Frage: Was ist Aufklärung?* (1784); *Metaphysische Anfangsgründe der Rechtslehre*, II, §§ 46, 47. B. Constant, *Principes de Politique* (1815), ch. i; *De la liberté des Anciens comparée à celle des Modernes* (1819). A. de Tocqueville, *De la Démocratie en Amérique*, First Vol. (1835), Introd.; Second Vol., iv, ch. 7 (Eng. trans. by H. Reeve, London, 1946, p. 584); *L'Ancien Régime et la Révolution* (1856). G. De Ruggiero, *Storia del liberalismo europeo*, Bari, 1925, p. 384 (Eng. trans. by R. G. Collingwood, *The History of European Liberalism*, London, 1927, p. 353).

On Mallet du Pan see the author's article 'Mallet du Pan, a Swiss Critic of Democracy' in *The Cambridge Journal*, I (1947).

For a balanced account of the discussions about Rousseau's alleged 'totalitarianism' see J. W. Chapman, *Rousseau—Totalitarian or Liberal?*, New York, 1956.

On the different 'meanings' of democracy, H. B. Mayo, *An Introduction to Democratic Theory*, New York, 1960; G. Sartori, *Democratic Theory*, Detroit, 1962.

The quotation from Sir Isaiah Berlin on pp. 211–212 is taken from his Inaugural Lecture, *Two Concepts of Liberty*, Oxford, 1958, pp. 14–16. His judgement of Rousseau, quoted on p. 215, is from his (unpublished) B.B.C. broadcast of 5 Nov. 1952, in the series *Freedom and its Betrayal*.

8

THE COMMON GOOD

The request for an exact definition of the 'good', or complex of 'goods', described as the 'common good' is not unlike another request we have met several times, but which has so far remained unanswered: the request for a definition of the 'principles of justice'. In both cases what is felt is the need of going beyond the purely formal approach to the problems of law and of politics. The common good, so the argument runs, must be the final aim of power if it is to be called legitimate; for law to be just, the legal system must conform to some basic principles of justice. We have noticed above, in discussing the value of order, the inadequacy of the pure and simple identification of order and justice. Order may well be in itself a good thing; but this hardly excuses us from saying what kind of order we have in mind; nor is it enough to say that justice consists in giving each man his due (*suum cuique tribuere*), unless we specify in what exactly the due of each man (the *suum*) consists, that due which is supposed to be guaranteed by the existence of law and order. Hence the ever-recurring desire to establish once and for all a substantial criterion of justice, to discover the 'true', the really 'just' law: what used to be called, and is still called by many, the 'natural law', from which positive law should derive its content and its value. Similarly, from the need of determining the actual scope of State action—not only the rules of the game, but its stake—the desire has arisen to establish once and for all the notion of the common good, a substantial criterion which should enable us to say, in any given circumstance: 'This, and this alone, is what ought to direct, and what justifies, the use of power.' The two notions, indeed, present a striking parallel: one would almost be tempted to say that the part played by the notion of natural law in legal theory exactly corresponds to that played by the notion of the common good in political thought.

The extraordinary fascination of the idea of the common good is fully evinced by the fact that, as I pointed out at the end of the last chapter, it is to be found in writers of the most different schools and with every kind of background. At the head of the list —if we were ever to try to draw one up—we should obviously have to put Plato. Plato, in the *Republic*, it will be remembered, entrusted the task of governing to the guardians, on the ground that they alone 'know' what is the good of the City. But if we leave Aristotle aside,[1] the author who laid more stress than anyone else on the importance of the common good for the definition of both law and politics was certainly St. Thomas Aquinas. For him the very idea of law presupposes that of the common good: 'Law, strictly understood, has as its first and principal object the ordering of the common good (*bonum commune*).' In keeping with the current medieval view, the task of establishing this law, 'of ordering affairs (*ordinare*) to the common good' belongs for Aquinas to the whole community or to those who 'represent' it. The common good consists in the achievement of temporal welfare (*utilitas communis in temporalibus rebus*), in the attainment of that worldly happiness (*beatitudo huius vitae*) which is compatible with the pursuit of a higher, other-worldly end. The instrument and guarantor of this achievement is the State, the most perfect form of society in the natural order. Ultimately, the State and the common good coincide, for it is impossible to conceive of the one without the other. This is still, as is well known, the teaching adhered to by the Catholic Church. With its emphasis on the common good as the basic value on which legitimation of power depends, the Thomist doctrine must once again be given the merit of having successfully grafted a classical conception on the main stem of Christian political thought.

But the idea of the common good is not the exclusive preserve of the Aristotelian and Thomist tradition. We can trace it as well in a very different line of thought, in writers of a strongly individualistic turn of mind, where we should least expect to find it. Hobbes, for example, lists the common good (or more exactly the 'good of the people') among the three requisites which make it possible to judge if a law is 'good'—the other two being that law should be 'needful' and 'perspicuous'. It is true, of course, that Hobbes invokes 'the good of the people' with a view above all to the 'good of the sovereign': 'the good of the sovereign and people,

[1] I have already discussed his views on the subject in Part II, ch. 2, pp. 71–72, and Part III, ch. 2, pp. 162–163.

cannot be separated. It is a weak sovereign, that has weak subjects: and a weak people, whose sovereign wanteth power to rule them at his will.' His appeal to a traditional concept is none the less significant, besides qualifying once again the current view held of him as the extreme champion of absolute power.

As for Locke, many of his readers must find it hard to reconcile the express mention of the 'public good', which is to be found in several passages of the *Second Treatise of Government*, with his conception of the State as an organization exclusively concerned with the protection of the 'rights' and 'interests' of individuals— a view which Locke also stresses most emphatically in the *Letter concerning Toleration*. Perhaps, as some interpreters suggest, this is merely an example of one of Locke's many contradictions.[1] Perhaps, as has also been maintained, we have here a typical illustration of what is often called the 'liberal fallacy': the belief that conflicts of interests can be solved, or at least ironed out, if left to themselves, owing to a kind of 'natural harmony', similar to that between conflicting forces in nature. At any rate, the tribute Locke pays to the notion of the common good is worth careful consideration. It shows how strongly rooted in political theory that notion still was in Locke's day.

Still more significant, however, is the fact that the notion itself, even though under a different name, still plays an active part in a theory wholly opposed to any abstract vindication of 'rights', to any high-flown metaphysic of 'goodness' and 'justice'. In its own way, the utilitarian doctrine paid the greatest possible tribute to the idea of the common good. Every 'measure of government' can, and indeed must, according to Bentham, be weighed in the scales of the 'principle of utility', that is, its capacity to contribute to the 'happiness of the community'. It is true that 'the interest of the community' is nothing but 'the sum of the interests of the several members who compose it'. But far from indulging in the liberal fallacy, Bentham drew the most radical inferences from his individualistic premiss. Thirty years after the publication of his greatest political work he himself underlined the consequences of maintaining that 'the only *right* and justifiable end of government

---

[1] The most notorious case is usually believed to be that which occurs in connexion with Locke's notion of natural law, in view of the alleged impossibility of reconciling the dogmatic statements of the *Second Treatise* with the philosophic standpoint which Locke takes up in the *Essay on Human Understanding*.

[is] the greatest happiness of the greatest number'. This doctrine, wrote Bentham, has been said to be a 'dangerous one': and 'dangerous it unquestionably is', but only to a government 'which has for its *actual* end or object the greatest happiness of a certain *one*, with or without the addition of some comparatively small number of others'. Once again we see the common good reaffirming its claims at the very time of the fullest flowering of Individualism and Liberalism.

If we now try to assess the merits of the notion in the light of the inquiry we have pursued so far, three different lines of approach seem to suggest themselves, each leading to some useful conclusions.

The first approach takes into consideration the possibility of restoring the notion of the common good without renouncing those individual values which, as we saw, constitute the premiss of the modern concept of the State. This is the problem crudely presented by Locke, a problem which was to involve the Utilitarians in no small difficulties, as indeed it still involves liberal theory today. The relation between the individual good and the common good is usually settled in everyday political practice by a skilful game of compromise. But clearly a decision must ultimately be reached about priorities, and unless we are prepared to take the plunge in favour of the ethical, or even the totalitarian, State, accepting the absolute priority of the whole over the parts that compose it, we shall always end by coming back to Bentham's common-sense conclusion that the interest of the community is nothing else than the sum of the interests of individuals, and that it is therefore dangerous to speak of the common good in cases where the good of the individual is blatantly threatened or sacrificed. The demand is that the claim of each individual should be carefully weighed and considered on its own merits. As Messrs. Benn and Peters have aptly remarked, to say that the State should seek the common good 'is to say only that political decisions should attend to the interests of its members in a spirit of impartiality'.

At this point it is worth while remembering that the problem was certainly not unknown to medieval political theory, where it aroused perplexities and tensions which are not unimportant, even to the modern theory of the State. Aquinas, for example, goes so far as to say that the common good has the value of an end for the individual, and that the 'goodness' of a citizen depends on his being 'well adapted' (*proportionatus*) to the common good. He seems to accept in its entirety the Aristotelian conception of the integration of the individual in the State as a part in a whole. If, however, we examine more closely the way in which Aquinas conceives of this integration, we soon notice his determination to protect the value of individual personality against the dangers of the Aristotelian, that is pagan, concept of the State. There is one part of man which is not, and cannot be, in any way subordinate to the interests of the community. The whole spirit of Christianity is opposed to the degradation of the individual to a simple means to an end, even if the end is the common good. In this respect the modern liberal theory of the State can claim in its turn to have inherited and to continue to uphold the purest Christian tradition.

A second possible line of approach might be the following. The idea of the common good implies, as we saw, the request to describe exactly the good, or complex of goods, which ought to constitute the final aim of power. Quite apart from the almost hopeless difficulty of an enterprise of this kind, the question arises: whose task could it be in the modern State to define the common good, and what position of power within the framework of the State would be held by the man or the men to whom this task was entrusted? The problem is not quite unlike that which faces all those who attempt to restore the concept of natural law in the field of legal theory. In fact, once natural law is conceived as a set of clearly ascertainable and definable propositions, which are also and at the same time unconditionally valid and binding, it is clear that those on whom devolved the duty of ascertaining and defining this law would be, and could not but be, the true 'law-givers'. Similarly, the 'technicians', the 'experts', or whatever their modern name might be, to whom the task of deciding on the common good was entrusted, and whose decisions would then be guaranteed and implemented by the power of the State, would obviously be, and could not but be, the true 'sovereigns', the ultimate holders of power.

Surely there is here some ground for the serious misgivings which have of late been expressed in different quarters about the drift of present-day politics towards 'government by experts', or, as it is also called, 'technocracy'. If these experts held the rudder of the ship of State and were invested with the power of final decision, would they not be disquietingly similar to Plato's 'guardians' or to Rousseau's 'guides', and would they not in the end be the real arbiters of our whole life and destiny? We should all certainly wish that the voice of wisdom and not that of fools should be listened to where decisions touching the general interest and its implementation are concerned. But no amount of wisdom is an excuse for absolute power. Let us be chary of sacrificing the ideal of self-government to that of 'good government', and of renouncing the right, which democratic institutions secure, to share in the basic decisions that affect the life and destiny of us all. It is not yet long since we saw how great is the price paid for such renunciations and sacrifices. This is a lesson which our generation does not forget, and we can only hope that it will never be forgotten.

Finally, there is a third comment to be made on the constantly recurring request to define the common good in such a way that it may serve as the basic standard for the legitimation of power. Perhaps this is also the most serious objection to the notion itself, and that of which least account is taken. Let us imagine that it is possible, in spite of all difficulties, to determine with a fair amount of accuracy what constitutes the common good at a given time and place, and to lay down a whole series of precise propositions about it. The question now is: what exactly does it mean to say that the holders of power are 'obliged' to turn these propositions into commands, and that those to whom these commands are addressed are 'obliged' to obey them? Ever since the beginning of our inquiry we have pointed out that it is not logically possible to derive a judgement of value from a judgement of fact, nor, accordingly, a prescriptive from a descriptive proposition. Now even if it were possible to determine exactly and in detail all that at a given time and place is supposed to constitute the common good, what else would this be but an account of a factual situation, a description of the presence of a set of conditions likely to achieve or defeat a particular end? The problem, in other words, has been shelved, not solved. It is a question first of choosing between 'wealth', 'power', 'glory', and any of the countless ends which the State can pursue, before listing the types of behaviour, the kind of institutions, the plans and provisions that are needed to turn these 'goods' into the 'common good'. Needless to say, it is possible to imagine the greatest variety of situations. In a 'peace-loving' State the common good will be found to consist in a flourishing trade and in material prosperity. In a 'bellicose' one, guns will be given preference over butter. In every case, however, a description of the common good implies the indication of a choice already made, and the evaluation on the basis of that choice of a factual situation. It implies adding a special qualification—a value-qualification—to a state of affairs, to a particular 'order', which in actual fact is dependent on, and conditioned by, our preferences.

At this point the parallel between the common good and natural law is once again helpful. It has been said that to conceive of natural law as a set of propositions which can be ascertained and defined almost as precisely as those of positive law is to conceive of it as something factual. It involves maintaining the contemporary existence of two different systems of law, in opposition to, or at any rate in competition with, each other. If this remark is correct, it is clear that the idea of natural law has a chance of surviving the positivist attack only if it is no longer conceived as a fact, but as a value: not as something 'given', for us to take or to leave, but as something 'giving' to the given a particular relevance and qualification. It may thus still provide a convenient term for indicating the price attached or denied to 'existing' law, and the eventual 'duty' of submitting to or disregarding its precepts. But this qualification is important, and in some sense decisive, even in regard to the law's very existence. For the 'obligatoriness' of the laws does not consist in their undoubted capacity to compel observance, but in the possibility, which does not belong to all laws, of being accepted and obeyed by the 'good citizen'.

The same is true of the common good. The evidence of 'experts' is not final. The real evidence, the evidence which counts, is that of the 'good citizen'. Just as natural law is a gauge of the obligatoriness of law, so the common good is a gauge of the authority of the State. The greater the consensus on the ends to be pursued, the sounder is that authority. On this point the last word is still that spoken by Rousseau. The only legitimate government is that where 'the public interest governs', where the *res publica* is felt to be the common concern of all. In the end, the common good is perhaps nothing else than the bond of solidarity and loyalty which holds the State together.

I have thus come to the end of my venture, and reached the point where the cards must be laid on the table, and the winnings, however modest, picked up. Does there exist in the modern State a principle of legitimacy, a set of conditions which must be satisfied for power to be invested with the chrism of authority? Or is such a principle redundant in a world where indifference and scepticism, especially in political matters, are the rule? The avowed purpose of this book was to show that there is such a principle, and that democratic legitimacy, by uniting the liberty of the ancients with that of the moderns, is the only device that can raise men from the condition of subjects to the dignity of citizens.

In order to prove my case I have tried as far as possible to use the language of my own time. But I have not hesitated when necessary to have recourse to an older vocabulary—one which was familiar to our forebears, but now sounds out-of-fashion and quaint. It will probably have come as a surprise to the reader to find such phrases as 'the good citizen' or 'the good State' still mentioned in a book on political theory. I should like to assure him that, in resorting to such expressions, I knew very well what I was doing, and cherished few illusions about the 'good State' having ever existed, except for a few brief happy moments, in the history of mankind.

But it was a great and wise teacher who taught me that models constructed on past experience can help us to establish a 'hierarchy' of past and future events, and that he who does not recognize, or has no wish to recognize, this hierarchy, is 'neither a good historian nor a good philosopher'. Neither by temperament nor by profession was Luigi Einaudi a man to indulge in flights of fantasy or to discard a healthy respect for reality. And yet I cannot offer a better ending to this book than by paraphrasing the admirable conclusion of one of Einaudi's most scholarly works on economic theory. I should like to apply to political questions what he said there about using the 'Periclean model' as a touchstone for measuring 'that most humble category of past events which are concerned with finance and taxation'.

It may well be, of course, that the glamour of the Periclean City has long been over-rated and that what comes to our mind is but its nostalgic apology in Thucydides' celebrated lines. Yet the words of the great Funeral Oration still linger in our memory whenever we think of a model democracy. Respect for law and order, government by consent, love of country, pride of liberty: all the elements are there which conjure up, even for us moderns, the image of the 'good State'. That image may be far removed from what the realists call 'the effectual truth'. But it may serve to account for many things which the realist does not explain. What has also been called the 'heavenly city of the philosophers' has proved to be far more effectual in shaping man's political destiny than the mere possession of force.

REFERENCES

Thucydides, 'Funeral Oration of Pericles' in the *History of the Peloponnesian War*, II, 37–41. St. Thomas Aquinas, *Summa Theologica*, I ª 2 ᵃᵉ, q. xxi, art. 2; xc, 2–4; xcii, 1; 2 ª 2 ᵃᵉ, cxlvii, 3. Hobbes, *Leviathan*, ch. 30. Locke, *Second Treatise of Government*, §§ 3, 131, 134, and *passim*; *A Letter Concerning Toleration* (1689). Rousseau, *Contrat Social*, II, 6. Bentham, *An Introduction to the Principles of Morals and Legislation* (1789), 2nd edn., 1823, ch. 1.

The quotation from L. Einaudi on p. 229 is taken from his book, *Miti e paradossi della giustizia tributaria*, 2nd edn., Turin, 1940, ch. xii. That from Messrs. Benn and Peters on p. 225 is from their joint volume, *Social Principles and the Democratic State*, London, 1959, p. 273.

On the notion of the common good in Catholic thought see H. A. Rommen, *The State in Catholic Thought*, St. Louis and London, 1955, and J. Maritain, *The Person and the Common Good*, Paris, 1947 (Eng. trans. by J. T. Fitzgerald, London, 1948).

For a recent discussion of a topic which is closely related to the old notion of the common good see the collective volume on *The Public Interest*, ed. by C. J. Friedrich, (*Nomos* V), New York, 1962.

INDEX

Acton, Lord, 140.
Aguesseau, H. F. d', 177, 180.
Akzin, B., 176, 181.
Alanus ab Insulis, 98.
Alfieri, V., 48, 158, 160, 177, 181.
Ambrose, St., 185, 190.
Aquinas, St. Thomas, 116–17, 122, 140, 165, 187, 190, 198, 200, 223, 225–6, 230.
Aristotle, 9, 18, 20, 28, 30, 71–74, 75, 79, 82, 87, 115, 120, 122, 161–3, 165, 166, 168, 191–3, 198, 199, 212, 221, 223.
Augustine, St., 22–27, 28, 29, 35, 41, 47, 76, 77, 154, 159, 160.
Austin, J., 108, 111, 113, 128, 147.

Bacon, Sir F., 41.
Barbeyrac, J., 33.
Barker, Sir E., 29, 72, 75, 81, 190.
Bartolus of Sassoferrato, 142, 150.
Bellarmine, St. Robert, 136, 140.
Benn, S. I., 200, 225, 230.
Bentham, J., 224–5, 230.
Bentley, A. F., 60–62, 65.
Berlin, Sir I., 210, 211, 215, 221.
Bloch, M., 190.
Bobbio, N., 57, 113, 128, 146, 210.
Bodin, J., 32, 45, 99–102, 103, 108, 110, 117, 118, 120, 123, 171, 174, 180.
Boniface VIII, 97, 135.
Bosanquet, B., 168.
Bossuet, J. B., 186, 190.
Botero, G., 49.
Bottomore, T. B., 57.
Bracton, 86.
Browne, R., 140.
Burckhardt, J., 38.
Burdeau, G., 149.
Burke, E., 178, 181, 193, 200.
Burnham, J., 58.
Bury, J. B., 140.
Burzio, F., 200.

Calasso, F., 95, 103.
Carlyle, A. J., 193.
Carlyle, R. W., and A. J., 27, 88, 168.
Cassirer, E., 42, 43, 160.

Catalano, P., 81.
Cavour, C., 137.
Chabod, F., 35, 39, 43, 176, 179, 181.
Chapman, J. W., 221.
Charlemagne, 189.
Charles V, Emperor, 198.
Chiappelli, F., 35.
Cicero, 7, 9, 24, 25, 27, 28, 75–78, 80, 81, 83, 84, 115, 116, 122, 164, 168, 176, 180, 193, 212, 221.
Coke, Sir E., 91, 122.
Constant, B., 150, 212, 215, 221.
Cornford, F. M., 20.
Cranston, M., 210.
Crick, B., 65.
Croce, B., 40, 43, 44, 49, 65, 208, 210.
Cromwell, O., 137.
Crosara, F., 35.
Crossman, R. H. S., 20.

Dahl, R. A., 58.
Dante Alighieri, 31, 107, 134, 154, 164, 172, 180, 187, 188, 190.
De Gaulle, C., 142.
Derathé, R., 35, 160.
De Ruggiero, G., 220, 221.
Deutsch, K. W., 181.
Diderot, D., 157, 158, 160.
Dowdall, H. C., 35.
Duverger, M., 149.

Easton, D., 63, 65.
Einaudi, L., 208, 210, 229, 230.
Elizabeth I, 174.
Emerson, R., 20.
Emerton, E., 150.
Engels, F., 50, 51, 54, 57.
Ercole, F., 35, 103.
Eulau, H., 65.

Ferdinand of Aragon, 39.
Ferrero, G., 149, 150.
Fichte, J. G., 47, 179, 181.
Figgis, J. N., 27, 35, 87, 88, 103, 140, 190.
Foltz, W. J., 181.
Fortescue, Sir J., 117, 123.
Frederick II of Prussia, 210.
Friederich, C. J., 11, 149, 150, 230.

Fuller, L. L., 8.

Gablentz, O. von der, 150.
Gaius, 77.
Gierke, O. von, 20, 35, 83, 84, 88, 93, 123.
Gobineau, J. A. de, 198, 200.
Gramsci, A., 52, 57.
Gratian, 84, 85.
Gregory the Great, St., 193, 199.
Grosso, G., 81.
Grotius, H., 45, 102, 111, 126, 131, 216.
Guicciardini, F., 48, 177.

Halévy, E., 160.
Hart, H. L. A., 113, 147, 148.
Hauriou, M., 131.
Hegel, G. F., 47, 48, 50, 166-7, 168, 179, 181.
Henry VIII, 135.
Hertz, F., 181.
Heydte, F. A., von der, 103.
Hinsley, F. H., 95.
Hobbes, T., 19, 20, 33, 97, 102, 104-13, 114, 117, 118, 122, 123, 124-8, 130, 132, 133, 135, 137, 138, 139, 140, 144, 153, 154, 155, 156, 158, 159, 167, 170, 171, 174, 180, 201, 202, 203, 204, 209, 210, 230.
Hobhouse, L. T., 169.
Holmes, O. W., 148.
Hooker, R., 45, 117, 123, 197, 200.
Hume, D., 196, 197, 200.

Innocent III, 189.
Isidore of Seville, 84.
Isnardi, M., 35.

James I., 33, 186, 190.
Jennings, W. I., 131.
Jolowicz, J. A., 145.
Justinian, 30, 31, 81, 184, 189.

Kaegi, W., 173, 181.
Kant, I., 211, 213, 214, 221.
Kantorowicz, E. H., 95, 190.
Kaplan, A., 63, 65, 149.
Kedourie, E., 181.
Kelsen, H., 147.
Kern, F., 88, 190.
Kohn, H., 181.

Lagarde, G. de, 103.

Lakoff, S. A., 200.
Laski, H. J., 131.
Lasswell, H. D., 63, 65, 149.
Lewis, E., 88.
Lincoln, A., 196, 200, 213.
Lipset, S. M., 149.
Locke, J., 33, 118, 121, 123, 165, 168, 197, 200, 204, 205, 207, 208, 210, 213, 221, 223, 225, 230.
Lukàcs, G., 150.
Luther, M., 23, 27, 41.

Machiavelli, N., 16, 20, 21, 30, 31, 32, 34, 35, 37-43, 44-48, 52, 55, 59, 63, 102, 117, 118, 120, 123, 124, 133, 158, 159, 170, 172, 173, 174, 177, 180, 201, 202, 210, 218.
Macpherson, C. B., 210.
Madison, J., 119, 123.
Maistre, J. de, 23, 54.
Maitland, F. W., 20, 33, 35, 88.
Mallet du Pan, J., 215, 221.
Mancini, P. S., 171.
Mandeville, B. de, 158, 160.
Mannheim, K., 20.
Manzoni, A., 21.
Marcuse, H., 169.
Maritain, J., 230.
Marsh, N. S., 146.
Marshall, R. T., 35.
Marx, K., 50-52, 54, 57, 157.
Mayo, H. B., 221.
Mazzini, G., 176.
McCloskey, H. J., 20.
McIlwain, C. H., 27, 75, 81, 88, 91, 95.
Meinecke, F., 40, 43, 44, 46, 47, 49.
Meisel, J. H., 57.
Mesnard, P., 103.
Mill, J. S., 204-5, 208, 209, 210, 215.
Mochi-Onory, S., 103.
Montesquieu, 33, 119-22, 123, 124, 127, 131, 155, 156, 160, 193, 200, 211, 221.
Mosca, G., 53-57, 200.
Müllejans, H., 81.

Namier, Sir L., 179, 181.
Napoleon III, 189.
Niebuhr, R., 27.

Papinian, 77.
Pareto, V., 53-57, 157.
Paul, St., 183, 185.

Peters, R. S., 200, 225, 230.
Piovani, P., 146.
Plato, 15, 17, 18, 20, 28, 55, 70–71, 74, 79, 115, 122, 223, 226.
Pollard, A. F., 95, 173.
Polybius, 115, 122.
Popper, K. R., 20, 169.
Post, G., 36, 49, 95, 103, 173, 181.
Pound, R., 144.
Pufendorf, S., 33.

Rainborough, Col., 213.
Ranke, L. von, 47.
Renan, E., 180, 181.
Renard, G., 131.
Ritter, G., 47, 49.
Romano, Santi, 131, 147.
Romano, Silvio, 81.
Rommen, H., 230.
Roosevelt, F. D., 209.
Ross, A., 20.
Rousseau. J. J., 9, 48, 90, 97, 111, 112, 132, 133, 137, 140, 156, 157, 160, 181, 214, 215–19, 221, 228, 230.
Ruffini, F., 140.
Rutilius Namatianus, 195.
Ruyer, R., 160.

Sabine, G. H., 70.
Salutati, C., 142, 150.
Sartori, G., 221.
Schmitt, C., 149.
Schramm, P. E.. 190.
Seneca, 193.
Shafer, B. C., 181.

Shakespeare, W., 174.
Siéyès, E., 138, 140.
Smith, Sir T., 117, 123.
Socrates, 15, 16.
Spinoza, B., 156.
Strauss, L., 203.

Theodosius, 79.
Thucydides, 229, 230.
Tierney, B., 103.
Tocqueville, A. de, 137, 138, 140, 198, 200, 216, 217, 221.
Treitschke, H. von, 47, 49.
Truman, D. B., 62, 65.

Ullmann, W., 103, 190.
Ulpian, 78, 80, 92, 94.

Valentinian, 79.
Victor Emanuel II, 189.
Vinogradoff, Sir P., 95.
Voltaire, 178, 180.

Waldo, D., 65.
Weber, M., 10, 11, 27, 141, 143, 144, 149.
Weldon, T. D., 7, 9.
Whitgift, J., 135, 140.
Wild, J., 70.
Wilks, M., 103, 135.
Wilson, Justice, 122.
Winch, P., 129.
Woodcock, G., 160.

Zuccolo, L., 49.

PRINTED IN GREAT BRITAIN
AT THE UNIVERSITY PRESS, OXFORD
BY VIVIAN RIDLER
PRINTER TO THE UNIVERSITY